A Critical Introduction to the Ethics of Abortion

ALSO AVAILABLE FROM BLOOMSBURY

The Aesthetics and Ethics of Copying,
edited by Darren Hudson Hick and Reinold Schmücker
Nietzsche and Kantian Ethics, edited by João Constâncio and Tom Bailey
Phantasia in Aristotle's Ethics, edited by Jakob Leth Fink
Advances in Experimental Moral Psychology,
edited by Hagop Sarkissian and Jennifer Cole Wright

A Critical Introduction to the Ethics of Abortion

Understanding the Moral Arguments

BY BERNIE CANTENS

BLOOMSBURY ACADEMIC
LONDON • NEW YORK • OXFORD • NEW DELHI • SYDNEY

BLOOMSBURY ACADEMIC
Bloomsbury Publishing Plc
50 Bedford Square, London, WC1B 3DP, UK
1385 Broadway, New York, NY 10018, USA

BLOOMSBURY, BLOOMSBURY ACADEMIC and the Diana logo are
trademarks of Bloomsbury Publishing Plc

First published in Great Britain 2019

Cover design: Irene Martinez Costa

A catalogue record for this book is available from the British Library.

Library of Congress Cataloging-in-Publication Data
Names: Cantens, Bernie, author.
Title: A critical introduction to the ethics of abortion: : understanding the
moral arguments / by Bernie Cantens.
Description: New York : Bloomsbury Academic, 2019. |
Includes bibliographical references and index.
Identifiers: LCCN 2018034770 (print) | LCCN 2018040102 (ebook) |
ISBN 9781350055889 (ePuB) | ISBN 9781350055896 (ePDF) | ISBN 9781350055872
(pbk.) | ISBN 9781350055865 (hardback)
Subjects: LCSH: Abortion–Moral and ethical aspects.
Classification: LCC HQ767.15 (ebook) | LCC HQ767.15 .C39 2019 (print) |
DDC 179.7/6–dc23
LC record available at https://lccn.loc.gov/2018034770

ISBN: HB: 978-1-3500-5586-5
         PB: 978-1-3500-5587-2
         ePDF: 978-1-3500-5589-6
         eBook: 978-1-3500-5588-9

Typeset by Integra Software Services Pvt. Ltd.
Printed and bound in Great Britain

To find out more about our authors and books visit www.bloomsbury.com
and sign up for our newsletters.

Contents

Preface

The purpose of this book is to provide a clear, accessible and impartial analysis of some of the most influential moral arguments that have been advanced in the past fifty years on the ethics of abortion. The abortion issue is at its core an ethical issue. This means that the moral arguments and the conclusions derived from these arguments are fundamental to the social, legal and political views on abortion. In other words, we should begin the study of the abortion issue from a moral perspective, and it should be this discourse that sets the foundations and guides the conversations for all of the further discussions on abortion from the various other perspectives.

There are several challenges to the thesis of this book. First, there are a lot of emotions and passionate feelings surrounding the abortion debate. As a result, much of the existing language and terms used in abortion contexts within mainstream popular culture, such as 'pro-life' and 'pro-choice', carry with them a lot of emotive baggage. In an effort to create a more neutral discourse, I will use David Boonin's terms 'abortion defender' and 'abortion critic' throughout the text to represent those who consider most cases of abortions to be morally permissible and those who consider most cases of abortion to be morally wrong, respectively.[1] I will use the terms 'pro-life' and 'pro-choice' when I am referring to the specific movements that identify themselves with these labels, or when I refer to persons such as politicians who identify with the one of these movements, or when it is part of the content of a citation.

Second, so much has been written on the ethics of abortion that it is impossible to cover all of the excellent publications on the topic. My selection process has been guided with two objectives in mind: first, to include essays that have had a significant influence on the development of the ethical thought and philosophical arguments on abortion. This means that I tried to select essays that have marked paradigmatic shifts in the conceptual frameworks, assumptions and arguments on the ethics of abortion. Second, I have tried to present a wide range of representative views that offer a neophyte to the ethics of abortion a well-rounded and diverse presentation of the topic.

A third challenge concerns the practical constraints in writing a manuscript of this nature, namely, the manuscript's limited space and the author's limited time. This, obviously, restricts the number of works I can include as part of our study. Despite these practical limitations, the book covers some of the most central and representative arguments that have been developed from some of the most important approaches and perspectives on the abortion debate during the past five decades (e.g. personhood arguments, a moral risk assessment approach, personhood as an essentially contested concept, women's rights arguments, ethics of killing arguments, feminist arguments, virtue ethics approach).

A fourth challenge concerns the inherent difficult nature of the moral issue of abortion. We must concede that abortion is one of the most vexing, challenging and intractable moral problems for ethicists to resolve. Part of this difficulty stems from the fact that it entails five essentially interrelated ethical quandaries: (1) the moral status of the foetus, (2) the rights of the pregnant woman, (3) the rights and social status of women in society, (4) the relationship between the foetus and the pregnant woman and (5) the relationship between the moral and legal aspect of abortion.

The moral status of the foetus

The problem of abortion requires that we address the ethical issues concerning the moral status of the foetus (i.e. Is the foetus a person? When does it become a person? Does it have human rights? Does it have the right to life? Does the foetus have intrinsic value? Does the foetus have any moral standing at all?). Some of the answers to these questions depend on our definition of personhood, and personhood is a difficult concept to define. Some philosophers make a distinction between a human being and a person. According to them, the former connotes the biological elements of the organism (i.e. its genetic structure) and the latter connotes the psychological, cognitive and social elements of the organism (i.e. its ability to be self-aware, communicate, reason etc.). Moreover, some philosophers argue that only persons belong to the moral community. Therefore, being a human being is *not* sufficient for personhood status or to be a member of the moral community. As a result, while it might be clear that a foetus is a human being, it is not so clear that it is a person.

The rights of the pregnant woman

The moral problem of abortion is also essentially intertwined with the issues of women's individual rights, particularly her right to control her body and reproductive choices. Many feminists argue that this dimension of the abortion issue is too often ignored and neglected. They argue that the traditional debate on abortion is disproportionately focused on the foetus's personhood rights rather than the rights of the pregnant woman, and thus the debate is skewed in favour of the foetus. A thorough philosophical investigation of the issue of women's rights requires that we also understand more basic underlying concepts such as the concept of rights, moral obligations and personal freedoms. It also requires an exploration into the ethical limits of human freedom and privacy in a democratic society: Should human freedom and privacy have legal and moral restrictions or boundaries? If so, how should such restrictions and boundaries be determined? One of the most influential and prominent essays on this topic is Judith Jarvis Thomson's 'A Defense of Abortion'. Thomson argues that even if the foetus is a person, with all of the legal rights ascribed to an adult human person, if a pregnant woman did not consent for the foetus to use her body for its survival, then it has no right to do so. In this case, if a pregnant woman decides to abort the foetus, it does not violate the foetus's right to life. Therefore, a pregnant woman who does not grant consent to a foetus to use her body for its survival and decides to abort the foetus does not commit an injustice against the foetus.

Women in society

In addition to women's individual rights, the moral problem of abortion requires that we also address women's rights at the institutional and societal level, that is, women's rights within the society at large. This raises more complex social justice issues involving gender, race, socioeconomic status, sexual orientation and ethnicity. Feminist philosophers have argued that Western democratic societies continue to be plagued with severe problems of gender inequalities, prejudice, discrimination, oppression and exploitation. These social injustices against women manifest themselves, in part, through existing legislation and policies. Moreover, they stem from patriarchal systems and worldviews that are predominantly male centric. Is a worldview that has been developed by men and through a 'masculine perspective' inherently biased against women? According to some feminist, the abortion issue is at its core a women's issue, and therefore it should be understood as forming part of the larger debate on existing cultural and social injustices against women in society.

The relationship between the foetus and the pregnant woman

To adequately investigate the moral problem of abortion, we must explore and try to understand the dependency relationship between a foetus and a pregnant woman. Is it a special familial relationship? Is it a standard relationship between two human beings? Is it a relationship between one human being and parts of her own body? Is the status of the relationship dependent on a pregnant woman's conception of it? Does the biological or psychological dimension of a relationship have moral relevance? Answers to these questions will have a significant effect on how we morally assess situations in which there is a conflict between the health and survival of the foetus vis-à-vis the pregnant woman.

The relationship between the moral and legal aspect of abortion

Finally, the moral problem of abortion connects the moral principles with the legal precepts in ways that other moral problems do not. For instance, one can argue for the position that gay marriage is immoral while consistently supporting the legality of gay marriage. However, a popular view among abortion critics is that abortion is immoral because it entails the killing of a person, and thus it is equivalent to homicide. As a consequence, with few and rare exceptions (e.g. self-defence), this abortion critic's moral view entails the illegality of abortion.

These five philosophical issues are complex dimensions of the moral issue of abortion, making it one of the most difficult moral problems of our day. Some philosophers believe that the issue is inherently irresolvable. Nevertheless, even if we hold a sceptical view about our ability to arrive at an ultimate and unanimous solution to the moral problem of abortion, we can still maintain that continued moral investigation, analysis and examination of the abortion problem can substantially contribute to the advancement of ethical, political and legal solutions to problems concerning and surrounding the abortion issue.[2] Thus, even for those who are sceptics about reaching any evidentially based and universally accepted answers to the moral questions on abortion, understanding the arguments presented in this book remains important, because they can give us an understanding of the rationale and merits of some of the most prevalent and well-argued positions on the ethics of abortion.

Philosophical methodology: Evidence and arguments matter

Given the strong feelings and emotions associated with the abortion issue, other important goals of this book are to present the arguments as fairly as possible, to even-handedly weigh the evidence and the strength of the arguments presented and *not* to advance or promote a particular view or hidden agenda. This, of course, does not mean that I am infallible in my assessment of the evidence nor that I have some privileged objectively neutral perspective. It is possible that my insights in my evaluation of certain arguments and in my assessment of the truth or falsity of certain premises might be different from other people's. Nevertheless, I have made a concerted and sincere effort to present the arguments in the most equitable and impartial manner possible. Consequently, I hope that this book can also serve as a resource for both abortion critics' and abortion defenders' positions, as well as a guide in philosophical methodology: teaching students that evidence and argumentation matter for deriving truth, and thus that evidence and arguments are foundational for judicious moral decision-making. I hope students will understand their moral obligation to be *evidentially conscientious* about their moral beliefs.

To be evidentially conscientious about our moral beliefs requires that we ask ourselves: Why do we believe what we believe? Are the moral beliefs we hold justified? An evidentially conscientious agent should maintain that the more evidence and justification one has for the truth of a proposition the more reason one has to believe that the proposition is true. In contrast, the more evidence and justification one has for the falsity of a proposition, the more reason one has to believe the proposition is false. By saying this, we are not committed to the view that there is absolute truth(s) or that for any given moral situation there is only one correct answer. We are simply committed to the view that we can be objectively mistaken about our moral decisions and that careful reasoning and evaluation of the evidence and arguments can help us distinguish between true and false moral claims. In addition, an evidentially conscientious moral agent who appreciates and understands the importance of evidence and justification for deriving truth will always remain open minded towards new evidence and new moral arguments, and this will keep us from becoming dogmatic, closing the door to new evidence and ending our moral enquiries prematurely.

I also hope to convey to the reader that part of being an evidentially conscientious moral agent includes being *clear* about the concepts we use, making sure that the claims that support our arguments are *true*, and knowing how to distinguish between sound and unsound as well as cogent and uncogent arguments. In other words, an evidentially conscientious moral agent needs to know how to construct good arguments and how to refute bad ones. When possible, I take the time to present the arguments in premise-conclusion format, assess their validity or strength and determine whether the premises are true or false. Once the prima facie soundness or cogency of an argument has been presented and defended, I go on to examine the most substantial and serious objections and counterexamples that I can think of against the argument.

The importance of the abortion issue

Social importance

The social contentiousness of abortion in the United States can be measured, in part, by how highly divisive and ambivalent it is in the minds of Americans. According to a 2017 national survey by the Pew Research Center, 57 per cent of Americans believe that abortion should remain legal in all or most cases, while 40 per cent believe that it should be illegal in all or most cases.[3] However, 52 per cent believe that abortion is morally wrong and 10 per cent believe that abortion is morally acceptable.[4] Despite this majority anti-abortion view among Americans, almost 69 per cent of Americans (i.e. seven out every ten Americans) do not want to see *Roe* v. *Wade* overturned.[5]

Therefore, most Americans believe that abortions should remain legal, and yet the majority also believe that abortion is morally wrong. This seemingly paradoxical view demonstrates the complexity of the abortion issue, its myriad perspectives and the public's insight to see that the issue does not need to have an all-or-nothing solution, leaving room for some middle ground and moderate positions. In fact, 60 per cent of Americans believe that there is a middle ground on the issue of abortion.

Despite the fact that it seems that most people support the legalization of abortion, some of those who do not support it have used extreme measures to undermine the practice. For instance, in 27 November 2015, John Dear Jr. shot and killed three people and injured nine at the Planned Parenthood facility in Colorado Springs. Since 1977, eight people associated with abortion facilities have been murdered and more than 200 attacks on abortion facilities have been carried out. Not many other contemporary moral and social issues in the United States have provoked this kind of passionate and extremely violent behaviour.

Political importance

In the political arena, we have witnessed many political careers fail and succeed because of a candidate's views on abortion. Moreover, in most cases, political discussions are not grounded in reasoned and logical argumentation but instead on emotionally charged rhetoric, which, in many cases, is grounded on religious or faith-based beliefs. Political debates on abortion are hardly ever fair and unbiased enquiries into truth; most of the time, they are carried on by ideologues who intentionally use incendiary language to persuade and to pander to their constituencies. Perhaps it is because of these rhetorical methodologies used by politicians that abortion remains one of the most politically charged issues of our day.

In July of 2015, a pro-life organization released a video showing a doctor from Planned Parenthood discussing the selling of aborted foetuses' body parts.[6] Later, a second video was released alleging to be footage from within Planned Parenthood showing how these procedures were performed.[7] Needless to say, these videos caused a moral uproar within some segments of the US population, particularly with conservatives and religious groups. The topic was eagerly taken up as a major item agenda on numerous Republican candidates' platforms during the 2015 Republican Presidential primary debates. As a result of these videos and the rise of anti-Planned Parenthood sentiment in the United States, on 30 September 2015, the US government was on the brink of shutting down. Republicans from the House of Representative were on a mission to defund Planned Parenthood, and they made this a top priority. A total of 151 Republicans voted against the budget on the basis of their strong opposition to Planned Parenthood's selling of aborted foetal tissues.[8] Just seven hours before the government shutdown, Democrats were able to muster the necessary votes to keep the government running.

More recently, in June of 2017, the Trump administration and the GOP, in their attempt to repeal the Affordable Health Care Act, focused on defunding Planned Parenthood, a move that has created some controversy and possible dissenters among the more moderate Republicans. The cuts are deep (40 per cent of Planned Parenthood's funding) and could jeopardize the existence of many Planned Parenthood offices and their services, including abortions. Of course, the majority of women who would be affected by this cut are black, Hispanic, and low-income, single-parent providers. The motivation for ending Planned Parenthood funding is spearheaded by pro-life movements that want to eliminate any federal funds being used for subsidizing abortions.

Thus, once again, the abortion issue seems to be at the centre of American politics. As Avantika Chilkoti from the *New York Times* put it,

> The fight over one provision – to cut off funding to Planned Parenthood for a single year – may be tangential to the wider war over the American health care system. But the Senate is narrowly divided, Mr. Trump's vow to repeal President Obama's signature domestic achievement could rest in the hot-button issue of abortion. The proposed healthcare bill is bringing a decades-old debate over abortion to something of a climax.[9]

Never in our history has the issue of abortion been so divisive, providing all the more reason why a rational dialogue on the moral status of abortion is so vital in our time.

Legal importance

Legally, abortion laws are disputed every year in the United States at the local, state and national levels of government, as well as in state and federal courts. For instance, in Kansas, in 2013, Governor Sam Brownback passed some of the most extensive and restrictive pro-life and anti-abortion legislations since *Roe*. Other states, such as North Dakota, Alabama, Arkansas, Wyoming and Mississippi, are moving in this anti-choice direction.[10] In fact, according to the Guttmacher Institute, in 2011 there were ninety-two provisions passed in states within the United States intended to restrict a woman's access to abortion services, the highest ever in US history. While this number went down to forty-three provisions in 2012, it still ranks as the second highest in US history.[11] Moreover, recently there have been unsuccessful attempts to pass personhood amendments in Nebraska, Alabama, California, Colorado, Florida, Michigan, Mississippi, Missouri, Montana, Nevada and Virginia. Similar attempts have also occurred at the federal level.[12]

On 27 June 2016 the US Supreme Court concluded in *Whole Woman's Health* v. *Hellerstedt* that the Texas law that required Texas abortion clinics to maintain hospital-grade facilities and for abortion doctors to have admitting privileges in local hospitals was unconstitutional. The high standards would have caused the shutdown of some thirty abortion clinics around the state of Texas, leaving only ten abortion clinics to serve the entire state. The intense battle over the legal issue of abortion is far from over, and we should expect to continue to see pro-life and pro-choice politicians debating this issue at the local, state and federal levels in the US legislature and courts.

Moreover, with President Trump's two social conservative appointments to the US Supreme Court – Justice Neil Gorsuch and Justice Brett M. Kavanaugh – the Supreme Court now has one of the strongest social conservative majorities since the 1930s (Gorsuch and Kavanaugh join fellow social conservatives Chief Justice John Roberts Jr., Justice Clarence Thomas and Justice Samuel L. Alito). Peter Baker from the *New York Times* describes the historical phenomenon as follows: 'Mr. Trump's nomination of Judge Kavanaugh culminates a three-decade project unparalleled in American history to install a reliable conservative majority on the nation's highest tribunal, one that could shape the direction of the law for years to come.'[13]

Finally, it is interesting how unfamiliar the younger generation are with some of the most pivotal Supreme Court decisions concerning the abortion issue. According to the Pew Research Center, only 44 per cent of Americans less than thirty years of age could identify *Roe* v. *Wade* as the 1973 Supreme Court case that dealt with abortion.

Religious importance

Religious groups, by far, are the most fervent and vocal abortion critics. For instance, 60 per cent of white Evangelical Christians and 53 per cent of Mormons and Hispanic Catholics believe that abortion should be illegal in all or most cases.[14] Members of religious communities make up most of the activists against the pro-choice movement, and they are primarily responsible for the activism found at and around abortion clinics. Their strong views on abortion stem from the religious belief that human life is sacred, because it is a gift from God and only God has the right to take it away. This religious argument (or arguments similar to this one) is part of and dependent on specific religious communities' faith-based religious beliefs, and they should *not* be part of philosophical arguments. In this text, in order to remain committed to the philosophical method, we will steer away from religious arguments or arguments that include premises that depend on religious dogma or religious beliefs grounded on revelation or faith-based sources.

In conclusion, there are deeply rooted social, political, legal and religious controversies surrounding the abortion issue, and this makes it one of the most intractable moral issues of our day. In addition, its myriad of ethical dimensions (i.e. personhood issue, women's individual right's, women's societal rights, the relationship between the foetus and the pregnant woman and the relationship between the moral and legal aspects) make it one of the most difficult contemporary ethical problems to resolve.

Overview of the chapters

In the Introduction, I provide the basic intellectual tools to help beginners have the resources to conduct good ethical evaluations. In the first part, I provide a basic introduction to ethics, including a brief description of some of the general ethical theories that will be encountered in the book. In the second part, I present a basic introduction to the logic of argumentation. We study the anatomy of arguments, valid and invalid arguments, sound and unsound arguments and cogent and uncogent arguments. Finally, we study basic embryological facts that will provide important information to maintain a common and consistent vocabulary and set of data, in order to develop good arguments based on true premises.

In Chapter 1, we examine personhood arguments defending abortion. We study two arguments in defence of the premise that the foetus is not a person and thus does not have a right to life: (1) the Argument from Personhood as Developed Cognition and (2) the Argument from Personhood as First-

Person Perspective. We look closely at how these different conceptions of personhood are related to and affect women's rights. In this section, we also raise the question of the ethics of infanticide and its relation to some of the views that defend the moral permissibility of abortion.

In Chapter 2, we examine personhood arguments critiquing abortion as morally wrong. We analyse the following arguments: (1) the Being a Person versus Functioning as a Person Argument, (2) the Probability Argument and (3) the Argument from Potentiality.

In Chapter 3, we raise the question as to what should be done if a common meaning of personhood cannot be determined. In other words, what should we do if we cannot answer the question 'What is a person?' in a way that both abortion defenders and abortion critics will agree with? Does this mean that we must become sceptics on the moral issue of abortion? Or are there arguments that prescribe a given course of action as the morally right action, given the unresolvable nature of personhood. First, we distinguish between unresolvable concepts based on epistemic limitations (i.e. due to the lack of evidence available to us) and metaphysical limitations (i.e. due to the nature of the concepts and thus even an omnipotent observer would not be able to resolve the dispute). We then examine an argument based on a woman-centred, relational conception of morality in which the conception of women's autonomy takes precedent. This view does not derive a conclusion on whether an abortion is morally wrong or morally permissible, it only argues for the view that, given the uncertainty surrounding the conception of personhood, the pregnant woman should be the only one with the moral authority over abortion decisions. Next, we examine arguments based on the conception of moral risk. The idea is that understanding moral risk can help resolve moral cases in which there are facets or elements essentially related to the moral issues that are unknown or unknowable. In cases in which the personhood issue is metaphysically irresolvable, moral risk theory might help us determine an ethical course of action. We examine what moral risk is, what are non-negligible possibilities of errors and how to calculate moral risk. We go on to analyse a moral theory for moral risk and then apply it to the abortion issue. Finally, we will consider plausible objections to the arguments presented.

In Chapter 4, we focus on the issue of women's rights. We begin with a general description of the concepts of liberty rights, claim rights, justice and moral obligation. We then analyse the relationship between consent and responsibility and how these notions might affect the abortion debate from a variety of perspectives. Next we examine arguments from the right of a woman to control her body. We then turn to a description of Judith Jarvis Thomson's influential 1973 argument for the permissibility of abortion. We analyse her violinist analogy and examine several related topics: the notion of rights and consent, cases of unconsented sex and pregnancies, cases of unconsented pregnancies and the case for third-party interference. We conclude by considering the notions and objections that arise as part of the arguments related to minimal sacrifice, good and minimally decent Samaritan, whether the mother–child relationship is a special one, and the distinction between not saving and killing.

In Chapter 5, we reexamine the ethics of abortion through the lens of the ethics of killing. We begin with an analysis of the standoff that exists between the abortion defenders' and abortion critics' personhood arguments. We then introduce another method of dealing with the abortion issue that circumvents the personhood debate. This new strategy begins by examining what makes killing wrong. If we can determine what makes killing wrong, then we can enquire as to whether killing a foetus is morally wrong. We critically assess Don Marquis's view that what makes killing a person wrong is that it deprives them of a future-like-ours, that is, Deprivation Argument. We analyse Marquis's arguments in support of the Deprivation Argument and compare his theory with competing theories. Finally, we consider various objections and possible responses to Marquis' Deprivation Argument.

In Chapter 6, we turn to a substantially different approach to the ethics of abortion by adopting a virtue ethics theory instead of the traditional consequentialist and deontological ethical theories. We begin by reviewing briefly the distinction between consequentialism, deontology and virtue ethics. We then consider the basic concepts fundamental to Aristotelian virtue ethics: *eudaimonia, arête*, character, habit, intellectual virtue, character virtues and the virtue of justice. We examine Rosalind Hursthouse's argument for a contextual and moderate position on the ethics of abortion from a virtue ethics perspective. Finally, we consider some plausible objections and replies.

In Chapter 7, we consider feminist arguments on abortion. First, we begin by noting the broad and complex research area that is covered by feminist thought and the myriad of perspectives and positions that such research has engendered. As a consequence, we present a general definition of feminism for purposes of the abortion issue. A central claim of feminism is that, in any society and in all areas of society, women's rights, interests and talents ought to be respected, valued and compensated equally to those of men. We then present a general description of feminist ethics using Karen Warren's 'boundary conditions'. We examine two feminist arguments on abortion. First, we analyse Celia Wolfe-Devine's 'Abortion and the "Feminine Voice"' in which she attempts to describe how the abortion issue ought to be morally assessed through a feminine voice. Second, we examine Sally Markowitz's 'Abortion and Feminism' in which she argues that the issue of abortion cannot be treated as simply an issue of individual rights; instead, it must be dealt with within the context of women's oppressive conditions and with an authentic commitment to a more egalitarian society.

In Chapter 8, we turn to abortion-related bioethical issue concerning prenatal screening, human embryonic stem cell research and cloning. Some forms of prenatal screening have become routine, standard procedure for pregnant women. Some philosophers argue that prenatal testing and screening is more about eliminating defective foetuses and disabled people than about giving women informed decision-making opportunities and expanding their liberties. In fact, some argue that the way prenatal screening is performed today limits rather than expands women's autonomy. Is prenatal screening encouraging abortions? Does prenatal screening limit or expand women's rights and freedoms? Next, we examine the ethics of human embryonic stem cell research. Human embryonic stem cell research has given the medical profession enormous hope that it will eventually be able to provide cures to many forms of genetically caused diseases as well as degenerative diseases. However, if human embryos are individual human beings, can we ever be morally justified in destroying them for the purpose of research and the well-being of others? Finally, we explore the ethics of cloning and whether cloning persons is intrinsically ethically permissible or ethically wrong.

In Chapter 9, we examine and analyse the legal consequences for the abortion law of five of the most influential Supreme Court cases in the United States in the past six decades: *Griswold* v. *Connecticut* (1965), *Roe* v. *Wade* (1973), *Webster* v. *Reproductive Health Services* (1989), *Planned Parenthood* v. *Casey* (1992) and *Gonzales* v. *Carhart* (2007).

Acknowledgements

The idea for this book began as I was teaching an online section of *Ethics of Abortion* at Moravian College. My students requested secondary literature to help them understand the assigned readings for the course. However, I had a difficult time finding a text that presented and explained the moral arguments without taking a pro-life or pro-choice position. All of the secondary literature I found on abortion vigorously defended one side of the debate. I realized there was a need for a book that could introduce the most prevalent arguments on abortion from an objective standpoint, a perspective that would responsibly explain the abortion critics' and defenders' arguments without taking a definitive stance on the issue. Therefore, I want to begin by thanking my students in this course and many other subsequent courses for their desire to understand in greater detail the arguments on abortion.

I began writing this book during a sabbatical leave, which allowed me to dedicate a substantial amount of time to this topic without the disruptions of committee meetings, course lectures and course preparations. I am grateful to Moravian College for their support.

Many colleagues have reviewed various drafts of the chapters of this book. I would like to especially thank Dr. Arash Naraghi, Dr. Vicente Medina, Dr. Joel Wilcox, Dr. Sandra Fairbanks, Kristian Cantens and Dr. Theodore Schick Jr. for their detailed reading of various chapters, excellent comments and helpful recommendations. I would especially like to thank Arash Naraghi and Carol Moeller for being wonderful colleagues at the Moravian College Philosophy Department. Our philosophical discussions are too many to remember, but they are an important ongoing source of creative philosophical wisdom. I also have to thank various blind reviewers and the editorial team at Bloomsbury Publishing who have provided invaluable suggestions that have, in my estimation, improved the final version of this book. I am fortunate to have had excellent professors in both undergraduate and graduate school who were instrumental in teaching me the value of rigorous and honest enquiry. I am grateful to have learned so much from Paul Draper, Ramon Lemos, Alan Goldman, Harvey Siegel, Risto Hilpinen and Susan Haack.

Finally, I would like to thank the unselfish help and support that I receive from my partner, Esther Daganzo-Cantens, and my children Kristian, Kaila and Karina. Their lively input and views on the ethics of abortion have presented me with different perspectives and challenges.

Introduction

This chapter aims at providing the ethical, logical and factual foundations necessary to engage in meaningful discussion and debate on the ethics of abortion. First, we briefly examine the discipline of ethics, its purpose and some of the central ethical theories that we will encounter explicitly and implicitly throughout our analysis of the moral problem of abortion. Second, we study the logic of argumentation. To meaningfully evaluate the abortion arguments in the chapters that follow, it is necessary to understand the anatomy of arguments, how to determine the strength and weakness of arguments and how to correctly develop, support and undermine arguments. Finally, we study some basic embryological facts. We cover the basic timeline of the development of the foetus, and we consider some of the more relevant moments of foetal development for the abortion debate, such as when a foetus is viable, sentient, conscious. This basic overview of embryology will allow us to begin our discussions with a common set of facts concerning the foetus and its development, and it will permit us to refine our terminology so that we have some common agreement on the meaning of certain terms such as zygote, embryo, foetus, viability.

Ethics

The discipline of ethics is concerned with determining right and wrong behaviour of conscious, self-aware and intelligent beings. Right and wrong actions are measured, in part, by how effectively they help the agent advance towards what is morally good and avoid what is morally bad. If we consider the etymology of the words 'ethics' and 'morality', we will begin to forge a common meaning of these concepts. Ethics comes from the Greek word *ethos* and it refers to a person's customs, habits and character. Morality comes from the Latin *moralis* and it refers to one's manner or character. In the middles ages, *moralis* was the Latin word used to translate the Greek word *ethos*. In modern day, we use ethics and morality interchangeably to refer to the discipline that studies right and wrong actions of intelligent beings.

When we consider right and wrong action within the discipline of ethics, there must be a *moral agent* that is the perpetrator of the actions being evaluated. Moral agency requires certain psychological properties such as consciousness, self-awareness and intelligence. These cognitive traits give agents the ability to understand the nature, significance and consequences of their actions. For instance, a hurricane might cause a great deal of destruction, harm and suffering to sentient beings, but we would not classify a hurricane as a moral agent, because it is not conscious, self-aware or intelligent. Therefore, the hurricane's destructive and harmful actions do not fall within the category of ethics and morality.

Similarly, if a vicious dog attacks and kills a human being, we certainly would consider this action a horrible tragedy, but we would not classify it within the realm of ethics and morality. We would not, for instance, claim that the dog has acted immorally or hold the dog to be morally responsible for its actions. Again, the reason for this is because the dog lacks the sufficient intelligence to understand its actions as good or bad. The same might also be said of actions perpetrated by human beings who are mentally incapacitated or who have not reached the sufficient age to have the necessary intelligence required for them to understand their actions and the consequences of their actions. Such beings, then, lack moral agency, and they should not be held morally responsible for their actions.

Moral agents must also act freely and deliberatively. As a consequence, an intelligent moral agent makes a moral decision when he or she deliberates and chooses his or her action voluntarily, purposefully and intentionally. The question of free will in philosophy is a complicated issue that philosophers continue to study and debate at length. Here we only need an elementary understanding of it and its importance for moral agency. For instance, if someone who is conscious, self-aware and intelligent commits a crime while sleepwalking, we would not hold him morally responsible because, even though he has all of the characteristics of a moral agent when he committed the crime, he did not do so freely; that is, he did not choose the action voluntarily, purposefully and intentionally.

By narrowing the scope of the field of ethics and morality to free actions perpetrated by conscious, self-aware and intelligent agents, we also introduce the notion of intentionality. Ethical and moral evaluations focus on the actions, but they also must consider the intentions and mental states of the agent performing the action. This is an important distinction to make when we evaluate moral issues. You might conclude that an agent has done a morally wrong action, even though he or she had good intentions or vice versa. In addition, it is possible that facts about a person's mental state can affect our conclusions about the rightness and wrongness of the action performed while in that mental state. For instance, consider a person who has just lost a loved one and falls into a severe depression as a result of it. To accurately evaluate the moral status of this person's actions, it might help to consider the severe depression he is suffering. Putting actions within a psychological context might influence our moral assessment of the act.

Another important distinction to keep in mind when undertaking an ethical examination of a moral issue is that ethical judgements are directed at the actions performed and not at the person performing them. We know from experience that good people sometimes commit morally wrong acts and that bad people sometimes commit morally right acts. It would be a mistake to infer that a person is morally bad from the claim that he or she has committed an ethically wrong action. It would be equally problematic to infer that a person is morally good from the claim that he or she has committed an ethically right action. These inferences are too simplistic, and the connection between one's actions and one's moral status is much more complicated than this and cannot be deduced from only one or several actions. For starters, an accurate assessment of the moral status of a person requires knowledge of the person's internal and private cognitive states, such as their desires, fears, intentions. And this is difficult to determine. For our purposes, with the exception of virtue ethics, we will focus on evaluating the moral status of actions and not of the persons who committed the actions.

The field of ethical studies can be divided into three branches: (1) metaethics, (2) normative ethics and (3) applied ethics. Metaethics is the foundation of ethics. In simple terms, it investigates whether there is an overall justification for ethics and morality. It questions the whole enterprise by examining whether things such as good and bad are real and part of the fabric of the universe, like chairs, tables, atoms or elements. It also attempts to categorize the meaning of ethical judgements by analysing the psychological ground of ethical language. Are ethical utterances, such as 'stealing is wrong', representative of one's beliefs (i.e. cognitivism) or are they representative of only one's feelings (i.e. subjectivism) or are they simply expressions of one's emotions and feelings (i.e. emotivism)?

Normative ethics investigates theories that can help provide a systematic method for determining right and wrong actions. This is essential for ethical studies, because if we can provide such a theory to determine what is right and wrong, then it can serve as a common standard for the ethical evaluation of all moral agents' actions. For instance, utilitarian theory proposes that the right action is the one that will maximize happiness. This theory, therefore, gives us a method to systematically determine what the right action is in any given moral situation. We simply have to look at the consequences of the alternative possible actions and try and calculate which one will result in the greatest overall balance of happiness for the greatest number of people. Below we will survey some of the more common ethical theories such as utilitarianism, deontology and virtue ethics.

Applied ethics is the branch of ethical studies that focuses on working out and examining the application of various ethical theories on an array of ethical problems, such as euthanasia, capital punishment, animal rights, abortion, pornography. This branch of ethics, then, studies and evaluates practical ethical issues and moral dilemmas that we face on a daily basis.

While normative ethics and metaethics are essential branches of ethical studies, in this book we will focus on applied ethics, specifically on the ethical problem of abortion. We adopt a realist metaethical view in which ethical claims represent beliefs about the world that can be objectively true or false. Moreover, we leave open the possibility about the kind of ethical theories that provide the best evidence and arguments for the truth or falsity of different positions on abortion.

Before we embark on our investigations into the moral problem of abortion, you should have some grasp of the traditional ethical theories and how they work. Recall that the task of ethical theories is to provide a systematic method or standard by which we can determine ethically right and wrong actions. There are three general categories of ethical theories: (1) consequentialism, (2) deontology and (3) virtue ethics.

Consequentialism

Consequentialist theories attempt to discern the right action by focusing on the consequences of the action. There are various types of consequentialist theories but the two most common ones are egoism and utilitarianism.

Ethical egoism

Ethical egoism states that the right action is that which produces the greatest amount of happiness for the agent performing the action. Egoists point out that their theory is not the same as acting selfishly. Being selfish is a simplistic view that states that we ought to gratify our immediate desires and wants. Ethical egoism, on the other hand, is a more complex view about acting in ways that will benefit one's long-term life goals and objectives, our long-term well-being and the well-being of our loved ones and our community insofar as they benefit us. According to an ethical egoist, in most cases, one's long-term interest will require that we sacrifice our immediate desires and wants. Moreover, since the well-being of our family and friends, as well as members of our community, will impact our well-being, it is important that we care for them and their interests as well. In addition, ethical egoism will require that we treat others as we would want them to treat us, and hence it requires that we treat strangers with a certain amount of consideration and respect.

Two common arguments supporting ethical egoism are the following. First, ethical egoists argue that the only one who can know what one truly wants and desires is oneself and no one else. Only we can know what makes us truly happy. As a result, when we act to 'help' other people, we make the mistake of thinking that we know what will make them happy or what is truly best for them. However, this assumption is ill-founded and, in most cases, leads to harming rather than helping others. Second, ethical egoists argue that altruism is a form of pity and denigrates others' human dignity. When we go out of our way to 'help' others we are implying that they are not self-sufficient and that they are lesser beings than us. In effect, we denigrate and belittle their humanity.

While these arguments provide some justification for ethical egoism they also have their weaknesses. First, while it is true that we cannot know the feelings, desires and thoughts of others first-hand, the way we know our own, there are some basic psychological facts that we share with all sentient beings. For instance, it is safe to say that we can know when other people are in pain and when they are suffering. We can also know when others are ill or are disease-stricken, and we have a very good idea of the human suffering that these illnesses and diseases entail. In addition, human beings can communicate quite effectively, and thus we can learn about others' desires and what makes them happy through language and interpersonal communication.

Second, helping others and providing assistance to the less fortunate is not necessarily a demeaning action, and it does not necessarily require the denigration of their humanity. We all understand that unfortunate events can happen to anyone. For instance, many people are born with disabilities, many get gravely ill and many get seriously injured. Having empathy for the suffering of others is not the same as pity, and it is understood that sometimes the difference between us and them might be sheer luck. Therefore, compassion for others' needs neither denigrates nor belittles their humanity; on the contrary, it is seeing the other as equal to oneself and as a fully rational human being who deserves to be treated with respect.

Utilitarianism

A second popular consequentialist theory is utilitarianism. The fathers of modern utilitarianism are Jeremy Bentham (1748–1832) and John Stuart Mill (1806–1873). Utilitarianism is based on the principles of egalitarianism and utility. The principle of egalitarianism claims that we should give equal consideration to the interest of all beings. The principle of utility claims that we should strive to produce the consequences that will maximize the overall balance of happiness over unhappiness. Act-utilitarianism claims that the right action is always that action which produces the greatest amount of happiness for the greatest number of people. One of the striking properties of act-utilitarianism is its impartial egalitarianism; it requires that we consider every sentient being's interests and happiness equally, including animals. The more sophisticated versions of utilitarianism make qualitative distinction between physical and psychological pleasures and pains, giving higher value to the latter.

Utilitarianism does not need sophisticated arguments to support it. Its basic principles of egalitarianism and utility are self-evident. First, the idea that we consider the interest (i.e. suffering, pain and joy) of beings equally seems prima facie true. Second, the notion that we ought to produce as much happiness as possible and reduce as much suffering as possible also seems obvious to any morally conscientious agent. What is not so obvious are the objections to act-utilitarianism. A common objection is based on counter-examples that can be lodged against the theory. Counter-examples to utilitarianism consist of actions that are prescribed by the theory and also appear self-evidently unjust and immoral. A counter-example, therefore, illustrates that the theory does not work for all cases and in all circumstances. At a minimum, then, counter-examples demonstrate that utilitarianism does not always work well in determining what is morally right. For example, according to act-utilitarianism, if you have five sick people who need different organ transplants, then we would be morally justified in kidnapping an innocent healthy person to steal his organs to give them to the persons who are in need of them. According to act-utilitarianism, this seemingly unjust act would not only be permissible, it would also be the right thing to do, because it would produce more happiness for more people. We can think of many other scenarios in which the minority's interests are sacrificed (unfairly and unjustly) for the sake of the greatest happiness principle.

To overcome these kinds of objections philosophers modified act-utilitarianism to rule-utilitarianism. Rule-utilitarianism is also based on the egalitarian and utility principles, except that instead of focusing on the particular action of specific individuals, it requires that we evaluate the actions as rules or as if everyone were to do this action on an ongoing basis. Rule-utilitarianism, then, states that the right action is that which can become a rule for everyone, and, as a rule, will produce the greatest amount of happiness for the greatest number of people. Going back to the counter-example, we might ask whether it would be morally permissible, as a rule, to sacrifice the lives of individual innocent people without their consent for the sake of other individuals. This rule would not create the greatest amount of happiness for the greatest number of people, because it would create panic and hysteria among all healthy people.

Deontology

Deontology claims that there are moral principles that undergird moral actions as valuable for their own sake and not for the consequences they produce. For instance, some deontologist might argue in support of the moral principle 'it is morally wrong to lie'. Based on this moral principle, one may argue that the action of lying is always morally wrong, regardless of the consequences. Deontology places value in the action itself rather than on the consequences of the action. Philosophers describe this by saying that certain actions have intrinsic moral worth, and thus they ought to be done for their own sake and not for the sake of the consequences they produce. As a result of the intrinsic worth of certain moral actions, deontology is couched in the language of moral obligations, imperatives and duties.

Rights-based approaches to ethics also fall within the deontological ethical framework, because they entail duties and obligations towards others. For instance, if I have a right to life, then this right entails that other people have a moral duty not to kill me. If I have a right to free speech, then this right entails that others have the duty not to interfere with what I say and write. Rights-based theories are commonly used in the abortion arguments, because a prevalent argument in the abortion debates concerns the rights of foetuses and the rights of pregnant women. We will consider in more detail the theories of rights in Chapters 1, 2 and 4.

We should distinguish between several types of duties: (1) absolute duties, (2) prima facie duties, (3) universal duties and (4) contextual duties. Absolute duties are moral obligations for which there are no exceptions. If you claim that we have an absolute duty to tell the truth, then we should always tell the truth, regardless of the circumstances or consequences. In cases of absolute duties, then, there are no cases in which you are morally justified in lying. The best example of absolute duties is Immanuel Kant's Categorical Imperative. According to this version of deontology, one's duty should always be performed without exception (i.e. it is absolute). Thus, if one has a moral absolute duty not to kill a human being, then killing a person can never be justified, even if doing so would save the lives of millions of people.

A prima facie moral duty is an action that one has an obligation to perform but not in all circumstances. If it is a prima facie duty rather than an absolute duty, then it is possible that there be overriding circumstances that would morally justify one in not preforming the action. Prima facie duties, therefore, assume that there are actions that have intrinsic moral worth but there can also be special circumstances that would morally justify one from not having to perform the action. For instance, it might be the case that a person has two simultaneous prima facie duties that conflict. In this case, he might not be able to perform both, and thus he is justified in performing only one and disregarding the other. Consider the following case. We have a prima facie duty to not kill an innocent person. We also have a duty to save lives and thus to prevent the death of millions of people if we can do so. If one finds oneself in a situation in which killing an innocent person can save the lives of millions of people, then one might be morally justified in killing an innocent person.

Third, universal duties are moral obligations that persist through time and transcend different cultures and contexts. They apply to all people at all times.

Fourth, contextual duties are moral obligations that arise out of particular circumstances. This way of looking at moral duties requires that we first understand the particular circumstances and the particular facts associated with it in order to develop the moral obligations that are pertinent to the particular situation. We cannot, as the universalist view of duty holds, begin with a set of moral obligations and simply apply them to particular situations; instead, moral obligations depend on place, time and context.

Virtue ethics

Finally, there is virtue ethics. In the *Nicomachean Ethics*, Aristotle develops a theory of ethics that focuses on developing a person's character as a way of arriving at right actions and moral duties. Aristotle claims that the central objective of ethics is to do well and live well, and this can only be done if we know the ultimate end of human beings and understand the nature of our humanity. He argues that the ultimate purpose of life is happiness or *eudaimonia*, that is, to live a flourishing life. With respect to the nature of our humanity, Aristotle argues that the essential function of human beings is to act in accordance with reason, understood broadly. Putting these two claims together, Aristotle inferred that the good life or the flourishing life is one that is lived in accordance with reason. (See Chapter 6 for a more detailed explanation of virtue ethics.)

An important difference between virtue ethics, consequentialism and deontology is that the latter two focus mostly on actions, hence they are act-centred, while virtue ethics focuses both on actions and on a person's character (i.e. mental states, attitudes, dispositions and habits), and hence it is agent-centred. According to the theory of virtue ethics, morality is not just about performing the right act, it is also about the disposition one is in *while performing* the right action. To be virtuous, one must do the right thing and be in the right state of mind while doing it. Consequentialism and deontology, on the other hand, are concerned with the acts themselves and not with a person's character. Virtue ethics, then, develops a holistic theory that entails what kinds of character traits one must develop in order to be good and live a good life.

Let's conclude this section on ethics by making an important distinction that many confuse when it comes to the issue of abortion. There is an important difference between the issues concerning the morality of abortion and the legality of abortion. The questions 'Is abortion immoral?' and 'Should abortion be illegal?' are two different questions, and we should not conflate the two. Our main focus is on the morality of abortion and not on the legality of abortion. Nevertheless, there are important connections between these issues that we will examine in the chapters ahead.

Logic

To fully understand and appreciate the arguments in this book you need to first understand some basic concepts about the logic of argumentation. First, an argument is made up of at least two propositions that are either true or false. An argument can only have one conclusion but may have one or more premises. The conclusion is the statement that is being defended. The premise(s) are the statement(s) that serve as evidence to support the truth of the conclusion.[1]

The first assessment one should conduct in the examination of an argument is the formal assessment of the relationship between the premises and the conclusion. The objective here is to ascertain the strength of the support the premises have for the conclusion. If the premises and conclusion are structured in such a way that the conclusion is intended to follow *necessarily* from the premises, the argument is a *deductive* argument. If the premises and conclusion are structured in such a way that the conclusion is intended to follow *probably* from the premises, the argument is an *inductive* argument.

Deductive arguments

In a deductive argument the conclusion is intended to follow necessarily from the premises. If the deductive argument is successful, then the argument is said to be a *valid* argument. If the form of the argument is unsuccessful, and the conclusion does not follow necessarily from the premise, then we say that the argument is *invalid*. If a deductive argument is valid, then it is logically impossible for the premises to be true and the conclusion false. If a deductive argument is invalid, then it is logically possible for the premises to be true and the conclusion false.

The next step in the evaluation of a deductive argument is to determine whether the premises of the argument are true or false. If the premises are all true, then the valid argument is *sound*. Thus, a sound argument is a valid argument with true premises. It is possible, however, for a valid argument to have a false premise, and, if it does, then the argument is *unsound* (or a bad deductive argument). A few examples might help in understanding validity and soundness.

The following argument structure is valid. Premise (1): All *y* are *z*. Premise (2): All *x* are *y*. Conclusion: Therefore, all *x* are *z*. Notice that I cannot determine if this argument has true or false premises or if the conclusion is true. In fact, I do not know anything about the content of the premises or conclusion. To obtain this information, I would need to be told what *x*, *y*, and *z* stand for. However, even though I cannot assess the content of the argument and thus the truth or falsity of the premises, I can still assess the form of the argument. In this case, I can determine that the argument is valid because the form of the argument is such that it supports the conclusion necessarily, meaning that if the premises happen to be true, then the conclusion is necessarily true (i.e. it is logically impossible for the conclusion to be false).

Imagine that that *x* = tigers, *y* = mammals and *z* = animals. The argument would read as follows: (1) All mammals are animals; (2) All tigers are mammals; therefore, all tigers are animals. This argument is valid and the premises are true; as a result, the argument is *sound*. Imagine, instead that *x* = reptiles, *y* = animals and *z* = mammals. The argument would read as follows: (1) All animals are mammals; (2) All reptiles are animals; therefore, all reptiles are mammals. This argument has the same valid form but premise (1) is false and therefore the argument is *unsound*.

Let us examine an *invalid* argument: Premise (1): Some *x* are *z*. Premise (2): Some *x* are *y*. Therefore, all *y* are *z*. Again, I cannot know anything about the content of the premises or the conclusion, but, given the quantifiers and the structure of the premises, I can determine that the conclusion does not follow necessarily from the premises, and therefore the argument is *invalid*. Invalid simply means that the conclusion does not necessarily follow from the premises. In other words, if the premises turn out to be true, it is logically possible for the conclusion to be false. Whereas, in the case of a valid argument, this is logically impossible. Consider the following: *x* = geometrical figures, *y* = quadrilaterals and *z* = squares. (1) Some geometrical figures are squares; (2) some geometrical figures are quadrilaterals; and (3) therefore, all quadrilaterals are squares. Notice that in this case the premises are both true and the conclusion is false. This would have been impossible had the argument been valid.

Why is understanding validity important for the abortion debate? First, we should point out that validity and invalidity are completely objective, similar to mathematical truths. So, if an argument has a valid form, then its validity is not something that can be denied. If you construct a valid argument, then the form of the argument is such that if the premises are true, then the conclusion is *necessarily* true. Therefore, if the form of the argument is valid, then truth and falsity of the premises become crucial. If the premises can be defended and they turn out to be true, then we have a *sound* argument. A sound argument is the strongest of all possible arguments, and if you have truly constructed a sound argument, then the conclusion is absolutely, universally and necessarily true, whether others accept it or not.

Here is an example of a valid argument on abortion: (1) All living things are sacred. (2) The foetus is a living thing. (3) A sacred being should never be killed. (4) Therefore, a foetus should never be killed. This is a valid argument, so if the premises are true, then it is also a sound argument and the conclusion follows necessarily. The only way to reject the conclusion is by arguing that one of the premises is false. Knowing this makes it easy to determine what should be the topic of heated discussion. In this case, it might be premise (1) 'All living thing are sacred' and premise (3) 'A sacred being should never be killed'.

Inductive arguments

Let us now look at inductive arguments. If an argument is inductive, then we know that the conclusion is intended to follow from the premises with some degree of probability and not necessarily. Therefore, the first step in evaluating the argument is to try to gauge the strength or probability with which the premises support the conclusion. Here we are analysing the likelihood that if the premises are true, then the conclusion will be true. To take a simple example that will illustrate the concept consider the following: Premise (1): Eight out of ten of the students in my logic course received an A grade. Premise (2): John is in my logic course. Conclusion: (3) Therefore, John probably received an A grade. In this argument if the premises are true, then there is an 80 per cent chance that the conclusion is true. In other words, given the truth of the premises, it is more likely that the conclusion is true rather than false. The formal assessment of the strength of this inductive argument, then, is that the conclusion follows with a probability greater than 50 per cent, and thus this invalid argument is *strong* (as opposed to *weak*). For strong invalid arguments to be good arguments we also have to defend the truth of the premises (just as with valid arguments). If we can demonstrate that the premises are true, then we have a *cogent* argument. If an invalid argument is weak or if it has at least one false premise, then the argument is uncogent.

One final word should be said about deductive and inductive arguments. Deductive arguments are arguments that have been developed to function as valid arguments. Therefore, if a deductive argument is found to be invalid it is said to be flawed. Inductive arguments are arguments that have been developed to function as probable arguments. Therefore, invalidity cannot be a flaw of an inductive argument. In this case, a flaw would be that the argument is weak and the premises do not show that the conclusion follows with a probability greater than 50 per cent. Moreover, it should also be noted that to have a good argument, whether deductive or inductive, all the premises must be true and thus one must provide evidence for the truth of all of one's premises.

Let us summarize this brief description of the logic of argumentation. First, the formal assessment of deductive arguments will tell us whether an argument form is valid or invalid. If the form of the argument is valid, then our next step is to assess the truth or falsity of the premises. If the premises are true, then we have a sound argument and the conclusion must be true. If one or more of the premises are false, then we have an unsound argument. Keep in mind that if an argument is unsound, it does not mean that the conclusion will be false; instead, it means that it is a bad deductive argument, and we should not believe that the truth of the conclusion follows necessarily from the premises.

Second, the formal assessment of an inductive argument will tell us whether an argument form is strong or weak. If an argument is weak, then the conclusion follows from the premises with a probability of less than 50 per cent. In this case the argument is bad, even if the premises are true. If the conclusion follows from the premises with a probability of greater than 50 per cent, then the argument is strong. In this case, our next step is to determine whether the premises are true or false. If all the premises are true, then we have a cogent argument. If one or more premises are false, then the argument is uncogent and it is a bad argument. A cogent argument is a good argument in support of the truth of the conclusion. In constructing arguments, then, our goal is to create a sound or cogent argument. In attacking arguments, our goal is to show that the argument is invalid or weak, or that one of the premises is false.

Embryology

Moral deliberation about any ethical issue requires a well-grounded understanding of the facts surrounding the issue in question. The abortion issue is no different. When considering the moral issue of abortion, understanding the facts concerning the development of the foetus is essential in coming to a reasonable conclusion that is supported by the best available scientific evidence. Embryology is the study of embryos, but the term also means the study of prenatal development in general, including foetuses. Human organisms are continuously developing, even after birth. Human development can be divided into prenatal and postnatal development. In this section, we will consider some of the most relevant and important stages of the prenatal development of a human being, focusing on developmental stages that could have the most impact on our assessment of the moral status of the foetus.[2]

There are two ways to talk about prenatal developmental periods: (1) trimesters and (2) weeks. Many physicians use the trimester method by dividing the pregnancy into three periods of approximately three months each. However, to speak more precisely and accurately about the important stages of prenatal development, we need to divide the process into weeks. In what follows, we will refer to both trimesters and weeks, depending on which seems most appropriate for the given context.

Foetal development is an extremely complicated biological process. However, we are not interested in the biological details of these various stages; instead, we are interested only in the relevant and consequential developmental stages that might affect the outcome of our moral assessment of the abortion issue. We will, therefore, try to limit the level of detail and the use of biological technical terms in the explanations. Greater knowledge of prenatal human development may or may not influence our thinking about the moral permissibility of abortion. What is certain, though, is that considering these facts is necessary to undertake a fair and complete enquiry into the moral issue of abortion.

We can divide the prenatal development into four parts: (1) The fertilization period (week one); (2) the blastocyst period (weeks two and three); (3) the embryonic period (weeks four through eight) and (4) the foetal period (weeks nine through thirty-eight).

Fertilization

First, we should keep in mind that there is a difference between the *fertilization age* and the *gestation age*. The gestation age is determined by the last day of a woman's last normal menstrual period (LNMP). Fertilization occurs approximately two weeks after that. Therefore, the gestation age will be two weeks longer than the fertilization age. For purposes of evaluating the moral question of abortion, what is relevant is the fertilization age, and thus we should keep this difference in mind.

Fertilization or conception occurs when a male sperm and a female oocyte fuse and become a *zygote*. A zygote is a one-celled, unique organism composed of the combination of twenty-three maternal and twenty-three paternal chromosomes. The process of fertilization is not instantaneous but rather a complex set of stages. As emphasized above, we do not need to engage in a detailed explanation of all the biological processes that occur during fertilization; all that we need to understand is that it is a complex process that occurs over time (about a twenty-four-hour period) and concludes with the formation of a one-cell human organism that has all of the necessary biological structure to develop into a full-fledged human being.

At the conclusion of this process, when the sperm and the oocyte fuse to form a zygote, certain facts are determined about the new organism. For instance, the chromosomal sex is determined. If the sperm has an X chromosome it will be a female embryo, and if it has a Y chromosome it will produce a male embryo. In addition, all of the physical and psychological human features determined by the organism's genetic code, such as eye colour, hair colour, some personality traits, are also determined at the time of fertilization. Most important, the zygote has all of the genetic material necessary to direct its future growth towards a full-fledged human adult person.

Blastocyst (weeks two and three)

Approximately thirty hours after the completion of the process of fertilization, and as the zygote moves through the uterine tube towards the uterus, *cleavage* begins. Cleavage consists in the rapid increase in the number of cells. The cells are of two kinds. One type of cell formation is destined to become the embryo and the other the placenta. The zygote starts off as a one-cell human organism and that one cell divides into two, then four and so on. These cells are called *blastomeres*. After about five days there are about 100 cells and the zygote becomes a 'ball of cells' called a *blastocyst*. All the cells in the blastocyst are the same; they are called stem cells or *totipotent* cells. These cells have the potential to become any of the 200 different types of cells in the human body.

At the end of the first week after fertilization, the blastocyst is implanted in the uterus. Implantation in the uterus is also a process that has various stages, and it takes all of the second week of foetal development for it to be completed.

The third week of the developmental stage of the blastocyst is important, because it is usually the first week after the missed menstrual period, and, in many cases, when a woman finds out that she is pregnant. This third week of the fertilization age is the fifth week of the gestation period. During this week, it is also the beginning of *morphogenesis*, or the beginning of the development of the body form. We also see rudimentary parts (embryonic *ectoderm*, embryonic *endoderm* and embryonic *mesoderm*) that will produce the human tissues needed for all of the human organs and structures (vessels, respiratory system, gastrointestinal tract, cardiovascular system, nervous system etc.). It is a critical period in which the biological foundation of the human organism is established. At the end of the third week, the embryo is 1 mm in size, and it is growing about 1 mm a day. There are no visible human features or organs at this stage of development.

Embryonic period (weeks four through eight)

From the fourth through the eighth week (the embryonic period) the embryo develops all the major internal and external structures. The primordial brain and nervous system begins its development. However, at this stage none of the organs, except for the cardiovascular system, are functioning. The cardiovascular system is the first organ to function, and a heartbeat can be detected at about the end of the third week of the fertilization age. Without studying the DNA, it would be impossible for anyone to determine if the embryo is a human embryo or an embryo of another animal such as a mouse or pig.

There are three phases to this stage of development: (1) growth, (2) morphogenesis and (3) differentiation. The growth refers to the rapid cell division that is taking place. The morphogenesis refers to the shape, size and organs that are forming. The differentiation is the organization of the different cells into the necessary categories to form the organs and other human structures necessary for the functioning of a human being. The embryo's limbs begin to move at the end of the eighth week.

This complicated developmental process is guided by the organism's genes, which serve as the blueprint of the organism's development. The development process is like a complicated orchestra in which each new cell development must be timed perfectly for the successful development of the human organism.

Foetus (weeks nine through thirty-eight)

After eight weeks the human organism begins to show some slight resemblance to a human, and it is now referred to as a foetus. The placenta is now mature, and it becomes the main source of nutrition and protection for the foetus.

Weeks nine through twelve

By the ninth week the head is so large that it constitutes about half of the length of the foetus. By the eleventh week the foetus has a basic human form and has all of the different types of cells and the basic organs such as stomach, kidneys and liver. At this stage, the foetus grows rapidly so that by the end of week twelve (or the end of the first trimester) it doubles in size. During these four weeks, the foetus's arms and legs grow. The arms will reach their final relative length. The bones begin to form. At week twelve, it is still only approximately three inches in length.

Week thirteen through sixteen

At about week fourteen, the foetus's eyes begin to move and limb movement becomes coordinated. By the end of week sixteen the foetus's skeleton is visible in an ultrasound. The kidneys begin to function and the foetus can produce urine. Between weeks twelve and fourteen the foetus's genitalia can be recognized. The foetus can make facial expressions, and it might even suck its thumb. At the end of week sixteen the foetus is approximately six inches in length.

Weeks seventeen through twenty

During this period quickening usually occurs. Quickening is when the pregnant woman feels the movements of the foetus. Eyebrows and head hair are visible by week twenty. The foetus's growth begins to slow down. The foetus can hear the pregnant woman's heartbeat and can hear voices from outside. The foetus is about nine inches long at the end of twenty weeks.

Weeks twenty-one through twenty-five

Between the weeks twenty-one and twenty-five the foetus begins to gain weight, and its body begins to become more proportional and more human looking. At week twenty-one the foetus has rapid eye movement. By week twenty-four foetus has fingernails. It is possible that a foetus that is twenty-two weeks old and born prematurely can survive with artificial assistance. However, at this age, foetuses may not have their lungs and respiratory system sufficiently developed, and they might also suffer from neurodevelopmental disability.

Weeks twenty-six through twenty-nine

During the weeks twenty-six through twenty-nine the foetus can survive with artificial assistance if born prematurely. Therefore, most foetuses are viable after the twenty-fifth week. The lungs and the nervous system are sufficiently developed so that it can control breathing and body temperature. In addition, the eyelids are open at twenty-six weeks. The foetus sleeps and dreams. Billions of neurons are developing in its brain. The foetus is about fifteen inches long and weighs about two-and-a-half pounds.

Weeks thirty through thirty-four

By week thirty-four the limbs have gained weight and the skin of the foetus has become pinkish colour. At the end of week thirty-four the foetus is eighteen inches long and about four-and-a-half pounds.

Weeks thirty-five through thirty-eight

These last few weeks the foetus gains weight and it is ready to be born. All of its organs are developed sufficiently to exist outside of the pregnant woman. The head remains the largest part of the foetus but the body is now larger than the head. A full-term foetus is about twenty inches long and seven-and-a-half pounds.

The brain and nervous system

The human brain is the organ that is connected to the essential properties that some philosophers normally attribute to personhood, such as consciousness, reasoning and self-awareness. Thus, we should focus on the prenatal development of the brain. Let's begin by reviewing the brain's anatomy in an adult human person. There are three major parts that make up the human brain: (1) cerebrum, (2) cerebellum and (3) brain stem. The cerebrum is the part of the brain that is responsible for the functions of thinking, reasoning, memory and feeling. The cerebellum controls the functions concerning motor skills and movements. The brainstem controls the vital function of the heart and breathing.

The foetal brain begins developing around the third week, when the neural plate forms. This eventually will develop into the foetus's brain and nervous system. The neural plate grows and folds, and this becomes the neural tube. At around week seven the neural tube curves and three parts are formed: the forebrain, the midbrain and the hindbrain. The first thing that develops is the brain stem and thus one of the foetus's first functions is to control its involuntary movement such as a heartbeat. During the second trimester (weeks thirteen through twenty-eight) the cerebrum develops to give the foetus a host of motor functions. Its nerves also develop and grow so that it can have many of its fundamental sensations. By the end of the second trimester, the foetus can have coordinated movements and basic sensations such as hearing and tasting. During the third trimester the foetus's brain grows rapidly, especially the cerebrum. The brain size triples its weight during the last trimester, from around three to ten ounces. The appearance of the foetal brain also changes significantly. It goes from a smooth surface to a curved one, looking more like an adult human brain. The cerebral cortex, which is the part of the brain responsible for consciousness, self-awareness, thinking and reasoning, is the last to develop and this development takes place after the foetus is born. The cerebral cortex is the most complex part of the brain and it continues to develop until twenty-five years of age.

Embryology and the ethics of abortion

What factors in the development of the foetus are important for its moral status? Is the size and weight of a foetus important? Is a foetus's resemblance to an adult human person important? Is the foetus's viability important? What about a foetus's developmental maturity and potential?

The size and weight of the foetus is not directly relevant to the moral status of the foetus. Whether a foetus weighs three pounds or eight pounds, or whether a foetus is twelve inches or twenty inches, is not directly relevant to whether a foetus is a person and has rights similar to those of an adult human being. For instance, a premature foetus that is born in week twenty-eight and only weighs three pounds and measures fourteen inches is more of a person than a full-term foetus with anencephaly (born without a major part of its brain). The rationale for this is that our ability to reason and to think, or the potential to do so – and not our size and weight – is the essential property that makes us a human person.

Does a foetus's resemblance to an adult human being affect its moral status? Should the foetus's rights grow proportionally to its growth in resemblance to an adult human being? The answer to this is no, because appearance does not grasp the essence of what it means to be a human person. It is conceivable that there might be things that resemble an adult human being, such as a robot, that do not have any of the functions relevant to the personhood traits of a human person. What makes a human being a person is not just its appearance but also its ability to be conscious, self-aware, reflective, and to think and act voluntarily.

What about viability? Should a foetus's ability to live independent of the pregnant woman serve as threshold of some sort to indicate the increased moral standing of a foetus? It does not seem that a foetus's ability to live independent of the pregnant woman can provide any evidence to support its moral standing. The fact that a foetus can live independent of the pregnant woman only means that the organs necessary for its biological survival have developed sufficiently to function independently. This, however, does not tell us anything of substance about the nature of the foetus as a moral being.

While viability might not indicate anything significant about the personhood of the foetus, it could indicate a change in the moral relationship between the pregnant woman and the foetus. First, if an abortion is seen as a procedure that separates a woman from its foetus – as opposed to the intentional killing of the foetus – then, after viability, an abortion does not necessarily require the killing or death of the foetus. As a consequence, abortions that kill the foetus, after the foetus is viable, might be considered as an unjustified killing of a human organism with the potential to become a person.

Second, contrary to common belief, from an abortion critic's perspective, viability might be a mark for the permissibility of abortion rather than a mark for the impermissibility of abortion. The reasoning behind this conclusion is that, before viability, if the mother separates herself from the foetus, the foetus will necessarily die. Therefore, one might argue that a woman has an obligation to stay connected to the foetus because the foetus needs her for its survival. However, after viability, the foetus no longer needs the mother for its survival, therefore, the mother should no longer be obliged to carry the foetus within her womb. Thus, an abortion critic might argue that an abortion is permissible after viability, if it does not kill the foetus.

What about a foetus's developmental maturity and potential? It does seem that the biological growth of the foetus is relevant to its moral standing. Even if we do not consider a foetus a person, we know that it is a human organism with a real potential to become a person. We also know that its becoming a person is a gradual process that requires complex biological growth that begins at fertilization. With the passing of each moment, therefore, a foetus gets closer and closer to becoming a person. We might conceive of the foetus's life as occupying a large temporal spectrum in which its personhood status and moral standing grow proportionally to its biological growth. If this is the case, then we can conclude that a nine-week foetus is less of a person than a thirty-two-week foetus. Therefore, a nine-week foetus has less of a moral standing than a thirty-two-week foetus. As a result, even though one might believe that it is morally permissible to have an abortion at nine weeks and at thirty-two weeks of pregnancy, one could also hold that it is less morally permissible (or one takes a greater moral risk) when one has an abortion at thirty-two weeks than at nine weeks.

Summary

In this chapter, we examined three facets essential to intelligibly discuss the abortion debate. First, we studied a basic introduction to ethical concepts and theories. We examined the importance of consciousness and rational understanding for moral agency. We distinguished between the moral status of a moral agent and the moral status of an action. We described the three most prominent theories in ethics: consequentialism, deontology and virtue ethics. Under consequentialism, we examined egoism and utilitarianism. Egoisms states that one should always act in one's own long-term self-interest. Utilitarianism states that the right action is always that which will produce the greatest amount of happiness for the greatest number of people. Deontology, on the other hand, focuses on the acts themselves and not on the consequences. It states that moral argents have certain duties and obligations, regardless of the consequences. Finally, virtue ethics centres more on the moral status of the person and the person's character rather than on actions. For this reason we refer to virtue ethics as an agent-centred theory and consequentialism and deontology as act-centred theories.

Second, we examined the anatomy of arguments and how to evaluate deductive and inductive arguments. Deductive arguments are arguments that are constructed so that the conclusion follows necessarily from the premises. First, we evaluated deductive arguments in terms of the form and structure. If they are successful and their form is such that the conclusion follows necessarily from the premises, or it is impossible for the premises to be true and the conclusion to be false, then the argument is valid. If the conclusion does not follow necessarily or if the premises can be true and the conclusion false, then the argument is invalid. Next we examine the truth and falsity of the premises: if the argument is valid and the premises are true, then the argument is a good argument and we call it a sound argument. Inductive arguments are constructed with the intention for the conclusion to follow with some degree of probability. If the conclusion follows from the premises with a higher than 50 per cent probability then the argument is strong. If the conclusion follows with less than a 50 per cent probability the argument is weak. We next examine the truth and falsity of the premises. If a strong inductive argument's premises are all true then it is a good argument and we call it a cogent argument. In any argument, whether deductive or inductive, if one of the premises is false then the argument fails.

Finally, we explored the different stages of foetal development and discussed how they might be relevant to the abortion debate. We divided prenatal development into four parts: The fertilization period, the blastocyst period (weeks two and three), the embryonic period (weeks four through eight) and the foetal period (weeks nine though thirty-eight). The purpose of this study is to highlight the stages and developments that might influence our moral decision-making concerning abortion. With this objective in mind we dedicated a section to the foetal brain and nervous system. We noted that the cerebral cortex, the part of the brain responsible for thinking and reasoning, is the last to develop and this does not occur until very late in the development process.

Study questions

1   What is ethics?
2   What are the main branches of ethics?
3   What are the main ethical theories?

4 What is a good deductive argument?

5 What is a good inductive argument?

6 Why is understanding foetal development important for the abortion debate?

7 What are some of the most relevant foetal stages for the abortion debate and why?

1

Personhood Arguments for the Moral Permissibility of Abortion

In this chapter we examine arguments that defend the position that abortion is morally permissible based on the claim that the foetus is not a person and thus does not have a right to life. We examine two arguments: (1) the argument from undeveloped cognition[1] and (2) the argument from first-person perspective.[2] The distinction some abortion defenders make between a person and a human being is crucial to properly understand these arguments. Some philosophers argue that the necessary properties for personhood are a complete or partial set of complex psychological properties such as consciousness, self-awareness, desires, reasoning and autonomy. They define a human being as a being that belongs to the species *Homo sapiens*, and this entails only a being's physical and biological composition. Therefore, according to these philosophers, being a human being does not guarantee personhood.

Personhood core argument for the moral permissibility of abortion

Let's begin by analysing the abortion defenders core personhood argument.

The first thing to notice about this argument is that the first premise is a moral principle, and it is expressed in an absolute and universal form. The second thing we should notice is that the argument is valid. Therefore, if the premises are true, then the conclusion follows necessarily and must also be

Personhood core argument for the moral permissibility of abortion

Premise 1:   Intentionally killing a non-person human being is always morally permissible.

Premise 2:   A foetus is a non-person human being.

Premise 3:   Abortion is the intentional killing of a foetus.

Premise 4:   Abortion is the intentional killing of a non-person human being (from 2 and 3).

Conclusion: Therefore, abortion is morally permissible.

true. The question that needs to be addressed, then, is whether the premises are true. If all the premises are true, then the argument is sound, and we can be certain that abortion is morally permissible. If one or more of the premises are false, then we can reject the argument as deductively sound; in other words, if one or more of the premises are false, then the conclusion does not follow necessarily from the premises.[3] Let us begin, then, by examining the truth and falsity of the premises.

Assessing the soundness of the argument: Truth and falsity of the premises

Premise (1) states that killing a non-person is always morally permissible. Why is killing a living non-person always morally permissible? The truth of premise (1) can certainly be challenged. The permissibility of killing a living non-person human being seems to depend on the idea that living non-person human beings lack the mental capabilities necessary for personhood, such as consciousness, desires, self-awareness, autonomy and rationality. However, consider the issue of the ethical treatment of animals. Most people would agree that the unjustified killing of a dog or a cat is morally wrong, and dogs and cats do not have the mental capabilities necessary for personhood. Therefore, we need to know on what basis do abortion defenders support the truth of premise (1).

They have at least three possible responses. First, they might claim that while animals are not persons and they do not have the necessary properties for personhood, they are, nevertheless, conscious and sentient beings. Foetuses, on the other hand, lack consciousness and sentience, at least in the early stages of the gestation period, and thus the two cases are not equivalent. However, this response will run into several problems. The first problem is that later foetuses do acquire some basic degree of sentience. More importantly, this response substantially changes the nature of the argument, because it changes the basis for the permissibility of abortion from non-personhood to non-sentience.

A second and more promising response is to change premise (1) and defend a weaker premise: (1.1) Killing a non-person human being is *sometimes* morally permissible. By modifying premise (1) to a weaker claim, the abortion defender is suggesting that it is only sometimes the case that it is morally permissible to kill a non-person human being. However, this solution will require the proponent of the argument to develop a defence of the view that abortions are instances in which killing a non-person human being is not morally wrong. They might, for instance, invoke the argument that the foetus depends on the use of a woman's body for its survival and thus killing it is not the same as killing an independent non-person human being. Let us refer to this as the *dependency principle*.

A third alternative available to the abortion defenders is to substitute premise (1) with the following two premises: (1.2) A non-person living thing does not have a right to life, and (1.3) killing a being that does not have a right to life is prima facie morally permissible. The argument now is grounded on both the conception of personhood and the right to life. Since a foetus is not a person, it does not have a right to life; therefore, an abortion does not violate a foetus's rights and thus does not commit a moral wrong.

This response seems vulnerable to several objections. First, one might point out that, according to this line of argumentation, it would be morally permissible to kill our pets and any other animal that lacks personhood and thus does not have a right to life. But this goes against some of our most basic moral intuitions about the ethics of killing. It raises questions about whether personhood is a necessary condition for a right to life and whether a right to life is a necessary condition for the moral wrongness of killing. Do animals have a right to life, even though they lack personhood? Is it morally permissible to kill animals even if they lack a right to life?

Second, one might be morally obligated not to kill a living thing, based on a criterion other than a living thing's right to life. For instance, one might argue that it is morally wrong to kill an animal that is on the brink of extinction even though it is not a person and even if it lacks a right to life. Furthermore, imagine that the species the animal belongs to plays an important environmental role, and killing it would create an environmental imbalance in the ecosystem that could severely harm the community of people living in its vicinity. In such a case, one might argue that, not only is it morally wrong to kill it, it is morally obligatory to try and sustain its existence. Therefore, it might be morally wrong to kill any non-person animal belonging to that species. These arguments demonstrate that a living thing's lack of personhood status and lack of a right to life are not sufficient to infer the moral permissibility of killing it.

In response, the abortion defender could invoke, once again, the dependency principle. She might, for instance, argue that the case of the foetus is different insofar as the foetus depends on the use of a pregnant woman's body for its survival and thus the pregnant woman's killing it is not morally wrong, if the pregnant woman does not want the foetus and she did not agree to support its life. We could use premise (1.2) and the dependency principle to defend the truth of premise (1). In this case, proponents of the argument might defend the truth of premise (1) based on the claim that the foetus is not a person and thus lacks a right to life. In addition, the foetus's life depends on the pregnant woman and thus the pregnant woman has the right to kill the foetus without violating the foetus's right to life. Notice, however, that this line of argumentation only gives the pregnant woman the right to kill the foetus and not necessarily the right to have a third person to kill the foetus for her.[4]

From this discussion, I hope it is evident that defending the moral principle in premise (1) is not as easy as it might seem. Another important insight from our analysis of premise (1) is that while the personhood of the foetus *seems* to be a sufficient condition to defend the abortion critic's position (i.e. if it can be shown that the foetus is a person, then killing it, without justification, would be equivalent to murder and morally wrong),[5] it is not a sufficient condition for the abortion defender's position (i.e. if it can be shown that the foetus is not a person, then it does not follow that it is morally permissible to kill it). For now, however, we will grant the justification of the truth of premise (1) based on (1.2) and the dependency principle. Therefore, if the foetus is not a person and it is dependent on the pregnant woman for its survival, then an abortion does not violate a foetus's right to life and the pregnant woman's killing it is morally permissible.

Personhood core argument for the permissibility of abortion restated

Premises 4 and 7 are not basic premises (meaning they are derived from other premises) and are derived from premises 1, 3, 5 and 6. We have accepted premises 1, 2 and 5 for now as true. The only basic premises remaining are 3 and 6. Premise 6 is simply the definition of an abortion so it seems incontrovertibly true. However, this premise can also be challenged. Other definitions of abortions are possible. For instance, one might argue that an abortion is not the killing of a foetus but rather the intentional separation of a pregnant woman from an unwanted foetus. The death of the foetus is an accidental result of the separation of the foetus from the woman. This

Premise 1:   A non-person does not have a right to life.

Premise 2:   Killing a being that lacks a right to life and is dependent on another person for its survival is prima facie morally permissible if the person does not want the being and does not agree to support its life.

Premise 3:   A foetus is a non-person human being.

Premise 4:   A foetus does not have a right to life (from 1 and 3).

Premise 5:   A foetus is dependent on a woman for its survival (dependency principle).

Premise 6:   Abortion is the killing of an unwanted foetus by the pregnant woman (by definition).

Premise 7:   Abortion is the killing of an unwanted being that does not have a right to life and is dependent on a woman's body for its survival (from 4, 5 and 6).

Conclusion: Therefore, abortion is morally permissible (from 2 and 7).

definition does not necessarily entail the death of the foetus, for if the foetus can survive without the assistance of the woman, the woman is not justified in killing the foetus.[6] Since cases in which a woman has an abortion and the foetus survives are rare, we will accept the notion that an abortion entails (or brings about) the death of the foetus, and thus it essentially constitutes the killing of the foetus.

The final premise remaining is 3 or *A foetus is a non-person human being*. If this premise is demonstrated to be true, then the argument is sound. Thus, we have a valid argument with all true premises, which means that the conclusion, 'abortion is morally permissible', is *true*. Recall that to undermine a deductive argument one must show that either the argument form is invalid or one of the premises is false. The Restated Personhood Argument for the Permissibility of Abortion is valid and thus the only way to reject it is to show that one of the premises is false. We have shown that the basic premises 1, 5 and 6 can be defended. This leaves the anti-abortion proponent in a difficult position, because the only way to reject the conclusion would be by showing that premise 3, 'A foetus is a non-person human being', is false.

Is a foetus a person? In this chapter, we study two arguments that attempt to demonstrate that the foetus is a human being but *not* a person. If they succeed, then the argument is sound and the conclusion that abortion is morally permissible is true. Therefore, there is a lot at stake in these arguments.

Personhood argument from developed cognition for the moral permissibility of abortion

Some philosophers view morality as a phenomenon that takes place within a society or community of persons. It is only within such a community of persons that moral concepts such as inalienable rights and the right to life, liberty and the pursuit of happiness make any sense. If one does not belong to such a community or society, then one cannot partake in the moral community. Moreover, if someone cannot partake in the moral community then the moral concepts of that moral community simply cannot be attributed to that non-member. For instance, Mary Anne Warren sees the moral community as 'the set of beings with full and equal moral rights'.[7] However, to participate in such a community the members must have cognitive powers that are sufficiently developed to carry on sophisticated forms of thinking. They must be able to understand and reason, and they must be able to make moral decision and communicate with other members of the moral community. It is only when members have this form of developed cognition that we can say that they are persons and they can be a part of the moral community.

This analysis of the moral community fleshes out what some philosophers believe is a serious fallacy of equivocation that is common in the abortion debate with the term 'human'. Before 1972, many philosophers used the terms 'human' and 'person' interchangeably to mean and refer to the same thing. However, doing so gives a certain hidden advantage to abortion critics and results in fallacious, question-begging arguments. The word 'human' has at least two significantly different meanings that get conflated within the abortion debate. For instance, consider the following argument:

1 Killing innocent **human** beings is morally wrong.
2 A foetus is a **human** being.
3 Abortion is the killing of a foetus.
4 Therefore, an abortion is morally wrong.

Notice that the term 'human' is used twice in premises 1 and 2. For the argument to be sound, it must be both valid and have true premises. However, some might argue that the term 'human' in the first and second premises are not being used consistently, which would make one of the premises false and thus the argument unsound. This is known as the fallacy of equivocation.

Let's look at this fallacy more carefully. In the first premise, human refers to a full-fledged adult human being that has the cognitive abilities we attribute to a person, such as consciousness, desires, self-awareness, rationality, communicative abilities and self-determination. However, in the second premise human refers to an organism that belongs to the species *Homo sapiens* but does not necessarily have the personhood traits of a full-fledged adult human being. If we use 'humans' consistently to refer to persons, then premise (1) will be true and premise (2) false and the argument unsound. If we use the 'humans' consistently to refer to a biological human non-person, then premise (1) will be false and premise (2) true and the argument unsound.

In the first premise, the term 'human' refers to the moral sense of human, that is, those members that make up the moral community that share the same full set of equal rights. In the second premise, the term refers to genetic sense of human, that is, those beings that belong to the human species. Many arguments for the moral impermissibility of abortion blur this distinction and assume that the term 'human' in both premises refer to one and the same kinds of beings and the same set of beings composed of exactly the same members. However, it is not the case that human beings in the genetic sense are the same as human beings in the moral sense. This requires further demonstration, and so one important factor in the abortion debate is determining who belongs to the moral community and who can be considered persons.

Warren, for instance, defends the view that the moral community should be defined to include only *persons* and not all human beings. If we can determine what is a person, then we can establish who belongs to the moral community. As a consequence, belonging to the human species is neither a sufficient nor a necessary condition for belonging to the moral community. Only persons are the kinds of beings with full and equal moral rights. Warren argues:

> Can it be established that genetic humanity is sufficient for the moral humanity? I think that there are very good reasons for not defining the moral community in this way. I would like to suggest an alternative way of defining the moral community, which I will argue for only to the extent of explaining why it is, or should be, self-evident. The suggestion is simply that the moral community consists of all and only *people*, rather than all and only human beings; and probably the best way of demonstrating its self-evidence is by considering the concept of persons, and what the decision that a being is or is not a person implies about its moral rights.[8]

How can we determine what is a person?

Criteria for personhood

Let us consider a thought experiment suggested by Warren. Imagine that you were to go to another planet where you encountered an alien race completely unlike yourself. Your mission is to determine what kind of beings they are and what kind of treatment they deserve. Are they the kind of beings that we should attribute inalienable rights to, such as the right to life and pursuit of happiness? If so, then we ought to respect their rights, even if they are not human beings. The purpose of this thought exercise is to try limiting our human bias, for we are strongly predisposed to think that human beings are persons in virtue solely of their belonging to the human species. But there is no reason why we should assume that these two concepts, human being and person, mean or refer to the same things.

This thought experiment will also force us to think outside of our commonly accepted categories, which we take for granted and accept out of habit and custom, even if they are improperly formed and inaccurate representations of reality. In this scenario, we cannot rely on the category of humanity; we are forced to look for properties that we believe would make these alien beings worthy of respect and membership in a moral community, despite their not being human.

What evidence would you look for in an effort to make conclusions about the aliens' personhood status? Warren argues that we can point to five traits that could roughly and approximately give us some conclusive evidence about whether the aliens are or are not persons and worthy of being attributed fundamental rights. The first trait is *consciousness*. Are the alien beings conscious? Are they sentient? Can they have experiences, feelings, desires, wants, intentions, thoughts and ideas? Can they experience pain? A second trait is *reasoning*. Do the aliens exhibit an ability to solve problems? Do they have artefacts that require thought and reasoning skills? The third trait is *self-motivated activity*. Do the aliens exhibit any form of autonomy in their actions? Do they behave in ways that would indicate to us that they are self-determined beings? Do they act towards certain goals and with specific intentions? The fourth trait is the ability to *communicate*. The form or method of communication is not important. What is important is that they can somehow form ideas and share those ideas with other members of their species. The fifth is the trait of *self-awareness*. Are the aliens self-aware? Can they make a distinction between themselves and others? Do they have some notion of personal identity? In summation, then, Warren claims there are five traits that are central to the concept of personhood: (1) consciousness, (2) reasoning, (3) self-motivating activity, (4) communication and (5) self-awareness.[9]

Does a being need all of these traits to be considered a person? Most would agree that they do not need all of these traits. For instance, Warren argues that if a being has consciousness, reasoning and self-motivation, then the being should be considered a person. Moreover, these intellectual and psychological traits seem to be related; it is difficult to imagine that one could be a conscious, reasoning and self-motivated being and not be self-aware or unable to communicate. It seems that some combination of these five psychological properties would point to a sufficiently sophisticated cognitive being that ought to be treated with the kind of respect we would attribute to human persons. Some combination of these traits would also demonstrate that these beings deserve to be members of our moral community. For instance, if the aliens were conscious and thus had feelings, experiences and desires, and if they could reason and make deliberative decisions, this would be sufficient for them to be worthy of our respect as persons. As a result, they should be considered the kind of beings that have inalienable rights such as the right to life, liberty and the pursuit of happiness.

What is also clear is that if the aliens lack all of these five cognitive capabilities and have nothing resembling them, then they are more like inanimate objects than like animals or persons. In other words, if they have no organs or systems through which they could have a semblance of consciousness, then they could not have feelings, wants, desires or experiences. They cannot suffer or feel pain, and they cannot be sad or happy. If they lacked these most basic cognitive abilities, then they probably will not be rational, self-motivated, communicative or self-aware. Warren argues with respect to a foetus:

> All we need to claim, to demonstrate that a fetus is not a person is that any being which satisfies *none* of (1)–(5) is certainly not a person. I consider this claim to be so obvious that I think that anyone who denied it, and claimed that a being which satisfied none of (1)–(5) was a person all the same, would thereby demonstrate that he had no notion at all of what a person is – perhaps because he had confused the concept of a person with that of a genetic humanity.[10]

Let us imagine, for argument's sake, that we can determine with certainty that the aliens lack all of these five cognitive abilities. What would our conclusion be with respect to their status as persons? It would be difficult to conceive how we could grant these aliens any kind of status other than that of a living thing. They might be considered the equivalent to a plant of sorts or an oyster. Plants and trees are considered living things, but some might argue that they should not be attributed the same rights as are attributed to animals and persons, because they do not have the same level of consciousness that animals and persons have. Thus, we might categorize these aliens to be at the level of plants and grant them a vegetative status. With this status, however, they could not be granted the right to life, and it would not be morally wrong to kill them. There might be other reasons why we ought not to kill the aliens, but these would be reasons not related to their status as persons. For instance, we might argue that all life should be respected or that all life has intrinsic value. But these are not personhood arguments.

An abortion critic might object that the list of cognitive abilities is vague and what is required is that the arguments further elaborate these mental capabilities. But this is incorrect. For our purposes, we simply need general descriptions and conceptions of these cognitive abilities. We do not need a sophisticated, scientific or a very precise definition of consciousness, reasoning, self-determination, communication and self-awareness. These abilities can easily be assessed through an individual's behaviour and determined through a community's rituals and history. We can observe and take notice of how the aliens behave, how they treat each other and what kinds of things they have produced throughout their history. This data would provide sufficient evidence to make an intelligible and informed opinion of these aliens' mental abilities. For instance, if they have sophisticated machinery, we can infer that they have reasoning abilities. If they have any structures or facilities that they have constructed, we can also make sound judgements about their level of mental abilities, depending on the sophistication of the structures and facilities. The community's governance, how they live and how they treat each other would also be sufficient signs of the level and kinds of mental capacities we ought to attribute to these beings. Thus, the argument only requires that we provide a mundane and approximate conception of these mental abilities.

The foetus is not a person

The next step in this argument is to put the foetus through a similar test. Abortion defenders argue that if we examine the foetus, especially at the very early stages of development, it lacks all five of these attributes. The foetus is not conscious, it cannot reason, it lacks the power of self-determination, it cannot communicate, and it is not self-aware. The foetus, therefore, lacks all of these five mental capabilities that we normally attribute to persons, and, as a result, a foetus cannot be a member of a moral community. Based solely on its intrinsic nature at the time of its foetal gestation, a foetus is not the kind of being that is worthy of inalienable rights such as the right to life, liberty and the pursuit of happiness. Warren concludes the following:

> Thus it is clear that even though a seven- or eight-month fetus has features which make it apt to arouse in us almost the same powerful protective instinct as is commonly aroused by a small infant, nevertheless, it is not significantly more personlike than a very small embryo. It is *somewhat* more personlike; it can apparently feel and respond to pain, and it can even have a rudimentary form of consciousness, insofar as its brain is quite active. Nevertheless, it seems safe to say that that it is not fully conscious, in the way an infant of a few months is, and that it cannot reason, or communicate messages of infinitely many sorts, does not engage in self-

motivated activity, and has no self-awareness. Thus, in the *relevant* respect a fetus, even a fully developed one, is considerably less personlike than is the average mature mammal, indeed the average fish.[11]

Notice that this argument does not deny that a foetus is a product of two human beings. It also does not deny that a foetus is a human being in the genetic sense, since it is alive and has a complete genetic code. Instead, it only denies that the foetus is a person. The foetus is in a similar situation to an adult human being who lacks all five of these traits and would still be considered human but not a person. For instance, a human being who, for whatever reason, has lost all of his or her mental capabilities would no longer be considered a person and a member of the moral community. Therefore, as premise 3 states, a foetus is a *non-person human being*.

If we accept this definition of personhood, then we must accept premise 3 as true, unless it can be shown that a foetus has some of these traits at some point during its gestation period, or unless it can be shown that a foetus deserves to be considered a person in virtue of its resembling a person or its potentiality to become a person.

Answering some challenges

Can't the foetus have some rudimentary degree of consciousness at a developed stage of gestation? If so, wouldn't this be sufficient to grant it some degree of personhood. According to the American College of Obstetrician and Gynecologist, at the end of the 8th week of gestation age, a foetus has already begun to develop all major organs and body systems, including the brain and the nervous system. Moreover, at the gestation age of 13–16 weeks, a foetus may be able to respond to sounds in a reflex manner, but it can't 'hear' them if hearing means being consciously aware of them. Between weeks 21 and 24 a foetus's brain is developing rapidly, and it can respond to sounds outside the womb. Consciousness is one of the traits to be considered for personhood, however, there are other traits that seem to be much more mentally complex and sophisticated such as reasoning, self-motivation, communication and self-awareness. Most abortion defenders do not believe that we need to demonstrate that a being has all five traits to conclude that the foetus is a person. For instance, Warren claims that if we could show the first three (i.e. consciousness, reasoning and self-motivation) that would be sufficient. A foetus, even if it has consciousness at a very basic level, is far from developing reasoning and self-motivation. Therefore, with consciousness alone it would not be considered a person. Warren does concede that, since the foetus is continuously developing and it is always moving towards personhood, there is something to be said about a foetus's rights evolving and gaining strength in a corresponding fashion.

What about the foetus resembling a human being? Is this enough for it to be included in the moral community? We have to be careful how we understand resemblance. Resemblance is important if we are considering the appropriate properties that make a being a person, that is, the five mental properties described above. Physical resemblance should not be a determining factor when considering the personhood of a being. However, it can be a very strong psychological factor that can have a strong influence in favour of the abortion critics' position. When the foetus begins to look more like a human being, killing it will seem more reprehensible, and it will appear that we are killing a person. Nevertheless, resemblance based solely on physical properties does not help the foetus gain access to membership in a moral community any more than an adult human who has lost all of his or her mental faculties.

The abortion critic might point out that there are essential differences between an adult who has lost his mental capabilities and a foetus. First, while a foetus does not have the traits of a person, it does have a real potential to acquire these traits; second, while the adult human person is defective, the foetus is not defective; its lack of mental capacities is a normal part of its developmental process. Shouldn't a foetus's potential to become a person be considered of great value? The argument from potentiality has some weight with many abortion defenders. For instance, Warren notes that certainly this is a possibility: 'It is hard to deny that the fact that an entity is a potential person is a strong prima facie reason for not destroying it; but we need not conclude from this that the potential person has a right to life.'[12] Therefore, the potentiality to become a human person is not sufficient for us to ascribe a being a right to life. The argument from potentiality is much more complex and an entire section has been devoted to it in Chapter 2.

Infanticide issue

There is one last major difficulty that this view needs to deal with. If Warren's theory on personhood is correct, then newborn babies and even young children might not be considered persons and thus might not have a right to life. As a consequence, it would be morally permissible to kill innocent healthy babies and young children. In other words, the killing of infants would not be considered murder or the taking of a person's life. But killing innocent and healthy babies and young children seems self-evidently morally wrong. In fact, many philosophers use this as the standard for determining when a theory has gone awry. Do abortion defenders who justify their view on the non-personhood status of the foetus also believe that it is morally permissible to kill infants?

One way to respond to this problem is to argue that while killing newborn babies or young children is not morally wrong based on the violation of their right to life, it is morally wrong based on some other reason. For instance, once a foetus is born, it no longer depends solely on the mother and therefore their value as potential persons no longer needs to be weighed against a woman's freedom over her reproductive choices. In other words, once a foetus has entered the world its value as a potential person can be considered in and of itself. Once the foetus is born, the mother, obviously, cannot terminate her pregnancy, and thus cannot have an abortion; consequently, she no longer has any right to kill the newborn child.

In addition, once the foetus is born and it becomes independent of the mother, it can also relate to other people in the moral community in a much more autonomous way. In other words, the child now has a robust independence from the mother, and members of the moral community can have an interest in the child as a potential person. Moreover, notice that the Personhood Argument in Defence of Abortion Restated will not work to defend infanticide because premise 2 (Killing a being that lacks a right to life and is dependent on another person for its survival is prima facie morally permissible if the person does not want the being and does not agree in support its life.) is no longer applicable.

Finally, there might be alternative reasons why it is wrong to kill infants. For instance, Warren points out that one reason why it might be morally wrong to kill infants is that many people in society value them; that is, they are the kinds of things that people want and confer great value on. In this sense, she argues, infants are like natural resources or great works of arts. In addition, most people do not want to see infants destroyed and thus society at large confers upon them a value and desire for their preservation. These reasons are all extrinsic and thus even though killing an infant may not be morally wrong in and of itself, it is wrong given the value our culture has conferred upon infants.

Personhood argument from first-person perspective for the moral permissibility of abortion

The main proponent of this argument is Lynne Rudder Baker. She is mostly interested in the question of personhood from a metaphysical perspective. She develops what she calls the *constitution view* of personhood. However, she also realizes that her metaphysical constitution view of personhood has important and relevant consequences for the abortion issue; therefore, let us examine these as they relate to personhood. She begins her metaphysical enquiry by addressing the question: When does a person begin? However, immediately she diverts this question into a more fundamental one: What is a person? Baker submits that this question has two different answers, one grounded in biology and another in ontology. The biological question can be answered through empirical facts. However, the ontological question is a philosophical question and while empirical facts are relevant they alone cannot provide an answer. Therefore, we can divide the question of personhood into two parts: (1) When does an organism begin? and (2) When does a person begin?

Biological question: When does a human organism begin?

The prominent position for when a human organism begins is at fertilization. However, there are two problems with this response: first, all human developmental processes are gradual, including fertilization, and thus we cannot provide a specific point in time when fertilization takes place. Instead, it takes place over a twenty-four-hour period. Second, when fertilization is completed there is some time after within which the fertilized egg can split and become two or more individual human beings. This possibility of twinning precludes us from identifying the zygote as an individual human organism.

Consider, for instance, that a zygote, call it A, divides and we then have two individual organisms. Let us call them B and C. There is, obviously, a causal connection between A and B and between A and C, however, we can say neither that A is identical to B nor that A is identical to C. For if we were to hold such identities, then we could conclude (from the principle of transitivity of identity) that B is identical (one and the same individual) with C, but this is logically impossible for they are two different human organisms. Therefore, it is logically impossible to hold that a zygote is identical with the resulting embryo(s), and, if that is the case, then it is also physically impossible. Therefore, we can safely conclude that a human *individual* organism begins approximately two weeks after fertilization, when the blastocyst is implanted in the womb. As in fertilization, this process is also a gradual one, and thus there is no discrete moment in time that we can demarcate as the cut-off for the beginning of a human organism. Nevertheless, we can conclude that a human organism comes into existence approximately fourteen days after fertilization.

Ontological question: When does a human person begin?

In an effort to determine when a person begins, two questions need to be addressed: (1) What is a human person? and (2) What is the relationship between a human organism and a human person? In answering the second,

Baker argues that the relation between a human organism and a human person is based on *constitution*. She defines it as follows: 'A human person is wholly constituted by a human organism, without being identical to the constituting organism.'[13] In other words, the fundamental and basic elements of human persons are the human organisms (i.e. the basic elements of human persons are the physical, material and biological stuff of human organism), but human organism and human persons do not necessarily overlap temporally.

To understand a little better Baker's proposal, let us consider her analogy with the statue. A statue is constrictive of the clay from which it is made; however, it is not just clay, it is more than that. Similarly, a human person is constitutive of a human organism, but it is not just a human organism; it is more than that. What is most important, for our purpose, is that when human organisms come into existence, human persons do not necessarily also come into existence. Human organisms and human persons can have different temporal existences.

Let us examine the first question: What is a person? To answer this we need to determine what are the essential properties of personhood, as we tried to do in the previous section. However, Baker has a different answer to this question. First, she takes personhood to be a 'primary kind' or an irreducible ontological entity. This means that persons refer to a kind of entity that cannot be reduced to another kind of entity. This is important because it marks an important difference between being a human organism and a human person. To say that a human person is a primary kind and that a human organism is a different primary kind means that human organisms and human persons are different kinds of things, and one cannot be reduced to the other. Moreover, they each have different essential properties. The essential property is a trait that makes the thing the kind of thing it is. A human person can only exist when their essential properties exist. It is impossible to have a human organism without the essential properties of a human organism. Likewise, it is impossible to have a human person without the essential properties of a human person.

The essential property of personhood is *first-person perspective*. A first-person perspective refers to the mental capacity 'to think of oneself without the use of any name, description, or demonstrative; it is the ability to conceive of oneself as oneself, from the inside, as it were'.[14] Therefore, a person is any being with a first-person perspective. There can be non-humans with first-person perspectives. For instance, an extraterrestrial person (i.e. an extraterrestrial being with first-person perspective) would be constituted in its particular extraterrestrial organism. To understand Baker's conception of human persons, we must get a better understanding of what is a first-person perspective.

Constitution view and first-person perspective

A robust first-person perspective is the cognitive ability that allows one to have a robust inner mental life; it is the mental capability to be self-aware and self-conscious. It allows one to assess and evaluate one's own thoughts, behaviour, experiences and life. It allows for moral agency and rationality. According to Baker, being conscious and having desires and beliefs is not sufficient for a first-person perspective. Animals such as dogs and cats may have this level of consciousness and yet not have robust first-person perspectives. A first-person perspective, therefore, refers to a very high-level state of consciousness in which one can reflect upon one's past and future and assess it based on various criteria, such as morality, happiness.

Baker also introduces the concept of *rudimentary* first-person perspective. She defines it as follows: 'A being has a rudimentary first-person perspective if and only if (i) it is conscious, a sentient being; (ii) it has a capacity to imitate; and (iii) its behavior is explainable only by attribution of beliefs, desires, and intentions.'[15] According to Baker, infants are a good example of beings that have rudimentary first-person perspective but not robust first-person perspective. First, they are conscious and sentient beings. They have feelings and sensations, and can feel pain and endure suffering. Second, psychologists have shown that infants have an endowed ability to imitate behaviour from the first days after their birth; therefore, they have the capacity to imitate. Third, infants are intentional beings because they can have basic desires, such as the desire to eat and drink. In addition to infants, many animals meet the criteria for rudimentary first-person perspective. For instance, primates are conscious and sentient beings, have the capacity to imitate and are intentional beings (i.e. they have desires, beliefs etc.). Therefore, some non-human mammals also have a rudimentary first-person perspective.

Baker goes on to draw an important distinction between non-humans with rudimentary first-person perspectives and humans with rudimentary first-person perspectives. She claims that the former exhibit this cognitive ability as their maximum and permanent state. However, in the case of humans, their rudimentary first-person perspectives are the building blocks for a robust first-person perspectives. Thus, for human infants this cognitive state is only a preliminary developmental stage that will continue to develop towards a robust version, as ascribed to mature adult persons. She also grants a privileged status to humans who are defective and whose rudimentary first-person perspective fails to develop into a robust first-person perspective. She explains:

> This is not to say that a person will develop a robust first-person perspective: perhaps severely autistic individuals, or retarded individuals, have only rudimentary first-person perspectives. However, they are still

persons, albeit very impaired, because they have rudimentary first-person perspectives and are of a kind – human animal – that develops a robust first-person perspective.[16]

Given the definition of robust first-person perspective, rudimentary first-person perspective and the distinction between non-human and human rudimentary first-person perspectives, Baker defines human person (HP) as follows: '(HP) x constitutes a human person at t if and only if x is a human organism at t and x has a rudimentary or robust first-person perspective at t.'[17]

According to Baker, therefore, a human person comes into existence at the time it develops rudimentary first-person perspective, which is around the time of birth or possibly a little before birth. We have already seen that a human organism comes into being approximately fourteen days after fertilization. Therefore, there is a period of time when the human organism is developing that it is not yet a human person.

Potentiality: Capacity for a rudimentary perspective

At this point, abortion critics will submit that we should extend the notion of personhood to include human organisms that have the capacity to develop rudimentary first-person perspective even though they have not yet acquired it. After all, rudimentary first-person perspective is not first-person perspective; it is only a potentiality for first-person perspective. Thus, it would make sense to assent to the personhood of the human organism from its very origin. Baker examines the possibility of HP*: '(HP*) x constitutes a human person at t if and only if x is a human organism at t and either x has a robust first-person perspective or x has capacities that, in normal course, produce a being with a robust first-person perspective.'[18] This captures the idea that personhood should be ascribed to organisms in virtue of their potentiality to develop a robust first-person perspective. Baker rejects this proposal for two reasons.

First, there is a metaphysical relevant distinction between having a capacity in-hand and having a remote capacity. A capacity in-hand refers to the ability to carry out a certain act or function in the present moment even though one is not carrying out such an act or function in the present moment. For instance, one may have an in-hand capacity to walk even though one is not walking in the present moment. This means that if one decided to walk, then one could do so; thus, one has an in-hand capacity to walk. For instance, a newborn infant does not have an in-hand capacity to walk. Instead, it has a remote capacity to walk, because it has a potentiality to develop such capacities in the future. The status of an in-hand capacity to walk in an adult and a remote capacity to walk in an infant are very different. We can also refer to these as first-order capacities and second-order capacities, respectively. Relating this to the abortion issue, we can argue that an infant has a rudimentary first-person perspective as a first-order capacity insofar as it has rudimentary first-person perspective in-hand. An embryo, on the other hand, has a rudimentary first-person capacity as a second-order capacity because it only has the potential to develop this capacity in the future, and thus they are essentially different.

The second reason that Baker rejects the potentiality argument concerns the nature and properties attributed to rudimentary first-person perspective. These properties are (1) sentience, (2) ability to imitate and (3) intentionality. Baker claims that these are specifically *personal properties* because they are what make an individual a person. These properties are morally relevant because they indicate an already existing degree of consciousness and some degree of personhood. A mere human organism that has not yet acquired rudimentary first-person perspective has none of these properties. For instance, the properties of an early human foetus resemble a human person only in its physical and biological properties but not in any of its personal properties (i.e. those which make an individual a person). According to Baker, then, it is the personal properties and not the biological properties (e.g. having a heart, lungs, limbs) that make a human being a human person. Under the constitution view, it is only when a human organism acquires these properties that a human person comes into existence. A human organism and a human person are two different kinds of things, and they each come into existence at different moments in the gestation period.

The constitution view and the abortion debate

The significance of the constitution view of personhood is unique and revolutionary. The view is different from other abortion defenders' views, such as Warren's, in that it clearly precludes the moral permissibility of infanticide. The conclusion that can be drawn from the constitutional view is that the human zygote and foetus, from its moment of conception and until it develops a rudimentary first-person perspective, is not a person. For simplicity, we will refer to the developing human organism during this period of time as the 'human foetus'. Baker's central thesis, which she refers to as thesis (O), is '*a human fetus is an organism that does not constitute a person*'.[19] What does this mean for the abortion debate?

First, we should be careful not to conclude that given that a human foetus is not yet a person, it is morally permissible to kill it, and thus abortion is morally permissible. One could have good reasons for not killing a non-person human organism, and one could uphold a system of values that ascribes a significant moral status to non-person human organisms.[20] Nevertheless, the constitution view has a significant influence on the kinds of arguments that will and will not succeed in the abortion debate. One important result of Baker's thesis (which it shares with other personhood arguments for the permissibility of abortion) is that it precludes any anti-abortion argument to use as a premise the claim that 'a fetus is a person'. This is significant because an argument based on this claim leads to the conclusion that an abortion is the killing of an innocent human person. Moreover, if the foetus is a person, then we must ascribe to the foetus the right to life (the same right to life that we would ascribe to an adult human person). Therefore, if we grant that the foetus is a person, it will be very difficult to justify an abortion. In almost all cases, abortion would be morally wrong, and a pregnant woman's circumstances, no matter how difficult and grave they may be, would be morally irrelevant. Baker describes the situation as follows: 'Morally speaking, the thesis that the fetus is a person renders the pregnant female invisible.'[21]

On the other hand, if we accept the metaphysical constitution view of human persons, then all arguments that rely on the premise 'a human fetus is a person' will be *deductively unsound* or *inductively uncogent* because the premise is false. The consequences of this are significant, because even though it does not lead to a specific conclusion in the abortion debate (it does not morally condemn or condone abortion), it opens the possibilities for discussing the abortion issue within a broader context, allowing for greater consideration of pregnant women's circumstances and the larger societal problems within each particular case. As Baker puts it so eloquently, 'Thesis (O) is, however, significant for thinking about abortion, because it removes a whole category of arguments that short-circuit careful moral thought.'[22] According to Baker, thesis (O) has three benefits for the abortion debate.

The first benefit is that it eliminates all anti-abortion arguments based on the right to life.[23] These arguments disregard all of the particular circumstances given in any particular case of abortion, except for, possibly, cases of self-defence, when the pregnant woman's life is in danger. Thesis (O) permits us to opens up the discussion and to give many other factors moral relevance in the deliberation over the moral status of an abortion decision. For example, issues such as the following become relevant and important to consider: the circumstances surrounding the pregnancy, that is, how a woman became pregnant? (e.g. incest, rape); the age of the pregnant woman; the health of the pregnant woman; the health of the foetus; a pregnant woman's financial circumstances; a pregnant woman's psychological condition; a pregnant woman's current family situation; a pregnant woman's religious beliefs etc.

A second benefit of thesis (O) is that it shifts the discussion from the morality of killing a person to the morality of bringing a person into existence. If we reject the premise that a foetus is a person, then abortion is not about the morality of killing a person. If we accept the constitution view, then the foetus is only a human organism and a person comes into being only when it has acquired rudimentary first-person perspective. Therefore, the central question for the abortion issue becomes, 'Under what conditions and circumstance is it morally acceptable to bring into existence a human person?' This is a very different way of approaching the abortion issue that entails very different considerations and moral assessments.

Finally, the third benefit of accepting thesis (O) is that it provides the right conditions to appreciate the complexity of the abortion issue. By precluding the anti-abortion right to life arguments, the abortion debate unveils a plethora of new morally relevant circumstances, conditions and situations that change and vary from case to case, forcing a moral assessment and evaluation of abortion issues at the particular level of individual cases. Thus, no general response to the abortion issue will be possible; instead, each case will vary given the particular facts surrounding it.

Objections

The most glaring problem with Baker's view for the abortion defender's position is not an inherent defect of her argument; instead, it is that her view does not deliver the conclusion that most abortion defenders desire. The only conclusion that the constitutional view of personhood claims is that an abortion is not morally wrong insofar as it does not violate the right to life of a person. However, it abstains from advancing further and committing to any particular conclusions about the morality of abortion. It leaves open the possibility that abortion is morally wrong for other reasons than the right to life of the foetus.

A second objection concerns Baker's treatment of mentally handicapped human beings. Baker provides a justification to make a morally relevant distinction between animals with rudimentary first-person perspective and human infants with rudimentary first-person perspective. She claims that for the former it is a final developing point in animals while for the latter it is only a stage of transition to a robust first-person perspective. However, this distinction is not applicable to humans who are permanently psychologically damaged and only have rudimentary first-person perspective as a final developing point. She wants to claim an exception for these human beings, but it is difficult to understand on what rationale such an exception should be based, except for arbitrary bias for our own species. Therefore, this seems to present a challenge to Baker's view.

Summary

In this chapter, we considered two personhood arguments in defence of the moral permissibility of abortion. We began by constructing the stem argument from which both burgeon, 'The Personhood Core Argument for the Moral Permissibility of Abortion Restated'. It goes as follows: (1) A non-person does not have a right to life. (2) Killing a being that lacks a right to life and is dependent on another person for its survival is prima facie morally permissible, if the person does not want the being and does not agree to support its life. (3) **A foetus is a non-person human being.** (4) A foetus does not have a right to life (from 1 and 3). (5) A foetus is dependent on a woman for its survival (dependency principle). (6) Abortion is the killing of an unwanted foetus by the pregnant woman (by definition). (7) Abortion is the killing of a being that does not have a right to life and is dependent on a woman's body or its survival (from 4, 5 and 6). Therefore, abortion is morally permissible (from 2 and 7). The goal of personhood arguments in defence of the moral permissibility of abortion is to demonstrate the truth of premise (3). The arguments assume that if we can show that a foetus is not a person, then we can conclude that abortions are morally permissible.

We examined two arguments that attempt to demonstrate that the foetus is not a person: (1) the argument from developed cognition and (2) the argument from first-person perspective. Both arguments depend on the distinction between being a person and being a human being. This distinction is based on certain cognitive functions that are essential to personhood. The argument from developed cognition emphasized the functions of consciousness, self-awareness, ability to communicate, autonomy and reason. And the argument from first-person perspective emphasized the function to understand oneself as oneself and as different from others.

The first argument takes for granted that a being's lack of personhood will provide sufficient justification for the moral permissibility to kill that being. As we have discussed above, this view can be challenged. It seems that the most epistemologically conservative conclusion we can draw from the arguments presented in this chapter (if they are indeed successful) are the following: (1) All arguments for the moral impermissibility of abortion that depend on the false claim that 'the fetus is a person' are deductively unsound. (2) Insofar as abortions are not the same as murder, they are morally permissible. (3) Given (1) and (2), even if abortions are found to be immoral, based on some other reason other than that of the personhood of the foetus and the foetus's right to life, it will be highly improbable that abortions should be illegal. This final conclusion can have important ramifications for the legal status of abortion in the United States.

Study questions

1 Explain the core personhood argument for the permissibility of abortion.

2 According to some abortion defenders, what is the difference between a person and a human being? Why is this distinction so important for the abortion debate?

3 Explain the 'personhood argument for the permissibility of abortion restated'. What is the major difference between this argument and the core personhood argument?

4 Explain the personhood argument from developed cognition for the moral permissibility of abortion. Consider several possible objections and criticisms of the argument. Do you think these objections are successful? Why or why not?

5 Explain the personhood argument from first-person perspective for the moral permissibility of abortion. Consider several possible objections and criticisms of the argument. Do you think these objections are successful? Why or why not?

6 Given the arguments discussed in this chapter, assess the relevance of the personhood issue for the abortion debate.

2

Personhood Arguments for the Moral Wrongness of Abortion

In this chapter we examine arguments defending the position that the foetus is a human person from conception, or close to the moment of conception, and that the foetus has a right to life. Therefore, all induced abortions are morally wrong. We examine three deontological arguments: (1) the argument from functioning as a person versus being a person,[1] (2) the argument from possibility and (3) the argument from potentiality.[2]

Abortion critics' personhood core argument

All three arguments begin with a similar form as follows.

Personhood core argument for the moral wrongness of abortion

Premise 1:   Intentionally killing an innocent human person is always morally wrong.

Premise 2:   A foetus at the time of conception or close to the time of conception is an innocent human person.

Premise 3:   Abortion is the killing of a foetus.

Premise 4:   Abortion is the killing an innocent human person (follows from 2 and 3).

Conclusion: Therefore, abortion is always morally wrong.

First, notice that this argument is valid, so if the premises are true, then the conclusion follows necessarily. In other words, the form of the argument is such that it is impossible for the premises to be true and the conclusion false. As a result, the issue that needs to be addressed is whether the premises are true. If all the premises are true, then the argument is sound, and we can be certain that all abortions are morally wrong. If one or more of the premises are false, then we can conclude that the argument is unsound. This, of course, does not mean that the conclusion is false; however, it does mean that the truth of the conclusion cannot be determined based on *this* argument or on *these* premises.

Another important aspect of this argument is that the justification for the view that abortion is morally wrong is based on the premise that it is an immoral act of killing an innocent person. This is essential because it also affects the legal issue on abortion. For instance, if one argues, instead, that abortion is morally wrong because it undermines societal values concerning the significance of living things, or because it denigrates the value of potential human life, then, even if we agree with these premises, it is not clear what are its implications for the legal status of abortion. However, if one argues that abortion is morally wrong because it is the killing of an innocent human person, then an abortion might also be considered murder. As a consequence, in addition to being morally wrong, we might also conclude that abortion ought to be illegal.

Assessing the soundness of the argument: Truth and falsity of the premises

Let us begin, then, by examining the truth and falsity of the premises. Premises 1 and 3 seem to be self-evidently true, or, at least, they seem to be much less contentious than premise 2. But let us look at premise 1 a little closer. First, notice that this premise is a deontological moral principle which seems self-evident. Most people would agree that intentionally killing an innocent human person is morally wrong. However, is it *always* morally wrong? Can we think of exceptions to this moral principle? If we can come up with one exception, then we have a counter-example that undermines the truth of the premise and the soundness of the argument.

Exceptions to the moral principle against intentionally killing an innocent person would require some extraordinary justification, such as the self-preservation of one's own life or the saving of many other people's lives. For instance, one might argue that it is morally permissible to intentionally kill an innocent human person, if doing so is the only way to save the lives of hundreds of innocent people. Similar cases, in which the life of one or a few individuals is sacrificed for the sake of the lives of many individuals (or the common good), might serve as counter-examples to the principle that it is always morally wrong to kill an innocent person. Given these counter-examples, we can conclude that premise 1 is false, and it is not the case that it is *always* morally wrong to intentionally kill an innocent person. This argument, therefore, is unsound.

The argument may be salvaged if we revise premise 1 to allow for certain extraordinary exceptions, while excluding abortion as one of them. For instance, the premise can be weakened to read as follows: 'Intentionally killing an innocent human person is *prima facie* morally wrong.' *Prima facie* means at face value, and thus it means that, in normal circumstances, intentionally killing an innocent person is morally wrong. This allows for the possibility that there might be extreme and unusual situations that might count as exceptions to this generally accepted moral principle, without having to deny the truth of the moral principle.

Premise 3, 'abortion is the killing of a foetus', also seems incontrovertibly true, since it is simply the definition of an abortion. However, even this premise can be challenged. Some might argue that there is a difference between killing someone and letting someone die and that the former is more morally problematic than the latter.[3] In the act of killing, an agent acts with the purpose of taking the life of the other person. In the act of letting someone die, an agent's intention might be other than taking the life of the other person; instead, the death of the person might be a secondary, unintended effect of the primary and intended purpose of the action. For instance, imagine a woman that is dying from cancer. Her son refuses to connect her to any type of artificial life-support system. The son's primary intention is to prevent his mother from suffering a long anguishing death. In such a case, even though we know that if the mother is not connected to a life-support system she will die, we would not conclude that the son has killed his mother.

Given this analysis, a pregnant woman might argue that her primary intention in having an abortion is not to take the life of the foetus but simply to disconnect herself from the foetus or to terminate her pregnancy. If there were some way in which the foetus could survive without the woman, the killing of the foetus would not be necessary or permissible. Moreover, if the foetus happens to survive its separation from the woman, the woman is not intent on killing the foetus. In fact, some philosophers have defined an abortion as the termination of a pregnancy rather than as the killing of a foetus.[4] This distinction is important and it raises some interesting questions as to the truth of premise 3. However, for our purposes, in this chapter, we will not engage further in this interesting debate. What is important to recognize is that justifying the truth of premises of an argument, even ones that might seem obvious at first, is not always an easy task. For the continuation of this chapter, we will accept premise 3 as true.

Premise 4 follows from 2 and 3; therefore, by process of elimination, it appears that the central difficulty concerns premise 2. Is the foetus a human person from the moment of conception? Below, we study three arguments that attempt to answer this in the affirmative. These arguments attempt to demonstrate the truth of premise 2. For these arguments to succeed, they need to provide evidence that support the claim that the early foetus is a person. If they accomplish this task, and we accept premises 1 and 3 as true, then the argument is *sound*, and the conclusion that abortion is morally wrong is true. Therefore, there is a lot at stake in these arguments.

The argument from functioning as a person versus being a person for the view that abortion is morally wrong

Many personhood arguments in defence of the moral permissibility of abortion distinguish between a human being and a person. For instance, Mary Anne Warren, Michael Tooley and Lynn Rudder Baker (see Chapter 1) argue that being a person is qualitatively different than being a human being. According to Warren, for instance, the term 'human' is ambiguous, because it can refer to (1) an organism that belongs to the human species but has not yet developed cognitively to become a full-fledged person; or (2) a human organism that is fully developed and has become a person and thus is conscious, rational, self-motivated, communicative and self-aware. The first is an organism that is only biologically or genetically human but is not yet a full-fledged human person and does not belong to the moral community. Being a person and belonging to the moral community, then, entails much more than just being human; it requires many sophisticated cognitive functions.[5]

If we make this distinction, we can then claim that a foetus is a human being in the biological and genetic sense (i.e. it is a living organism that belongs to the human species); however, it is not a human person and it does not belong to the moral community. The distinction highlights the fact that a foetus has none of the mental capabilities that a human person has, and some of these cognitive capabilities (e.g. sentience, consciousness, reasoning, self-awareness) to some degree are deemed necessary if we are to include the foetus in the moral community and attribute to it personhood rights. While abortion defenders will differ in terms of the cognitive capabilities and their degree of development necessary for personhood, they all agree that there is a difference between a human living organism and a human person. They argue that this distinction is crucial for determining the rights that belong to a living human being and the obligations others have towards it. For instance, some abortion defenders argue that when considering an agent's rights, we must also consider the mental states its nature is capable of, such as its desires, intentions and wants. According to this view, it makes little sense to attribute rights to an entity that not only has no capacity to desire the object of such rights in the present, but also that will never have capacities to desire them in the future.

For instance, it is absurd to suggest that a sheet of paper has the right not to be written on, scribbled on or torn into little pieces. The reason it makes no sense to attribute such rights to a piece of paper is because the paper does not have and cannot have a desire not to be written on, scribbled on or torn into little pieces. Consider the rights of an animal such as a dog. It would make sense to attribute to a dog the right not to be tortured, because, as a sentient being, a dog has a desire not to feel pain. However, it would make little sense to attribute to a dog the right to attend college or university, because a dog not only has no such desires but also, given the nature of a dog, it cannot attain such desires or wants.[6]

Stephen Schwarz's anti-abortion argument claims that the central notions of personhood that are used in these abortion-defending arguments are based on the idea of how a person functions and not on what a person is. For instance, it is true that human persons have the following functions: consciousness, sentience, thinking, autonomy and rationality. Indeed, these are proper and essential functions of human adult persons. However, the function of something and what the thing is, while related, are different concepts. What a thing is is not necessarily the same as the functions of a thing. Schwarz claims that the personhood arguments in defence of abortion conflate these two concepts, and they make the mistake of trying to reduce the central notion of personhood or the necessary conditions for personhood to certain basic cognitive functions. Schwarz says: 'The failure of Warren's argument can be seen in light of the distinction between being a person and functioning as a person.'[7] This mistake is made evident by showing that we have a strong intuition to consider non-functioning human beings as human persons. In many cases, our intuition to consider non-functioning human beings as human persons is just as strong as our intuitions to consider functioning human beings as human persons. But, if this is true, then either our strong intuitions must be wrong or our necessary criteria for personhood based on cognitive functions must be wrong.

Sleepers, unconscious and comatose persons

According to Warren, functioning as a person means that a being's brain and nervous system are developed sufficiently for the being to be conscious, rational, self-motivated, communicative and self-aware (or at least some combination of these). For instance, Warren claims:

I suggest that the traits that are most central to the concept of personhood, or humanity in the moral sense, are, very roughly, the following: (1) Consciousness (of objects and events external and/or internal to the being), and in particular the capacity to feel pain; (2) reasoning (the developed capacity to solve new and relatively complex problems); (3) self-motivated activity (activity which is relatively independent of either genetic or direct external control); (4) the capacity to communicate, by whatever means, messages of and indefinite variety of types, that is, not just with indefinite number of possible contents, but on indefinitely many possible topics; (5) the presence of self-concepts, and self-awareness, either individual or, or both. ... We needn't suppose that and entity must have *all* of these attributes to be properly considered a person; (1) and (1) may well be sufficient for personhood, and quite properly (1)-(3) are sufficient. Neither do we need to insist that any one of these criteria is *necessary* for personhood, although once again (1) and (2) look like fairly good candidates for necessary conditions, as does (3), if activity is construed so as to include the activity of reasoning.[8]

Therefore, according to Warren, necessary conditions for personhood are the cognitive attributes of consciousness, reasoning and, possibly, self-motivated activity. However, there are times when a person's brain is shut-off, and during this time it does not function. During these moments a human being is not conscious, rational, self-motivated, communicative or self-aware. For instance, consider Schwarz's example:

Imagine a person in a deep dreamless sleep. She is not conscious, she cannot reason, etc.: she lacks all five of these traits. She is not functioning as a person. But of course she is a person, she retains fully her status of being a person, and killing her while asleep is just as wrong as killing her when she is awake and functioning as a person.[9]

When a person is asleep or is put under anaesthesia, she is no longer functioning as a person. Would it be morally permissible to kill these human beings, because they are asleep and thus not functioning as persons? An affirmative answer to this question seems self-evidently absurd, because it would run contrary to our strong moral intuition that killing people while they are asleep is morally wrong. Moreover, the fact that they are not functioning as persons seems morally irrelevant in our assessment of their personhood status. Therefore, there must be something wrong with the personhood arguments in defence of abortion that are based on the idea that foetuses are not persons because they are not functioning as persons.

Abortion defenders might respond by arguing that there is a morally relevant difference between a human being who has never functioned as a person and one who has a history of functioning as a person. So, for instance, in the case of an adult person who is temporarily asleep and not functioning as a person, it would be morally wrong to kill them because they have a past history of functioning as a person. In the case of a foetus, however, we would not be morally prohibited because the foetus does not have a history of functioning as a person. The foetus has never functioned as a person.

But is having a history of functioning as a person a morally relevant difference? Let us examine Schwarz's response:

> Imagine a case of two children. One is born comatose, and will remain so until the age of nine. The other is healthy at birth, but as soon as she received the concept of continuing self for a brief time, she, too, lapses into a coma, from which she will not emerge until she is nine. Can anyone seriously hold that the second child is a person with a right to life, while the first child is not? ... If this distinction is absurd when applied to the two born human beings, is it any less absurd when applied to two human beings, one born (asleep in a bed), the other preborn (sleeping in the womb).[10]

The abortion critics, then, may argue that our moral intuitions and common sense tell us that these two cases are morally equivalent, and that we ought to value the lives of both human beings, regardless of their history as functioning human beings. But, if this is true, then this thought experiment demonstrates that having a history of functioning as a person is not a morally relevant factor when it comes to determining the status of personhood.

Abortion defender's response: Immediately present capacity to function as a person

The abortion defender might respond that both nine-year-old children should be considered persons because they both have a *present immediate capacity* to function as a person. This means that if any of these two children were to wake up, they would be able to exert their capability to function as a person immediately. In other words, they would be able to actualize this potentiality in the present moment, because they already have all of the necessary biological hardware to perform such sophisticated mental actions such as self-consciousness, rationality, self-motivation, communication and self-awareness. Therefore, both nine-year-old children have all of the physical attributes they need to function as a person. Thus, even though this capacity has not been actualized in one of them, they both have the present immediate capacity to have it actualized. Moreover, this can also be said about people who are sleeping, in a coma and under anaesthesia. However, the abortion defender's argument continues; a foetus, particularly in the early stages of its development, does not have the present immediate capacity to function as a person, because its physical attributes, such as its brain and nervous system, are not fully developed. Therefore, it seems that the present immediate capacity to function as a person is a morally relevant necessary criterion that the abortion defender can use to distinguish sleepers and unconscious human persons from foetuses.

Abortion critics' reply: Basic inherent capacity and latency 1 and 2

Schwarz responds that while it is true that the nine-year-old comatose children may have the physical make-up for the present immediate capacity to function as a person and a foetus does not, the foetus has a *basic inherent capacity* to function as a person. A basic inherent capacity is the rudimentary biological make-up that underlies the present immediate capacity to function as a person; it is the primary cause of an agent developing the capacity to function as a person. He explains it as follows:

> The objection claims that the being in the womb lacks the capacity to function as a person. True, it lacks what I shall call *the present immediate capacity* to function, where responses may be immediately elicited. Such a capacity means the capability of functioning, where such a capability varies enormously among people, and normally develops and grows (as a result of learning and other experiences). The capability of functioning as a person is grounded in the *basic inherent capacity* to function. This is proper to the being of a person and it has a physical basis, typically the brain and nervous system. It is a capacity that grows and develops as the child grows and develops.[11]

Another way to understand the conception of basic inherent capacity is to comprehend the two forms of latency associated with it. First, there is *latency 1*. Latency 1 means that a being has a basic inherent capacity to develop as a person, but its biological material cannot develop further into present immediate capacity because it is either damaged or its development path has been blocked. Second, there is *latency 2* and this means that a being has a basic inherent capacity, but it is still in its natural developmental stages towards present immediate capacity. To understand these distinctions better and their relevance for the abortion argument, let us examine Schwarz's spectrum of developmental stages and their relation to the abortion debate.

Schwarz asks us to consider human beings at different stages of its development: (a) a sleeping adult person, (b) a comatose adult person, (c) a newborn baby, (d) a foetus about to be born, (e) a seven-week foetus and (f) a zygote. Most people would agree that (a) a sleeping adult is a person. Schwarz proposes that the remaining cases, (b) through (f), share an essential similarity and thus should also be granted the status of personhood. If this is true, then, returning to our original abortion critics' argument, premise (2) 'A foetus is an innocent person' is true.

But on what grounds can we maintain that a sleeping person and all of the other examples share a common essential similarity? Schwarz expresses the argument as follows: 'The beings on our list, (a) through (e), differ only with respect to their present immediate capacity to function. They are all essentially similar with respect to their basic inherent capacity, and through this, their being as persons.'[12] Schwarz leaves out the zygote from this first group since the zygote does not have a basic inherent capacity to function as a person. Nevertheless, Schwarz wants to also argue that

> the zygote does not lack this physical basis; it is merely that it is now a primitive, undeveloped form. The zygote has the essential structure of this basis; a structure that will unfold, grow, develop, mature, which takes time .... Thus, the zygote has, in primitive form, the physical basis of his inherent capacity to function as a person. In the adult this same basis exists in developed form.[13]

See Table 2.1 to get a clearer picture of Schwarz's spectrum of developmental stages of the human beings.

Table 2.1 Schwarz's spectrum of developmental stages of the human beings

		Present immediate capacity	Basic inherent capacity	Latent 1 (Damaged or blocked)	Latent 2 (Undeveloped)
	Stages of Human Development				
A	Adult asleep	Yes	Yes	No	No
B	Adult in coma (will wake in 6 months)	No	Yes	Yes	No
C	A newborn	No	Yes	No	Yes
D	A foetus about to be born	No	Yes	No	Yes
E	A 7-week foetus	No	Yes	No	Yes
F	A zygote	No	Yes	No	Yes

Challenges to the argument from functioning as a person versus being a person

There are some serious challenges to the argument based on the distinction between being a person and functioning as a person. Here we will examine two. First, the argument is based on the idea that being a person and functioning as a person are two distinct concepts, and that the former does not depend on the latter. However, if we examine the argument a little closer it appears that the concept of functioning as a person cannot be separated from the concept of being a person.

Consider the concepts of *present immediate capacity* and *basic inherent capacity*. These two categories refer to human beings who can function as persons in the present or immediate moment, and who can function as persons at some time in the future, respectively. Consider, also, the concepts of latency 1 and 2. These refer to groups of human beings who do not have the capacity to function as persons in the present or immediate moment, because, in the case of latency 1, they have a defect or a blocked capability, and in the case of latency 2, their capacity to function as persons has not yet been fully developed.

In other words, the conception of being a person remains intimately connected to the idea of functioning as a person, and even when we attempt to separate these, as Schwarz tries to do, we seem to fall back on them as an essential property of being a person, and as the ultimate foundation of the concept of personhood. For instance, according to Schwarz, what makes a zygote a person is that the zygote has a basic inherent capability to *function as a person*.

This inability to separate the concept of personhood from the idea of functioning as a person should not be surprising because their intricate connection goes as far back as Aristotle. Without getting into complicated Aristotelian metaphysics, we can simply observe that for Aristotle the notion of what a thing is and its essential function are inseparable.

The point of invoking Aristotle in this debate is not to attempt to undermine Schwarz's argument based dogmatically on Aristotelian authority, but rather to show that the intricate connection between the concepts of what makes a thing the kind of thing it is and the thing's functions has a very long history.

In an attempt to find what is the ultimate best good for persons (i.e. *eudaimonia*), Aristotle claims that we must first determine the function of a person. This connection highlights Aristotle's belief that to discover what is good for a person, we first must know what the essence of a person is, and this can only be determined through the function of a person. He writes:

But presumably the remark that the best good is happiness is apparently something [generally] agreed, and we still need a clearer statement of what the best good is. Perhaps, then, we shall find this if we first grasp the function of a human being. For just as the good, i.e., [doing] well, for a flautist, sculptor, and every craftsman, and, in general, for whatever has a function and characteristic action, seems to depend on its function, the same seems to be true for a human being, if a human being has some function.[14]

If it is true that the function of human beings is pivotal to the concept of personhood, then the central premise of Schwarz's argument fails.

A second objection that can be raised against Schwarz's argument is that it seems to be a sophisticated argument from potentiality. The argument claims that a zygote is a person because the zygote has a basic inherent capacity to develop in the future the capabilities of functioning as a person. This argument will have little effect on any philosopher who maintains an abortion defender's position. From their perspective, this argument is the same thing as saying that the zygote has a real potentiality for becoming a person. No abortion defender denies this claim; they agree that the zygote is a human being, with the biological and genetic capacity to develop as a person. Therefore, except for the introduction of new terminology and a shift in semantics, the argument does not seem to provide any new position for the progress of the abortion debate. We are back to the original question: What constitutes personhood? The anti-abortionist answer to this question – namely, having a basic inherent capacity to function as a person – will not persuade abortion defenders such as Warren or Tooley. The abortion defender will respond by noting that it is precisely because zygotes have *only* a basic inherent capacity and latency 2 that they cannot be considered persons.

Probabilities argument for the view that abortion is morally wrong

The abortion critics' argument from probability claims that the high probability that a fertilized embryo will become an adult human person represents a morally relevant fact that should make abortion a morally wrong action. The argument states that at conception, something significant happens, which can be best captured through the morally relevant distinction between a spermatozoon, an ovum and a zygote. The zygote is an essentially different sort of biological organism than the spermatozoon and the ovum, and these biological distinctions can be best described through an analysis of actual probabilities each of them has, as it relates to personhood. John Noonan, who is a major proponent of this argument, explains it as follows:

Consider for example, the spermatozoa in any normal ejaculate: There are about 200,000,000 in any single ejaculate, of which one has a chance of developing into a zygote. Consider the oocytes which may become an ova: there are 1,000,000 oocytes which may become an ova: There are 100,000 to 1,000,000 oocytes in a female infant, of which a maximum of 390 ovulated. But once a spermatozoon and ovum meet and the conceptus is formed, such studies as have been made show that roughly in only 20 per cent of the cases will spontaneous abortion occur. In other words, the chances are about 4 out of 5 that this new being will develop.

The argument from probability suggests that if one were to destroy a spermatozoon, one would destroy an organism that has a 1 in 200 million chance of becoming a full-fledged adult human person; if one were to destroy an ovum, one would destroy an organism that has a 1 in 1 million chance of becoming a full-fledged human person; however, if one were to destroy a zygote, one would destroy a being that has 4 in 5 chances of becoming a full-fledged adult human person. This distinction grounded in significantly different probabilities should result in different moral judgements with respect to the destruction of each of these entities. We ought to judge the destruction of the spermatozoon and ovum as morally permissible, and the destruction of the zygote as morally wrong. Ultimately, what seems to be providing the force of the argument is that we ought to value the zygote much more than a spermatozoon or ovum, in virtue of its actual probability to become a full-fledged adult human person. Consider the analogy Noonan provides to defend his view.

The appeal to probabilities is the most commonsensical of arguments, to a greater or smaller degree all of us base our action on probabilities, and in morals, as in laws, prudence and negligence, are often measured by the account one has taken of the probabilities. If the chance is 200,000,000 to 1 that the movement in the bushes into which you shoot is a man's, I doubt if many persons would hold you careless in shooting; but if the chances are 4 out of 5 that the movement is a human being's, few would acquit you of blame.

If we agree with the intuitions of this example, we can safely transfer such intuitions to the issue of abortion. If we do this, then destroying an embryo, any time after conception, would be like shooting into bushes where we know for certain that there is an 80 per cent chance that the motion in the bushes is being caused by an adult human person. Clearly, then, with this knowledge, the shooter's action would be morally reprehensible; likewise, someone who has an abortion and knows that there is an 80 per cent chance that the aborted foetus will become an adult person commits a morally reprehensible action.

Before we proceed to discussing the challenges to Noonan's argument, we should clarify that he does not argue that the zygote is a person, and thus the success of his argument is not dependent on proving the personhood status of the foetus. Nevertheless, he does argue that the foetus deserves to be treated as a person and that the foetus ought to be ascribed all of the rights we ascribe to a full-fledged person. He explains his positions as follows:

> It might be asked, What does the change in biological probabilities have to do with establishing humanity? The argument from probabilities is not aimed at establishing humanity but at establishing an objective discontinuity that may be taken into account in moral discourse.

Challenges to the argument from probability

The abortion critics' probability argument concludes that at conception we have a morally significant shift in probabilities that ought to cause us to make morally significant changes in our attitude towards the zygote. Based on the known fact that a zygote has four out of five chances to become an adult human person, we ought to respect its right to life the way we would respect the right to life of an adult human person. How can an abortion defender respond to this argument?

First, it is important to note that implicit in this argument is the fact that a foetus is not a full-fledged human person. In other words, the fact that an organism has any probability whatsoever, even 99.99 per cent, *to become* a full-fledged human person concedes that the organism is *not* a full-fledged human person. Therefore, we can re-describe the zygote's status to the category of potentiality, so that what is at stake is the zygote's potential to become a full-fledged human person with the right to life. But, if this is true, then we also have to acknowledge that there is a morally significant difference between taking the life of a being that will become a full-fledged human person and taking the life of a full-fledged human person. This leads to a further difficulty with Noonan's analogy of the person shooting into the bushes.

Noonan suggests that if one is told that there is an 80 per cent chance that the movement in the bushes is being caused by an innocent human person, and we have good reason to believe that this claim is true, then if one were to shoot in the bushes and kill an innocent person, one would be held morally responsible for homicide. Given the background knowledge that there is an 80 per cent chance that our target in the bushes is an innocent person, one's decision to shoot at the target in the bushes is grossly negligent. One's action would be equivalent to murder. However, if we change the probabilities to 1 in 200 million, and if one shoots into the bushes and kills a person, one would not be held responsible or culpable for murder. Instead, it would best be categorized as a freak accident.

This demonstrates that probabilities can and should affect our moral judgement. Noonan wants his analogy to do more than highlight the importance of probabilities for moral decision-making; he also wants us to compare it with the abortion issue and conclude that when a pregnant woman has an abortion any time after conception, and she knows that the foetus has an 80 per cent chance of becoming a full-fledged human person, she should be held morally responsible for killing an innocent person or for committing homicide. According to Noonan, the pregnant woman is as morally reprehensible as the negligent shooter, because they both have knowledge that what they are destroying has an 80 per cent chance of being a human person.

This analogy can be challenged because the 80 per cent chance applies to different categories in each of the analogues, and thus it commits the fallacy of weak analogy. In the shooter's case, the 80 per cent relates to the existence of full-fledged human person and therefore there is real negligence on the part of the shooter for shooting a person. Moreover, whether or not the shooter kills an adult human person, the shooter's actions are morally reprehensible because he shoots knowing that there is an 80 per cent chance of killing an adult human person. However, the case of the pregnant woman is very different. She is not being told that there is an 80 per cent chance that the foetus is not really a foetus but rather a full-fledged human person; rather, she is being told simply that the foetus has an 80 per cent chance of, someday, in the future, becoming an adult human person. To see more clearly why Noonan's analogy fails to make the point that he intends to make, let us reconstruct his own analogy to represent more accurately the pregnant woman's situation as described here.

Imagine that you have a rifle in your hand. You are about to shoot into the bushes. Your friend intervenes and stops you from shooting. He warns you that in the bushes there is a rabbit. He informs you that this is not just any rabbit. This rabbit has been injected with a special human serum, which will, in the future, immediately convert the rabbit into a human person. Moreover, there is an 80 per cent chance that this conversion from rabbit to person will be successful. Imagine that you disregard your friend's admonishment and shoot into the bushes. Imagine also that you kill the rabbit. We cannot conclude that you have killed a person, as Noonan's analogy suggests; rather, we can conclude that you have killed a rabbit that has a strong possibility of one day becoming a person. As a consequence, if you shoot and kill the rabbit, you do not kill a person; instead, you kill a rabbit, albeit a rabbit that might convert to a human person. This demonstrates that Noonan's probability argument will not convince an abortion defender that killing a foetus is morally negligent or equivalent to homicide. The fact that a foetus has a high probability of becoming a person at some point in the future does not entail that killing it is the same as killing a person.

Even though Noonan's analogy is problematic, and it does not support the view that an abortion is the killing of a human person, it does provide a weaker sort of argument in support of the abortion critics' position. An abortion critic could argue that an organism that has a strong probability of becoming something so intrinsically valuable as an adult human person has value in virtue of this possibility. Therefore, while we cannot equate it with killing an adult human person, we can equate it with killing a very valuable living organism. There is an argument, therefore, for regretting such a death and for preserving its life. One might argue, for instance, that a shooter should respond differently if he is told that there is an organism that has a strong probability of becoming a person than if he is told that there is an organism with no probability of becoming a person. Therefore, Noonan's analogy might suggest that while an abortion is not the same as killing a person, it is also not the same as killing an organism that has no personhood possibilities; for killing an organism with a strong possibility of becoming an adult human person is killing something of value.

The argument from potentiality

Related to the question of personhood is the concept of potentiality. This notion plays an important role in abortion arguments because many abortion critics' arguments rely on the principle of potentiality as the justification for their position. Even if the foetus is not considered a person, it cannot be denied that it is a living human organism that will probably develop into a person. Moreover, as we have seen in the previous section, the probabilities that it will develop into a person are very high. So, even if the foetus does not have a right to life, it has a potentiality for the right to life. Abortion critics argue that, in virtue of this potentiality, it is morally wrong to destroy the foetus. They will also point out that the potentiality to become a person also gives the foetus a high degree of intrinsic value, making it morally wrong to destroy it. Before we get any deeper into the arguments, let us first understand the concept of potentiality properly.

What is potentiality?

Potentiality is best understood when it is contrasted with actuality and possibility. Something is actual when it exists in the present moment. So, for instance, if there is a glass of water in front of me at time t, we would say that the glass of water is actual at time t. When we refer to capabilities or functions, such as the capability or function of speaking, we say that anyone that has the capability to speak in the present moment, whether or not they are speaking, has this capability and function in actuality. So, even if Joy, who is ten years old and loves to tell stories, is sleeping and thus is not speaking at the present time, she still has the capability and function to speak in actuality. Her capacity and function to speak is actual (i.e. present), because even though it is not being used, it is ready to be used.

On the other hand, consider Mary, who is only three months old and does not have the capability to speak. However, if she continues to develop normally, she will have this capability in the future. Therefore, she has a potentiality for the capability to speak. Mary does not have this capability in actuality, because she does not have it at the present time. However, she does have it in potentiality because it is an attribute that she will acquire as part of her normal developmental process.

Notice also that potentialities are not the same as possibilities. Philosophers will point out that the ontological status of possibilities is much weaker than that of potentialities. This is a fancy way of saying that potentialities are much more real than possibilities. Let us consider some examples that will help clarify this distinction.

Think of a human being's genetic code. A human being's genes provide the colour of eyes, the colour of hair and many other traits the being will develop in the future. These attributes do not exist in the present in their completed state, but they have, in some sense, already been designed. So, they exist in potentiality. We can think of potentiality as a reality that exists in the present but will manifest itself in the future. It is analogous to the plans or designs of a building before the building exists.

Possibilities, on the other hand, are only possible realities and not real potentialities that exist in the present. For instance, a newborn baby has the possibility of catching a virus immediately after her birth. She also has the possibility of getting into a car accident on her way home from the hospital. These are real possibilities, but they are different from potentialities. They are not pre-designed realities that will develop naturally as part of the organism; potentialities are pre-designed realities that currently exist and that will develop naturally as part of the organism.

Potentiality argument for the view that abortion is morally wrong

A foetus from the moment of conception has the potentiality for the cognitive traits of consciousness, self-awareness, rationality, communication and self-determination. A zygote does not have this rich cognitive consciousness in actuality, but, as it develops its mental capabilities, it will acquire them. In other words, a zygote will develop the capability of reasoning and of having a desire to continue to live, and thus it will have a right to life. Shouldn't we, therefore, grant zygotes a right to life in virtue of such potentiality?

Remember that a zygote's potentialities for a desire for its continued existence and for the aforementioned cognitive traits are real and present, and not just possibilities. Abortion critics argue that if we carry this argument to its logical conclusion, we should accept the claim that zygotes have a real and actual potential for a right to life. At a minimum, it appears that potentiality is a morally relevant factor that needs to be considered in our ethical deliberations on the ethics of abortion.

Objection 1 against the potentiality principle

Here we will consider several arguments against the view that the potentiality for personhood provides sufficient justification to conclude that abortions are morally wrong. First, we will explore Michael Tooley's argument against the potentiality principle. Tooley's argument has two parts. First, he defends what he calls the 'moral symmetry principle' with respect to action and inaction.[15] The symmetry principle refers to the idea that positive and negative duties are equally obligatory. What this means is that we have an equal moral obligation to perform an act as we do to not perform an act that will result in the same consequences. For instance, our positive duty to feed a person who is dying of starvation is just as obligatory as our negative duty not to kill that person.

Tooley notes that our intuitions tell us that negative duties (e.g. do not kill) are stronger than positive ones (e.g. feed the starving person). However, he argues that our intuitive perceptions are incorrect, mostly because positive duties are usually accompanied by motivational and sacrificial elements that create the illusion that they are less morally critical than negative duties. For instance, consider the intentions of a person, Joe, who does not feed a person who is dying of hunger. Let's assume that Joe's intentions are not malicious because his non-action is not directed at killing the other person; that is, his goal is not to kill the starving person. Consider another scenario where Mark stabs to death a person. Joe's breach of his positive moral duty to feed the starving person does not appear as morally reprehensible as Mark's action of stabbing the person to death. But this is true only because the two moral agents have two very different intentions, one is not malicious and the other is.

Consider another case in which Joe wants to kill the starving person. He decides to let the person die slowly of starvation and refuses to feed him. If we compare Joe's breach of his positive duty to feed the dying person with the case of Mark stabbing the person to death, they appear equally morally reprehensible. Therefore, to properly compare positive and negative duties we need to assume that the intentions are the same. We need to imagine a scenario in which the positive duty is performed with the same malicious intention as the negative duty.

A second problem in trying to compare positive and negative duties is that positive duties require some degree of sacrifice on the part of the moral agent. In addition, it is also a commonly accepted moral judgement that as one's sacrifice increases, one's moral obligation to perform a positive duty decreases. For instance, if to save the life of a person one needs to sacrifice his or her own life, one is probably not morally obligated to perform the positive duty of saving the person's life. Therefore, to level out the playing field between positive and negative duties, we need to assume that the sacrifice required of the moral agent to perform the positive duty is minimal.

Given these two assumptions, it should be evident that positive and negative duties carry the same moral weight. For instance, consider case 1: You want to see Betty dead. You intend to kill her by poisoning her. Fortunately, for you, she mistakenly picks up the wrong bottle, thinking that it is a soft drink when in fact it is a poisonous chemical. Instead of warning her, you sit back and watch her drink the deadly drink. Now consider case 2: You want to see Betty dead. You decide to pour poison in her coffee, then you sit back and watch her drink it to her death. Tooley would argue that, in both cases, you would be equally morally culpable for killing Betty, and both actions are equally morally wrong. What this example demonstrates is that the symmetry principle with respect to action and inaction is true.

The next step in the argument requires us to consider a hypothetical case in which scientists have discovered a new chemical that enhances the brain function of cats. When this new chemical is injected into a kitten it changes the physiological development of the kitten and the result is a cat with all of the cognitive apparatus necessary for personhood. The important point for our example is that once a kitten has received this injection it has a real potential (just like a zygote) to become a person. Let us call this injection the 'personhood serum'. Scientists have also discovered a chemical that can neutralize the personhood injection and thus cancel out the potentiality created by the personhood serum. Let us call this injection the 'the neutralizing serum'. So, if a kitten has received a personhood serum and later receives a neutralizing serum, it will not develop as a cat with the sufficient cognitive apparatus for personhood.

The first question is whether we have a moral obligation to inject kittens with a personhood serum. Tooley believes that the intuitive right answer to this question is that we have no moral obligation to go around injecting kittens with this new personhood serum. Moreover, our *inaction* is not morally wrong. Thus, we may conclude that our inaction of not injecting kittens with the personhood serum, even if our intention is that we do not desire for the kitten to become a person, is not morally wrong.

Now, imagine that we were to inject a kitten with the personhood serum. From this moment forward this kitten has the potential to become a person. If we allow the kitten to develop naturally from this moment on, it will become a person with a desire to continue to live, the psychological traits of persons and a right to life. The second question is whether we commit a morally wrong action if we inject the kitten with a neutralizing serum that destroys its potentiality for personhood. Does this action commit a moral wrong? Tooley's hypothetical scenario asks us to consider two events, an inaction and an action that fall under the symmetry principle. The first is the inaction of not giving a kitten the personhood serum and thus not initiating the personhood process in a particular kitten. The second is the action of giving a kitten, which received a personhood serum, a neutralizing serum.

Notice that the inaction and action result in the same end of not producing a person, and they have the same intention. Moreover, recall that the symmetry principle states that positive and negative actions are morally equivalent if they result in the same consequences and have the same intentions. Above we argued that a moral agent who performs the inaction of not giving a kitten a personhood serum does not commit a morally wrong action. If we accept the symmetry principle, and we do not believe that we did anything morally wrong when we did not initiate the personhood process (inaction), then we also do nothing morally wrong when we act to end the personhood process (action).

Therefore, a person who performs the action of injecting a kitten that has previously received the personhood serum (and thus has a real potential for personhood) with a neutralizing serum does not commit a morally wrong action. If this true, then a moral agent who terminates the potentiality of a kitten to become a full-fledged person does not commit a morally wrong action. If this is morally acceptable, then it is also morally acceptable that we end the potentiality for personhood in any species, whether it is a cat, lion, primates or humans, and the potentiality argument fails. Therefore, it is morally acceptable to have an abortion if the foetus is not a person and only has a potentiality to become a person.

Objection 2 against the potentiality principle

First, we must highlight and emphasize that potentiality alone does not give a foetus a right to life. It is commonly accepted that persons, in virtue solely of being persons, have certain basic personhood rights, such as the right to be treated with respect and dignity, the right to basic freedoms and liberties and the right to life or the right not to be killed unjustly. One does not have to earn these rights; instead, they are derived from the nature of personhood. Some philosophers will refer to these as innate or natural rights. Now, it is important to note that beings that have a potential for personhood do not participate in these natural or innate rights. Having a potential for personhood may confer upon a being a more valuable ontological status than not having the potential for personhood, but it is not the same as being a person.

Second, we must remember that whatever value (whether ontological or moral) one places on a foetus for being a potential person, this value must be weighed against the value we attribute to a woman's freedom and control over her reproductive choices. The pregnant woman is a person and does (and ought to) participate in all of the natural and innate rights attributed to persons. Some abortion defenders do not deny that potentiality gives a foetus some moral standing. However, they argue that the value of the potentiality of a foetus simply does not outweigh the value of a woman's freedom to choose to have an abortion. The abortion defender argues that, in all cases, a woman's right and liberty outweighs the rights of a potential person (if it has any rights at all). For instance, Warren presents the follow hypothetical scenario to support this argument.

> Suppose that our space explorer falls into the hands of an alien culture, whose scientist decide to create a few hundred thousand or more human beings, by breaking his body into his component cells, and using these to create fully developed human beings, with, of course, his genetic code. We may imagine that each of these newly created men will have all of the original man's abilities, skills, knowledge, and so on and also have an individual self-concept, in short that each of them will be a bona fide (though hardly unique) person. Imagine that the whole project will take only seconds, and that its chances of success are extremely high, and that our explorer knows all of this, and also knows these people will be treated fairly. I maintain that in such a situation he would have every right to escape if he could, and thus to deprive all of these potential people of their potential lives. ... even if it were not his live which the alien scientists planned to take, but only a year of his freedom, or, indeed, only a day.[16]

This example might seem strange but remember that examples like these do not need to be realistic in any way. They are constructed simply to make a very specific point by appealing to our common sense and intuition about certain moral sensibilities. In this case, the point Warren wants to make is that a potential person is not actual or real, no matter how likely and quickly its potentiality can convert into actuality. So, even if the potential person has a high chance of becoming an actual person and this can happen in a matter of seconds, the fact remains that the potential person is not a person. In contrast, the explorer and a pregnant woman are actual persons. As a consequence, it is irrelevant if there are 1 or 1 million potential persons; their reality as persons is non-existent until they are actualized. It would be like multiplying many large numbers by zeros, the answer would still be zero. The important point in this argument is that, in the case of the abortion, we cannot simply consider the value of the foetus as a potential person in a vacuum; instead, we must always consider it against the rights and wishes of the pregnant woman who is not a potential person but an actual person.

Summary

In this chapter, we investigated three personhood arguments for the view that abortion is morally wrong. We began by constructing the stem argument from which all three arguments burgeon: The Personhood Core Argument for the Moral Wrongness of Abortion. The argument goes as follows: Premise 1: Intentionally killing an innocent human person is prima facie morally wrong. Premise 2: *A foetus at the time of conception or close to the time of conception is an innocent human person.* Premise 3: Abortion is the killing of a foetus. Premise 4: Abortion is the killing of an innocent human person (follows from 2 and 3). Conclusion: Therefore, abortion is prima facie morally wrong. We then examined three arguments defending premise 2 that the foetus is a person: (1) the argument from functioning as a person versus being a person, (2) the argument from probability and (3) the argument from potentiality.

The argument from functioning as a person versus being a person attempted to show that there is some essential property that the zygote shares with an adult human person. It tried to demonstrate that the notion of 'functioning as a person' should not be an essential part of what constitutes personhood. However, the argument faces many challenges, because it defines a zygote as a being with the basic inherent structure to *function* as a person, and this seems to go contrary to the very thesis of the position being advanced. It also seems to fall back to the question of personhood and the notion of potentiality, because the claim that a zygote has a basic inherent capacity to develop in the future the capabilities to function as a person is the same as saying that the zygote has a real potentiality for becoming a person. But this introduces nothing new about the concept of personhood, and we are back to the original question: What constitutes personhood?

The abortion critics' argument from probability argued that the probability that a fertilized embryo will become an adult human person is 80 per cent.

This represents a morally relevant fact that should make abortion a seriously morally wrong action. The argument uses an analogy with a person shooting into the bushes, after being told that there is an 80 per cent chance that the movement in the bushes is being caused by a person. If the shooter takes a shot into the bushes and kills a person, the shooter should be held morally blameworthy for murder. Similarly, then, when a pregnant woman who knows that the foetus has an 80 per cent chance of becoming an adult person has an abortion, she should also be held morally blameworthy for murder. We discussed several flaws with this argument. The most glaring is the problem with the analogy upon which the argument is based. The analogy assumes that the percentages are related to killing an actual person, while, in the abortion issue, the percentage is related to a foetus becoming an actual person. This difference is morally essential, because there is a morally relevant difference between shooting a non-person with a high possibility for becoming a person and shooting an actual person.

Finally, we discussed the argument from potentiality. A foetus has a real potentiality for the cognitive traits of consciousness, self-awareness, rationality, communication and self-determination. A foetus, therefore, has a real potentiality for personhood and a right to life. It is undeniable, the argument goes, that this potentiality for personhood is extremely valuable and thus if we destroy the foetus, we destroy a potential person and a valuable being. Thus, abortion is morally wrong. We considered two objections. The first was based on Tooley's symmetry principle that states that positive and negative moral duties are morally equivalent. The apparent difference is caused by the psychological phenomena of intention and sacrifices related to positive duties. Then we considered if there existed a personhood serum for cats, whether we would have the positive duty to use it to convert cats into persons. The common sense intuition is that we would not be morally obligated to do so. But if this is the case for the positive moral question, and the symmetry principle is true, then it will also work for the negative question: Would it be wrong to neutralize the personhood serum in cats that have been injected with it and thus have a real potential to become persons? In this case, we would be neutralizing or destroying a being's real potential for personhood. Given our first answer, the answer here would be that it is not morally wrong. The second objection highlights the difference between actuality and potentiality. In this case, we were asked to imagine a space explorer who is captured by aliens. The aliens are about to create hundreds of new persons using the space explorer's genetic code. Even if there is a real potential for these new persons, the space explorer does nothing morally wrong if he escapes and precludes the potential persons from being actualized.

Study questions

1 Explain the personhood core argument for the moral wrongness of abortion. Is this argument sound? Why or why not?

2 Explain the argument from 'functioning as a person versus being a person' for the moral wrongness of abortion. Is this argument sound? Why or why not?

3 Explain the argument from probability for the moral wrongness of abortion. Is this argument sound? Why or why not?

4 Explain the argument from potentiality for the moral wrongness of abortion. Is this argument sound? Why or why not?

3

What If We Cannot Determine the Concept of Personhood?

From Chapters 1 and 2, we have learned that the concept of personhood is extremely controversial, and that a consensus as to what constitutes a person is not likely any time soon. What if the concept of personhood cannot be determined? If we cannot know what a person is, then we cannot know when a foetus becomes a person, and as a consequence the disagreements about the moral status and rights of a foetus will persist, with little hope of being resolved. In this chapter, we consider this alternative. We explore what moral obligations arise, if any, given the uncertainty surrounding the concept of personhood and the resulting scepticism about the moral status of the foetus.

First, we examine Susanne Gibson's view that personhood is an essentially contested concept, and thus one that will remain genuinely debated for years to come with no resolution in sight.[1] Gibson argues that the essentially contested status of personhood leads to a feminist and particularist perspective on the issue of abortion, and this ushers us to a relational view of moral status. We explore and critically assess her arguments that, given the essentially contested nature of the concept of personhood, the decision to have an abortion should always be left up to the pregnant woman.

Next, we turn to Dan Moller's theory on how to think ethically about situations that remain morally uncertain and that present an inherent risk of moral wrongdoing.[2] We evaluate his view that, with respect to the abortion dilemma, given the difficulty of the moral issue and the resulting high probability that we could make a grave moral mistake, it is morally preferable, in most cases, for a pregnant woman not to go through with an abortion, even if she has good reasons to believe that an abortion is morally permissible.

Gibson and personhood as an essentially contested concept

Susanne Gibson describes the traditional discussions on the abortion issue as being framed too narrowly, usually through a non-feminist approach that considers a situation involving only a pregnant woman's right to privacy, self-determination and bodily integrity versus a foetus's right to life. There is wide agreement about a woman's right to her body, but there is wide disagreement as to the moral status of a foetus and, as a result, as to the rights of a foetus.

Three traditional positions exist within the non-feminist perspective: (1) the conservative position claims that the foetus is a person at conception, or sometime close to the time of conception, and therefore all abortions are immoral; (2) the liberal position states that the foetus is not a person, and it does not have a right to life at any time during the gestation period, and therefore all abortions are morally permissible; (3) the moderate position states that the foetus becomes a person at some time during the gestation period, and therefore before this time abortions are morally permissible and after it abortions are morally wrong.

There is an irresolvable standoff among the conservative, liberal and moderate positions. Moreover, these views are grounded on the conception of personhood, and any headway in resolving disagreements among these positions requires some resolution of the personhood issue. However, according to Gibson, the standoff is inevitably and hopelessly irresolvable, because the concept of personhood is an *essentially contested concept*.

Essentially contested concept

An essentially contested concept is not simply a concept that cannot be defined or one that is the centre of controversy. Instead, according to Gibson, an essentially contested concept is a concept that is inherently indefinable and has several other specific attributes. First, it is a term that is used differently by different groups. Second, the concept lacks a generally agreed upon definition. In other words, there is no proper or standard use of the term that transcends the use of the different groups. Third, the disagreeing parties are not relativists; they believe that their definition of the concept is true and that all other definitions are false. Fourth, each group has a sophisticated, coherent and reasonable justification for their definition and use of the term. They each have a 'sustainable argument' defending their use of the term. Fifth, they all acknowledge the disagreement and take it seriously; as a consequence, there is a 'genuine disagreement'.

Finally, to show that they are not simply talking past one another, and that this is not merely a simple misunderstanding, there exists an exemplar that all the groups agree represents the ideal meaning of the concept. In the case of personhood, the exemplar is an adult functioning person. The adult functioning person is an exemplar for conservative, liberals and moderates, because they all agree that an adult human person exemplifies the essential attributes and traits of personhood. Gibson describes it as follows:

> An essentially contested concept is a concept over which there is disagreement regarding its proper use and where 'there is no one clearly definable use ... which can be set up as the correct or standard use.' ... The dispute over an essentially contested concept, although irresolvable, is a genuine dispute; that is, it is characterized by coherent and sustainable argument. It is not the case, for example, that the same term is being used to refer to two different concepts such that there is no real contest over the true meaning.[3]

To further understand the meaning of an essentially contested concept, let us distinguish it from disagreements that arise based on value and empirical differences. In the case of value disagreements, what is at stake is not the meaning of a given concept but rather the weight or importance such a concept ought to be given when compared to other important concepts or ideas.

For instance, if two people agree on the concept of person, and they both claim that the foetus is a potential person, they might disagree about the *value* we should attribute to the rights of a woman vis-à-vis the rights of a potential person. The abortion defender will argue that a woman's rights should override the rights of a foetus, because the foetus is only a potential person and not yet a person. As a consequence, it is morally permissible to have an abortion. Abortion critics will argue that the value of the life of a potential person should override the rights of a woman to control her body, and thus it is morally wrong to have an abortion. This disagreement is not about the concept of personhood but rather about the value we should ascribe to the life of a potential person.

The disagreement might be about an empirical claim. For instance, two people might agree that a foetus becomes a person when it has consciousness, but they may disagree as to when this occurs. This disagreement seems to have more chances of being resolved as science and technology enhance our abilities to learn more about the foetus's development. An empirical disagreement, then, is a disagreement about the facts of the matter and can probably be resolved with the proper scientific information.

An essentially contested concept, however, is a conceptual disagreement and not a value or empirical disagreement. It is difficult to see how a conceptual disagreement can be resolved by changes in one's value system or the addition of new scientific information. Therefore, neither value adjustments nor scientific advances can help resolve a conceptual disagreement.

If there are disagreements on a given topic and the disagreements are based on differences about the meaning of a fundamental concept, and the fundamental concept is an essentially contested one, then the disagreement will be irresolvable. According to Gibson, this is what has occurred with the abortion debate. What are the implications for the participants of such a debate? Should they simply suspend further enquiry into the issue?

On the contrary, in the case of the abortion issue, Gibson argues that it is precisely because personhood is an essentially contested concept that we can conclude that a woman ought to have the right to an abortion.

> If the concept of personhood is an essentially contested concept, and if it is fundamental to the abortion debate, then that debate is and will remain irresolvable. At the same time, it remains a genuine debate and one with which there is reason to engage. Further, the claim that it is irresolvable does not imply that we cannot reach a conclusion over whether or not women have a right to choose abortion, or over what this right consist in. Indeed, it is my argument that women have the right to choose abortion just because of the essentially contested nature of the concept of personhood.[4]

In the abortion debate, the participants of the debate acknowledge that there is a genuine disagreement, while maintaining that their position is correct and their opponents' incorrect. Abortion defenders and abortion critics each have a justified and coherent conception of personhood, and thus they have good reasons to maintain and defend their views and to stay engaged in the debate. However, Gibson argues that if we also accept that the abortion debate and controversy are at a standoff because personhood is an essentially contested concept, then there are further conclusions that can be drawn from this fact.

An expanded feminist account: A woman-centred and particular *moral account*

One of the central ideas of the feminist view on abortion is to broaden the scope of moral consideration from a pregnant woman's right to privacy, self-determination and bodily integrity versus a foetus's right to life, to include many other factors relevant to the pregnant woman such as age, how she got pregnant, financial situation, psychological condition, family situation and other unique and particular factors relevant to any woman's life.[5] Feminists find that these important factors are discarded when the issue is treated within the traditional framework. Gibson writes:

> If the non-feminist account can be characterised in terms of its focus on the moral status of the foetus, then the feminist alternative can be distinguished by the effort to broaden or indeed to shift this focus. ... Putting women at the centre of the abortion debate has a number of implications. At one level, abortion is put in its social and political context. In societies in which women are oppressed, and in which women's options are limited by the structure of patriarchy, abortion becomes a means of responding to the consequences of male domination as well as a means of breaking from it. ... However, what is more important for the purpose of this paper is the implication of a woman-centred account for an understanding of the nature of the abortion decisions as it is made by particular women in particular circumstances. Here the difference between the feminist and non-feminist approaches lies in a shift away from an abstract account of abortion that can be applied to any woman and any foetus, to a more contextual understanding that recognises the uniqueness of each pregnancy. The abortion decision is still a moral decision, but one that resists formulation in abstract, generalised terms.[6]

Gibson claims that a logical consequence of accepting personhood as an essentially contested concept is this more feminist perspective on abortion; that is, an approach to moral deliberation that is much more woman-centred, and thus much more open to consider particular issues affecting women in their unique circumstances and in consideration of their quality of life. This also would include the political and social context within which a woman lives and will have to give birth and raise her child.

In addition to shifting the emphasis from a foetus's right to life to the pregnant woman and the morally relevant issues in her life, the feminist account also shifts the emphasis from the general abstract moral view to the particular view of each specific abortion case. Gibson argues that once we begin to focus more on the pregnant woman, we are also forced to consider the specific circumstances of the woman in question. No two cases will ever be the same, so we cannot draw any general conclusions about the ethics of abortion that can be applied to all women, in all circumstances.

When assessing the ethics of abortion, therefore, we should take into consideration the contexts and situation of each individual woman. It is important to point out that the inclusion of relevant, morally related circumstance of a pregnant woman, in the evaluation of the moral issue of abortion, is consistent with maintaining consideration for the foetus. In other words, by broadening our scope of moral relevancy, we do not necessarily exclude the foetus as an important moral aspect of the abortion debate. However, within this new feminist paradigm, the foetus will be considered within a relational context.

Relational conception of moral status

Gibson argues that moral obligations are fundamentally based upon relationships. Without social relationships there would be no morality. Moreover, personhood entails the capacity to enter into such social relationships, and therefore a foetus cannot be considered a person until it has these relationship-forming social abilities. As the foetus develops and obtains the cognitive capacity to form human relationships, it moves closer towards personhood.

The foetus can only have one relationship with one person and that is with the pregnant woman on whom it is dependent. However, the relationship is merely a biological one and not a social one. As a consequence of the foetus's special circumstances, Gibson draws two conclusions: first, the value of the foetus is dependent on the pregnant woman, and, second, the choice of an abortion ought to be solely up to the pregnant woman.

Gibson argues that the feminist account takes into consideration this special dependency relationship the foetus has with the woman. The foetus's existence is brought about within a relationship with the pregnant woman; its existence is inherently relational and all moral obligations arise from this relationship. Therefore, the foetus and the woman should not be treated as two independent and separate persons; instead, the foetus should be considered as an inherently relational being. Any moral analysis of the abortion issue should take this relationship as fundamental. According to Gibson, therefore, the foetus cannot be assigned any kind of absolute value 'because they have no existence independent of this one relationship'.[7] She also concludes that 'the specific status of a foetus will vary according to the value ascribed to it by the woman in whose womb it is developing'.[8]

Gibson's view seems to be a compromise, insofar as it considers the foetus as a relational human being that can have value for the pregnant woman, but it does not have an absolute value as an independent human adult person. Therefore, this view also recognizes that the status of the pregnant woman's particular situation is essential in determining whether it is morally permissible or not to have an abortion. In addition, Gibson claims that since a foetus's only relationship is with the pregnant woman, it is only the pregnant woman who can make the decision to have an abortion.

One concern and possible objection that Gibson addresses is the seemingly conflicting positions that, on the one hand, personhood is an essentially contested concept and, on the other hand, that personhood is fundamentally a relational concept. So, while she concedes that the concept of personhood is not universally definable, she also attempts to objectively define the concept of personhood.

Gibson argues that taking a particular position with respect to the concept of personhood does not contradict the view that personhood is an essentially contested concept. Recall that the notion of an essentially contested concept entails both the view that one's position on personhood is the correct position while also maintaining that there are other competing positions that one takes seriously. Therefore, Gibson claims she can consistently maintain that personhood entails the capacity to enter into social relationship, and also that personhood is an essentially contested concept. We will revisit this objection below.

The logic of moral agency: Relational autonomy

At times, Gibson sounds like a relativist, arguing, for instance, that the pregnant woman ultimately determines the value of a foetus. Also, she seems to advocate a relativistic view when she claims that the decision to have an abortion should rest ultimately with the pregnant woman. However, Gibson is not a relativist; instead she defends a Kantian ethical view she calls 'relational autonomy'.

First, we should understand that, according to Gibson, a woman can make a moral mistake with respect to the issue of abortion. In other words, a woman might decide to have an abortion, thinking that it is morally permissible for her to do so, in her particular circumstances, when in fact it is not the case that it is morally permissible for her to do so.

If moral mistakes are possible, then Gibson must accept the idea of an objective external standard to which a woman's moral decision on abortion can be assessed and evaluated. She explains, 'The concept of a moral mistake implies a set of standards against which the judgement can be assessed external to the woman herself, even if it the same woman who later comes to think that it is she who has made a mistake. In this respect, it might be said that there is no such thing as a private morality.'[9]

Another important aspect of Gibson's realist moral view is that a pregnant woman, when she makes a moral judgement on whether to have an abortion, in her particular situation, she is also making a general claim to the same effect. In other words, she is also stating that any woman, in her particular situation, is morally permitted to have an abortion. Gibson is attempting to fuse Kantian abstract moral theory with a feminist contextual moral theory based on relationships. She explains her view's connection with Kantian ethics as follows:

> In the traditional Kantian conception of moral autonomy, the moral agent is self-legislating, but in such a way that when she legislates for herself she legislates for all others in relevantly similar circumstances. There is not a sense in which one can make a moral judgment regarding one's own actions without making a judgment regarding the actions of others, real or hypothetical.[10]

According to Gibson, a pregnant woman is a relational autonomous agent. She is relational insofar as she is a person that lives and acts within particular social, political and personal circumstances, and she is autonomous insofar as she is a self-legislator in the Kantian sense. Gibson argues that given the moral nature of moral agents, a woman has 'the right to act as a relationally autonomous moral agent, participating in membership of a network of moral relationships'.[11]

Relational autonomy is connected to the notions of responsibility, self-worth and moral identity. Autonomy refers to the individual freedom that one exercises in his or her moral decisions. When one exercises these autonomous decisions among members of the moral community, one should also be held responsible for the consequences of one's actions. The notions of blame, praise and responsibility arise from autonomous action within a social and relational context.

Moreover, one's moral identity is created within such a moral community and in dialogue with the members of the community about the justification for one's moral decisions. Reluctance to engage in such dialogue cuts one off the moral domain, because moral relationships and moral agency cannot function in isolation or non-relationally.

Evaluating and overruling

One final point requires greater clarification. On the one hand, Gibson claims that there is an objective morality so that a pregnant woman can make a mistake with respect to her moral judgement on whether it is morally permissible to have an abortion in her particular circumstances. On the other hand, Gibson also argues that the value of the foetus is determined only by the pregnant woman and the decision to have (or not to have) an abortion should be left up to the pregnant woman.

These views seem to conflict. For instance, if a woman, Joan, decides to have an abortion during her seventh month of pregnancy, because she really wants to try out for the cheerleading team, we might argue that this abortion, under these circumstances, is unethical. Let us assume, for argument's sake, that this ethical conclusion is true. Given that we have objectively determined that her decision is mistaken, does Joan still have the right to go through with the abortion? According to Gibson, yes, she does.

Gibson makes a distinction between 'overruling judgements' and 'evaluating judgements'. She argues that outsiders do not have a right to overrule a woman's decision to have an abortion. As an autonomous moral agent, a woman has the authority over her own moral decisions and actions. Nevertheless, even though outsiders cannot interfere in a woman's decision and action to have or not to have an abortion, her decision, insofar as it is a moral decision, can be objectively evaluated by outsiders as either morally good or bad. Gibson says, 'Whereas, in the case of abortion, it can be argued that no one has the authority to overrule a woman's judgment, it does not follow that it cannot be evaluated. Indeed, insofar as a judgment regarding an abortion decision is a moral judgment, then it is necessarily evaluative.'[12]

Challenges to Gibson's essentially contested concept view

Gibson presents an original and interesting view that does not depend on the personhood status of the foetus. However, it does depend on the notion that the concept of personhood is an essentially contested concept. The first challenge to Gibson's argument requires that we investigate further the meaning of an essentially contested concept, and that we revisit the seemingly inconsistent positions that, on the one hand, personhood is inherently indefinable and, on the other hand, that the definition of personhood entails the capacity to enter into a social relationship.

An essentially contested concept cannot mean that the concept is indefinable *per se*, since by definition an essentially contested concept requires that there are several inconsistent definitions. Moreover, according to the notion of an essentially contested concept, these definitions are well supported and can be defended. So, what exactly does an essentially contested concept mean? It can mean one of three things: (1) that, while there is a correct definition, no definition can be demonstrated to be *the* correct one; (2) that there is no one correct definition and thus there are more than one true definition and (3) that there is no correct definition and thus all definitions are false.

We can easily eliminate (3), since Gibson believes that there is a true definition of personhood. If we interpret essentially contested concept as (1), then we would have to concede that one of the conceptions of personhood is the right one and the others are all wrong, but none of them can be rationally justified. However, this is precisely the view that she rejects, since, according to Gibson, it is possible for many concepts of personhood to be rationally justified, including the conception she herself proposes. Therefore, we must also eliminate interpretation (1).

It seems, then, that Gibson would like to maintain the claim (2) that personhood has no correct definition. Gibson notes that people tend to believe that they have defined personhood correctly, and they also believe that all the other definitions are incorrect; and, moreover, they are committed to a realist metaphysical view about the conception of personhood; however, according to the notion of an essentially contested concept, there is no correct definition of the concept of personhood. There are reasonable, consistent and defendable definitions of the concept of personhood, but there will never be one that is the true definition or that can be proven to be the true definition. As a result, the people that believe that they hold the true definition of personhood must hold a false belief.

The problem for Gibson ensues once we understand what an essentially contested concept is, and we believe that personhood is such a concept. At this point, it seems contradictory to keep maintaining one's confidence in one's conception of personhood. Consider propositions 1 through 3.

1   Personhood is the ability to establish social relationships (Gibson's definition).

2   The definition of personhood stated in (1) above is true.

3   Personhood is an essentially contested concept, meaning there is no true definition of personhood.

These are the propositions a realist, must hold. But it appears that propositions (2) and (3) are clearly contradictory.

A second problem with Gibson's view is that it will have very little effect, if any, on the positions of abortion critics. Her view, in some strange way, seems to support rather than undermine the view that the foetus is a person from the moment of conception. Since, according to Gibson, the abortion critics' view of personhood is just as justified as her view of personhood. What prevents the abortion critics from arguing, then, as Gibson does, that while personhood is an essentially contested concept, personhood begins at conception, and thus the foetus from the moment of conception is a person and ought to be ascribed all of the rights of personhood, including the right to life?

Moller and moral risk in the abortion debate

Moller presents a two-part argument defending the view that, in some cases, moral risk might provide good moral reason not to perform an abortion, even if one has good arguments for the moral permissibility of abortion. First, he argues that it is possible for us to make non-negligible moral mistakes at the first-level of moral reasoning. By non-negligible, Moller means that the moral mistake is not due to any negligence on the part of the moral agent. In other words, the moral agent has deliberated correctly, has good intentions and is not corrupted by bad desires or vices. By first-level deliberation, Moller is referring to the arguments one has for or against the moral permissibility of performing the act.

In the second part of the argument, Moller explores what moral obligations, if any, we have from second-level deliberation or meta-deliberation. By second-level deliberation, Moller means our assessment of how certain we are about our first-level deliberation; second-level deliberation on ethical decisions is not ethical deliberation *per se*, but rather epistemological deliberation about first-level deliberation about ethical issues. The concern at the meta-level is focused on how certain we are about the conclusion derived at the first-level and how this ought to affect our moral decisions. Moller argues that, in some cases, even though one may conclude from first-level deliberation that a certain act is morally permissible, the moral risk of being wrong, derived from second-level deliberation, may be sufficient to override and reverse the conclusion derived at the first-level of deliberation. He writes:

> On this view, the mere *risk* of making a deep moral mistake rules out certain acts. If this were true, first-level deliberation about one's actions would not be enough; we would need to proceed to second-level deliberation about the risk of being mistaken at the first-level, and doing so might rule out or at least count against [an act one is contemplating in performing].[13]

What is non-negligible error? Moral fallibilism

To better understand a non-negligible moral mistake, consider an analogy with a non-negligible medical mistake. Doctors are human beings, and they can make negligent and non-negligent medical mistakes. In cases of negligent medical mistakes, we might argue that a doctor's mistake could have been prevented and, more importantly, should have been prevented. We can attribute the mistakes to poor performance or decision-making on the part of the doctor.

In these cases, the doctor is blameworthy for his or her mistake, and if the patient has suffered harm as a consequence of the mistake, he may be entitled to some form of recompense. However, some mistakes may be considered non-negligible. In these cases, medical errors are not caused by the doctor's poor performance or decision-making. It might be caused by the rarity of the disease or the complexity of the medical situation or the lack of information (no fault of the medical staff). In these cases, we should not blame the doctor for the error, and if the patient suffers any harm as a result of the mistake he is not entitled to indemnification.

Similarly, then, there are negligible and non-negligible moral mistakes. Moller wants to focus on the possibilities of making non-negligible mistakes in moral deliberations about abortion. Thus, these are mistakes that are not blameworthy. In other words, we should consider the possibility that we might be mistaken about the moral principles that we use to determine the status and treatment of a foetus and upon which we derive our moral decisions concerning abortion. Moller claims that we ought to be careful not to equate a moral mistake with a mistake over the status of the foetus. For it is possible that we come to the conclusion that we have made a mistake by believing that the foetus was not a person (i.e. later you determined that the foetus is a person) and not have made a moral mistake. The former is a conceptual or factual mistake and not a moral or axiological mistake.

Can we be mistaken about our conclusions at the first-level of moral consideration in the case of abortion? If so, why? Moller claims that the most sophisticated and clear-minded philosophers and ethicists can be mistaken about their conclusions on the abortion topic. He argues that, given the recondite nature of the subject matter, arguments are intrinsically fallible. There are many arguments that are based on value intuitions and vague concepts. In addition, there are many approaches and perspectives that result in different evaluative frameworks. In short, it is a difficult topic in which there are many opposing arguments; moreover, certainty with respect to any position is highly unlikely. He presents two prominent arguments in the ethics of abortion to demonstrate the complexity and uncertainty of any conclusion on the abortion issue. He tries to show that there can never be a high degree of certainty in one's first-level deliberation on such a complicated topic, no matter how careful one deliberates on the issue.

First, Moller considers Don Marquis's Deprivation Argument (see Chapter 5). It goes as follows:

1 Killing a person is morally wrong because it deprives the person of a future like ours.
2 Killing a foetus would deprive it of a future like ours.
3 Therefore, killing a foetus is morally wrong.

Moller points out that good and evidentially sound objections can be raised against premises 1 and 2, causing doubts about whether they are true. For instance, premise 1 requires that we assume that every case in which we deny a being a future like ours is morally wrong. But, of course, there are obvious cases where this is not true, such as in the case of self-defence. If we are defending ourselves for our life, killing someone and depriving him or her of a future like ours is morally justified and thus not morally wrong.

Next, Moller considers Judith Jarvis Thomson's violinist case (see Chapter 4). Imagine that you are kidnapped during the night as you sleep, and the next day you find yourself attached to a violinist. The violinist is dying, and he needs the use of your kidney for the next nine months to survive and continue living. The violinist is innocent, and he had nothing to do with the kidnapping. The question is whether you are morally obliged to remain connected to the violinist against your will for nine months. If you detach yourself, the violinist will die for certain. In effect, if you leave the hospital, you will kill the innocent violinist. We can adopt the same argument form for the moral wrongness of abortion and substitute the violinist for the foetus. The only difference is that there is no uncertainty at all about the personhood status of the violinist, for he is a full-fledged adult person.

1   Killing an innocent person is always morally wrong.
2   The violinist is an innocent person.
3   Killing the violinist is morally wrong (from 1 and 2).
4   Therefore, you ought not detach yourself from the violinist.

Thomson wants to show that this argument is not as clear-cut as we all tend to think. We have a strong moral intuition that the conclusion is false, because you never consented to be attached to the violinist. Therefore, the violinist has no right to use your body for his survival. Thomson argues that the abducted individual has no moral obligation to remain attached to the violinist, and thus detaching herself from the violinist is morally permissible, even if doing so will guarantee the death of the violinist.

Moller notes that this argument has many challenges. To begin with, it is not clear that the relationship between you and the violinist, and a pregnant woman and a foetus are morally equivalent. In addition, while this analogy works well with cases of rape, in which a woman gives no consent for sexual intercourse, it is not so clear that it will work for all cases of pregnancies. In addition, there are questions about the symmetry that is implied here between rights and moral obligations. The important point that Moller wants to make does not concern our assessment of the arguments, and he does not want to perform a deep analysis of these arguments; instead, he simply wants to demonstrate that there are very good arguments that seem persuasive on both sides of the abortion debate. Moreover, both arguments are open to reasonable challenges and objections.

Moller concludes that the task of analysing these arguments is extremely difficult and requires difficult abstruse argumentation and some degree of moral intuition. All of these strategies and methodologies leave some room for non-negligible mistakes. Philosophers have written hundreds of pages of detailed and rigorous analyses supporting and rejecting these arguments. Given the difficulty of the subject matter and the rigour of analysis entailed in the argumentation, it is conceivable that we can make mistakes that are invisible to our mind at the time we deliberate about these moral questions. Moreover, it is not simply that there are differing opinions among professional ethicists but rather that 'the subject matter involved is the sort of thing it is too easy for people like us to be mistaken about; abstruse moral reasoning involving far-out cases and complex principles is something we find very difficult and are disposed to get wrong reasonably often'.[14]

Moller claims that conceding that there is a high probability of non-negligible moral error about a given moral issue does not necessarily mean that one must change their moral belief or remain sceptical about a given moral topic. Instead, it means that there is some chance that the moral belief one maintains is mistaken. Moreover, we are not aware of our mistake, since we have no reason to believe that we are wrong. Also, given the difficulty of the subject matter and the deliberation process, we may never come to realize that we are mistaken or what the mistake is. As a result of this high probability of non-negligible moral error, there is a high risk that the agent performing this action is committing a moral mistake. Moller argues that our first-level moral deliberation ought to acknowledge and account for this moral risk.

Another important point Moller makes is that having all of the facts in a particular moral case does not guarantee that one is not mistaken in one's moral argumentation and conclusion. There can be many reasons, other than the facts of a case, that lead one to an incorrect and mistaken moral appraisal of a particular issue. There might be new insights that are difficult to explain that could provide new conclusions about the same existing set of facts. Moller uses the example of John Newton, the author of Amazing Grace. Newton was a slave trader who after many years came to find his actions as morally repugnant. His change of heart and change in his moral views on slavery cannot be explained by any changes of the facts that were known to him. For Newton had the same set of facts when he was a slave trader and when he came to morally reject slave trading.

If we admit that moral reasoning about difficult moral issues are inherently risky insofar as we could be mistaken about our conclusions, no matter how certain we believe to be about our arguments at the time, what are we to do?

Moller suggests that we need not suspend judgement or become sceptics. But then how should we conform to or account for this moral risk? Specifically, in the case of abortion, if our conclusion from our first-level deliberation on the abortion issue is that abortion is morally permissible, and we know that we could be mistaken about this belief, then what should be our attitude towards abortion?

Norms for moral risk

There are three general positions with respect to moral risk. The first occupies one extreme and that is to simply ignore it. This position states that moral risk should have no influence in our beliefs and actions. But this position seems terribly problematic. Imagine a person faced with a moral decision to do A or not to do A. His view is that A is morally permissible at time t, but he is also a moral fallibilist with respect to A, and thus believes that he could be wrong about his moral conclusion (that A is permissible) at time t. Imagine also that if he is wrong about his moral conclusion that A is permissible at time t and does A, then the consequences will be morally devastating. In addition, not doing A has no foreseeable negative consequences. In such a case, it is inconceivable that anyone who is sensitive to morality and the good could possibly ignore the moral risk; in other words, given the moral risk of being wrong, coupled with the grave negative consequences that could occur if one is wrong, and the fact that not doing A has no foreseeable negative consequences, it seems that doing A should no longer be morally permissible, or at least one should be much more apprehensive about doing A.

Consider the following example. Imagine that you are a manager of a store. Part of your responsibilities as a manager is to oversee the store's financial success and supervise its employees. This includes hiring and firing employees. In the past months, the store's revenues have declined slightly and the store has seen a small dip in its bottom line. However, the store remains financially viable and successful. One way to cut cost and increase your bottom line quickly is to terminate one of your employee's contracts. All your employees are excellent workers, and they give 100 per cent of their time and effort to the company. At the time, you believe that it is morally permissible to terminate an employee, because one of your duties and obligations is to increase the profitability of the company. On the other hand, a friend you trust and respect brings up concerns that such an action would be unfair and morally wrong, especially given the store's overall current positive financial condition and the lack of no serious threat to its ongoing success. You do not agree with your friend's assessment and remain confident that you are correct about the moral permissibility of firing an employee.

If you are mistaken, however, the moral mistake would be a serious one because you would be committing a terrible injustice to a valued employee. Moreover, you also will cause that employee and his family a great amount of stress, hardship and suffering. On the other hand, if you refrain from terminating an employee, you are not in danger of committing any morally wrong action (i.e. the risk is asymmetrical), and there are no foreseeable negative consequences, except a temporary small dip in the store's net profit. The question is whether or not the moral risk ought to be a factor in your moral decision-making process. Consistent moral reasoning requires that this moral risk not only be a factor but also, given the specific facts in this case, a determining factor in refraining from terminating an employee. Many other examples can be constructed showing that comprehensive and consistent moral decision-making cannot ignore moral risk.

The second position occupies the other extreme in which, given any degree of moral risk, we suspend our moral beliefs and actions. In this case, it does not matter if an action is morally permissible or obligatory; if there is a chance that your moral conclusion is wrong, then you should refrain from acting. This extreme view results in absurdly counter-intuitive situations. Let us consider the situations above once again, but instead let us imagine that the stores' financial situation is in much worse conditions. In this case, you are the manager of a failing business in which there are only two alternatives: (1) bankruptcy and thus the closing and firing of all the employees or (2) the termination of one employee. The moral risk that terminating an employee is morally wrong remains because it could be unfair and unjust. However, in this case, not firing an employee also has moral risks, in that you could be putting the livelihood of many other people in jeopardy (i.e. the risk is symmetrical). Nevertheless, even though the consideration of such moral risk remains part of the moral decision-making process, in this case, it should not be a determining factor as in the previous case. In this case, the existence of moral risk should not change our moral decision that firing of an employee is morally permissible.

Moller argues for a middle ground in which 'we have reason to avoid moral risk, variable in its strength, but not necessarily a decisive one, since it may be overridden by other considerations depending on the circumstances'.[15] This moderate position takes moral risk into consideration and allows the moral agent to assess it within the context of the overall moral situation. As a result, this middle position on moral risk neither ignores it nor makes it an absolute value.

If you are not convinced that moral risk is real, Moller presents one final blanket argument from the perspective of hindsight. It is common to think back on our past actions and to have moral regrets about many of them. In essence, a moral regret is an admission that some past action we performed and believed to morally permissible, we now consider to be immoral and a moral mistake. Moral regrets are common and in many cases they are based on value changes we have made in our moral thinking. These value regrets demonstrate that we have made moral mistakes and that we are morally fallible. But if this is true of many of our past actions, then they are also true of our present actions. Moller argues, 'Since we can envision the possibility of regretting our actions later due to our getting questions about value wrong, we seem to have a reason in the present to take seriously that possibility – not (merely) to avoid the pain of the future regret, but to avoid the moral or axiological mistakes that we might be making.'[16] Therefore, not only are moral regrets proof that we make moral mistakes, there is a proportional likelihood between moral regrets and moral mistakes in the present and future.

Moral risk and abortion

How does moral risk affect abortion defenders' and abortion critics' views? Adopting the moderate position on moral risk would mean that we ought to seriously consider the possibility that we are mistaken about the position we hold. This introduces a meta-level of analysis to the abortion debate that most arguments never consider. Moller claims that moral risk mostly affects the abortion defenders' position in a significant way.

Moller does not propose a full-fledged theory of moral risk; instead, he argues 'there is a reason to avoid certain acts such as abortion, often ignored, stemming from moral risk, and that reason seems to be a non-trivial one'.[17] Therefore, according to Moller, even if a woman believes that abortion is morally permissible, and she has arrived at her belief through cogent arguments, she still might have a moral obligation to refrain from having an abortion given an assessment of the moral risk involved in having the abortion. Notice that there are two levels of argumentation here, and that the moral risk argument supervenes on the first-level of arguments for or against the moral permissibility of abortion.

Moller provides five factors we need to consider when formulating an assessment of moral risk.

1 The likelihood that an action involves wrongdoing.
2 How wrong an action would be if it were wrong?
3 The costs the agent faces if she omits performing the action.
4 The agent's level of responsibility for facing the choice of doing the action.
5 Whether *not* doing the action would also involve moral risk.

Let us frame these factors within the abortion context.

(a) The likelihood that an abortion involves wrongdoing.

(b) How wrong is an abortion if it were wrong?

(c) The costs the pregnant woman faces if she refrains from having an abortion.

(d) The pregnant woman's level of responsibility for facing the choice of having an abortion.

(e) Whether *not* having an abortion would also involve moral risk.

Let us consider each of these in more detail.

(a) The likelihood that an abortion involves wrongdoing.

The likelihood that an abortion involves wrongdoing depends on the specific position one holds for the permissibility of an abortion. For example, consider the following three views for the moral permissibility of abortion: (1) abortion is morally permissible during the first twelve days of gestation before the possibility of twinning occurs; (2) abortion is morally permissible before the foetus is viable and (3) abortion is morally permissible at any time during the gestation period before the foetus is born. These views have different inherent probabilities associated with them as to how likely it is that an abortion involves wrongdoing. For instance, imagine that the view that abortion is permissible is wrong and that all abortions turn out to be immoral. In this case, people who hold the first view are less likely to commit a moral mistake than people who hold the third view. So, the probability that a view on abortion is wrong will depend on the specific details of the view. In addition, it is difficult to measure the probability that a given view on abortion might be wrong. But, if this is true, then it supports the claim that we ought to increase the moral risk involved in moral decisions concerning the abortion issue in virtue of its inherent difficult nature. In other words, Moller might argue that given the abstruse nature of the moral and metaphysical subject matter of abortion, the likelihood that we make a mistake and commit a morally wrong action is high for *all* views that defend the moral permissibility of abortion.

(b) How wrong would performing an abortion be if it were wrong?

Moller claims that if abortion were wrong it would be a moral travesty. If the abortion critics' arguments are correct and the abortion defenders are wrong, the moral wrong would be tantamount to murder or depriving an innocent human being of a future of like ours. This seems to be one of the most powerful factors in the moral risk argument against abortion. Moller thinks that the moral risk is so grave that it should serve as a strong reason for a woman to avoid abortion despite her believe that abortions are morally permissible.

To understand this factor better consider the following example. Imagine a demolition crew shows up to perform a scheduled destruction of a building. They do the routine precautionary drill, and they give out loud warnings to make sure the building is empty. Along comes a drunken person who walks up to the demolition leaders and tells them, in his slurred speech, that he saw a woman and a child walk into the building early in the morning. Let's say that the demolition leader has little reason to believe this drunken person. The drunken person is not a credible witness. Moreover, if there were a woman and a child in the building, they would have heard the warnings and evacuated. Thus, the likelihood of the demolition leader being mistaken is very low. Nevertheless, even though the risk is very low, if the demolition leader is mistaken, the moral wrong that would transpire – the killing of a woman and child – is so gravely horrific that it provides sufficient reason to cancel the demolition and order another thorough investigation of the entire building.

(c) The costs the woman faces if she refrains from having an abortion.
Here we need to consider what happens if a woman does not have an abortion. The particular situation of every woman will be different, and as a result it would be very difficult to derive any sort of general principle in this matter. We can, for instance, imagine a thirteen-year-old girl who is pregnant and for which the cost of going through with a pregnancy and having the baby would be so high that it could even cost her her life. On the other hand, we might imagine, at the other extreme, a mature woman who is financially well-off, has stable and healthy family life and only one child. For her, refraining from having an abortion might not entail the extreme sacrifice and suffering that it would for the 13-year-old girl. There are objectively identifiable factors that can help determine the cost of taking a pregnancy to term. However, there are also many other factors involved in taking a pregnancy to term that are subjective and personal. This aspect of pregnancy can only be assessed and evaluated by the pregnant woman herself.

(d) The agent's level of responsibility for facing the choice of having an abortion.
Another factor that Moller asks us to consider is the degree of responsibility that can be ascribed to a moral agent for ending up in the moral situation she is in. The idea here is that there seems to be a morally relevant relation between the degree of responsibility of the agent and the cost the agent is expected to endure in avoiding the moral risk. In other words, if an agent has been thrown into a particular situation, we would not expect her to sacrifice as much as someone who was responsible for getting into a similar situation. Here again, in the case of abortion, there are a plethora of situations and every case will be different, having their own unique facts and circumstances.

However, as in the other factors, we can describe some extreme views that will illustrate the relevancy of the responsibility criterion. At one extreme, we can imagine a woman who is raped and gets pregnant. In this case, we can argue that, for this woman, the threshold of the cost she faces ought to be less for avoiding the moral risk associated with an abortion than a woman who consents to unprotected sexual intercourse. At the other extreme, we might imagine a woman who wants to get pregnant and sets out to do so. She is successful, but after several months of being pregnant she changes her mind. In this case, we might expect the woman to be held to a higher threshold of the costs she should endure in an effort to avoid the moral risk associated with having an abortion.

(e) Whether not having an abortion would also involve moral risk.

Finally, Moller recognized that moral decisions have symmetrical or asymmetrical moral risks. If an agent faces symmetrical risks, then an agent will face a moral risk both in performing an action and in not performing it. In these cases, what is important is the net moral risk. If an agent faces an asymmetrical moral risk, then the agent will face moral risk in only one of the choices and no moral risk in the opposite choice. For instance, if an agent faces moral risk in performing action A and no moral risk in not performing A, we have a case of asymmetrical risk. In these cases, moral risk will be a factor that will carry much greater weight in the moral arguments. Moller presents the example of vegetarianism. Eating meat presents a moral risk for an agent, because when we eat meat we are accomplices to the harm that sentient animals suffer as part of the meat industry, but refraining from eating meat presents no moral risk for the agent.

Moller argues that the case of abortion is asymmetrical as well, so that while an agent faces moral risk in having an abortion, she faces little to no moral risk in not having an abortion. Moller says, 'Abortion seems to present us with the requisite asymmetry, as there is usually little to be said for thinking that having an abortion might be morally required. That view would entail that it was generally wrong to give birth!'[18] Of course there are exceptions to this as when the mother's health is in danger if she carries the pregnancy to term. In this case, if she does not have an abortion, then she could die or suffer some serious health problem. Also, this could put at risk the rest of her family. According to Moller, however, these cases are few and far between. He argues that the *net* moral risk involved in cases of abortion is much greater on the side of having an abortion. Moller summarizes his view as follows:

> Suppose that all this were right. How strong of a case against abortion would it yield? The main point is simply that agents should consider

something like 1–5 [(a)–(e)] when making abortion decisions; I will not try to show what exactly agents should conclude. In any case, as I have argued, the force of the risk-based point will vary with things like costs and facts about responsibility, which means that the force of this argument will vary from agent to agent. Clearly, then, the argument does not generate a blanket all-things-considered objection to abortion; it does seem to suggest, however, that there is a moral reason – probably not a weak one – for most agents to avoid abortion.[19]

Challenges to Moller's moral risk argument

How might abortion defenders respond to Moller's argument from moral risk? First, the conception of moral risk or the conception of meta-deliberation itself is not necessarily something that abortion defenders would object to. This is an important part of moral evaluation that ought to be present in all of our moral deliberations. However, what they might object to is that the result of meta-deliberation about the abortion issue will lead one to refrain from having an abortion. An abortion defender might have every different insight into (a) and (c) above.

First, if an abortion defender believes that the foetus is not a person, and she has good justification and a strong defence of this view based on a solid understanding of the conception of personhood, then she will have no doubts or worries about making a non-negligible mistake. She would have internal certainty about her position, as certain as she is about any well-justified belief. Therefore, even if she also believes that she could be wrong about beliefs she feels certain about, such fallibility would not (and should not) be sufficient to make her refrain from having an abortion. If the probability of being mistaken exists, it would appear to be very low for her. Thus, for such an abortion defender the likelihood that an abortion involves wrongdoing would be low to non-existent.

Second, an abortion defender might also argue that Moller has understated and underestimated the costs the pregnant woman faces if she refrains from having an abortion. It seems that people might view the costs and sacrifice of bringing a child into the world very differently. One could realistically argue that the psychological, emotional and physical impact of carrying the pregnancy to term and having and raising a child could be monumental and would last a lifetime. It's not simply an illness that interfere in one's life for nine months; instead, it is a lifelong responsibility to care, nurture and raise another person. Appraising one's responsibility and assessing the cost and sacrifice entailed in giving birth requires that a woman also consider her responsibility towards the newborn child, not only for the immediate future but also for the long-term future of the child. It is a decision that will

Table 3.1 Moral risk assessment

Criteria	Abortion Critic	Abortion Defender
The likelihood that an abortion involves wrongdoing.	Likely	Unlikely
How wrong is an abortion if it were wrong?	Very wrong	Very wrong
The costs the agent faces if she refrains from having an abortion.	In most cases, cost is not great.	In all cases, the cost is great.
An agent's level of responsibility for facing the choice of having an abortion.	Depends	Depends
Whether *not* having an abortion would also involve moral risk.	In most cases, no moral risk or little moral risk.	In most cases, there is moral risk of not caring for the child properly.

substantially change one's life in essential ways and these changes will last for one's entire life.

Given an abortion defender's assessment of factors (a) and (c), they might maintain that, while moral risk is something that one ought to consider in one's evaluation of moral issues, in the case of abortion, when a woman is certain that the likelihood of wrongdoing is low, and she understands well the sacrifice of bearing and raising a child, moral risk ought not change her view that having an abortion is morally permissible. Table 3.1 summarizes Moller's moral risk argument as applied to abortion. In this chart, we can also see how an abortion defender might respond to Moller's view.

Summary

In Chapters 1 and 2, we saw that the concept of personhood is an essential concept for the abortion defenders' and abortion critics' personhood positions. However, we also saw that arriving at a precise definition of personhood is challenging, to say the least. This chapter has provided two interesting positions that deal with the indeterminacy of the foetus's personhood status. In the first view, Susan Gibson directly addresses the issue by arguing that personhood is an essentially contested concept. In other words, it is a legitimate concept of debate, but one that is logically impossible to define in a universal manner. She then prescribes the logical consequences of personhood's status as an essentially contested concept.

First, she argues that one's view of personhood should not be abandoned but rather sustained and defended. Second, she argues that the foetus no longer occupies centre stage of the abortion debate; instead, we ought to adopt a feminist perspective, in which we consider the pregnant woman and her circumstances just as relevant as the foetus and its circumstances. Third, as a result of the feminist perspective, we can no longer consider the abortion issue from a general abstract model; we must consider the concrete and particular situation of each woman. Fourth, another consequence of the feminist perspective is that we must reconsider our paradigm of moral assessment from one based on independent individuals to one grounded in *relations of* individuals. As a consequence, the status of the foetus cannot be considered in and of itself, but rather as it relates to the pregnant woman. The central moral category of value is this relationship. Gibson concludes that the abortion decision should always be the right of a woman to decide and that no one should ever interfere in a woman's decision to have an abortion. However, she also argues that a woman can be morally mistaken about her decision to have an abortion, and therefore not all cases of abortion are morally permissible. Moreover, an objective third-party moral evaluation of a woman's abortion decision is possible. The conclusion of a third-party moral evaluation may be legitimate and applicable not only for the evaluator but also for the woman.

In the second part of the chapter, D. Moller addresses the difficult task of defining personhood indirectly through the concept of moral risk. Moller argues that the moral issue of abortion is inherently difficult, and thus there is a high probability that even the most intelligent philosophers and ethicists can make undetected mistakes in their arguments. Knowing that our arguments for or against the permissibility of abortion (i.e. first-level deliberation) can be mistaken and that these mistakes can remain undetected creates moral risk for the agent performing the action. Moller proposes a formula for determining the degree of moral risk involved in any particular moral dilemma. In the case of abortion, the criteria are the following: (a) the likelihood that an abortion involves wrongdoing, (b) the degree of wrongness of an abortion if it were wrong, (c) the costs the pregnant woman faces if she refrains from having an abortion, (d) the pregnant woman's level of responsibility for facing the choice of having an abortion and (e) whether *not* having an abortion would also involve moral risk.

According to Moller, in the case of people who believe that abortion is morally permissible, the risk that their moral conclusion is wrong has serious consequences; this risk could offer evidence for tilting the scales on whether it remains morally permissible. On the other hand, those who conclude that abortion is immoral in all circumstances also face similar challenges to their conclusions, once we allow moral risk to factor into their moral calculations.

Study questions

1 What is an essentially contested concept?

2 Is personhood an essentially contested concept? Why or why not?

3 How are the feminist and non-feminist perspectives on abortion different?

4 What is a Kantian conception of moral autonomy and how is it related to Gibson's view of rational autonomy?

5 What is the difference between overruling and evaluating another agent's action and how does this apply to abortion?

6 Gibson argues that the issue concerning the ethics of abortion is irresolvable because its resolution relies on an essentially contested concept, namely, personhood. Explain what conclusions, according to Gibson, we ought to derive from these arguments. Do you agree with her assessment? Why or why not?

7 What are non-negligible errors?

8 What is the difference between first-level and second-level deliberation?

9 What is moral risk?

10 What are the criteria for determining moral risk?

11 What are the criteria for determining moral risk in the abortion issue?

12 Moller argues that some moral choices entail an inherent non-negligible moral risk. What does this mean? How should we assess moral risk? If he is right, what are the consequences for the abortion issue?

4

Women's Rights and Abortion

Most of the traditional arguments on the ethics of abortion focus on the moral status of the foetus. One reason for this is because most abortion critics believe that if it can be shown that the foetus is a person, then we can ascribe to it all of the rights we ascribe to adult human persons, including the right to life. Therefore, abortion critics hold that demonstrating the personhood status of the foetus is a sufficient condition for concluding that all or most abortions are seriously immoral and are equivalent to homicide. But Judith Jarvis Thomson begs to differ. She argues that even if we grant that a foetus is a person at the moment of conception, it is not always the case that an abortion is morally wrong. In this chapter, we explore Thomson's argument that an abortion, in some cases, commits no injustice against the foetus, even if the foetus is considered a person. She bases her argument on the view that, in some cases, the right of a woman to detach herself from a foetus outweighs the right to life of the foetus.[1]

Personhood argument for the moral wrongness of abortion

Premise 1: Intentionally killing an innocent human person is always morally wrong.

Premise 2: A foetus from the time of conception or close to the time of conception is an innocent human person.

Premise 3: Abortion is (or entails) the intentional killing of a foetus.

Premise 4: Abortion is (or entails) the intentional killing of an innocent human person (follows from 2 and 3).

Conclusion: Therefore, abortion is morally wrong.

Let us begin by looking at, once again, the personhood argument for the moral wrongness of abortion.

Traditionally, the focus of the abortion debate has been on the truth status of premise (2). The abortion critics' arguments defend the truth of the premises and the validity of the argument, and thus the argument's soundness. In contrast, the abortion defenders' counter-arguments attempt to show that premise (2) is false, and as a result the argument is unsound and fails. In this chapter, we take a completely different perspective on the abortion issue by analysing an argument that does not focus on premise (2) or on the question of personhood. Instead, Thomson argues that a pregnant woman has a right to terminate her pregnancy even if it means the foetus will die and even if we grant that the foetus is a person. Thomson writes:

> Opponents of abortion commonly spend most of their time establishing that the fetus is a person, and hardly any time explaining the step from there to the impermissibility of abortion. Perhaps they think the step too simple and obvious to require much comment. Or perhaps instead they are simply being economical in argument. Many of those who defend abortion rely on the premise that the fetus is not a person, but only a bit of tissue that will become a person at birth; and why pay out more arguments than you have to? Whatever the explanation, I suggest that the step they take is neither easy nor obvious, that it calls for closer examination than it is commonly given, and that when we do give it this closer examination we shall feel inclined to reject it. *I propose, then, that we grant that the fetus is a person from the moment of conception* [my emphasis].[2]

Before we begin an analysis of Thomson's argument, let us explore the notion of rights and their relation to ethics and morality.

Rights and moral obligations

The notion of rights is an essential part of the abortion issue. One major issue associated with rights is whether the foetus has a right to life. Another is a woman's right to the use and control of her body and her rights over her reproductive choices. There is also the issue of how we balance a foetus's right to life, if it has a right to life, and a woman's right over her body and reproductive choices. Finally, there is also the issue of the father's rights and if he has any rights at all over a woman's choice to have an abortion. To understand how to evaluate the moral significance of these rights and how they play out in the moral debate on abortion, we need to understand more about the notion of rights and moral obligations.

Rights refer to basic freedoms and liberties human beings have within a society or community. Moreover, rights are an essential part of any successful democratic community, because they are what provide the members of that community the liberties to express their freedom and autonomy. Two of the important functions of governments are to provide security for its citizens and to guarantee its citizens' individual rights. The existence of basic individual rights and their protection, therefore, are a necessary part of a politically successful democratic society. Rights grant us the basic liberties that lead to a high standard of living and quality of life; they are essential for any successfully functioning democracy.

We can speak of *claim rights* and *liberty rights*. Claim rights are rights that create duties and obligations on others towards the right holder. In other words, a right holder of a claim right can legitimately demand that an agent act (in the case of positive rights) or refrain from acting (in the case of negative rights) towards the right holder. So, for instance, if person A has a claim right against person B to do (or not to do) x, then person B has a duty to do x (or refrain from doing x) for or to A.

Consider concrete examples. If I purchase a property, then I have certain claim rights related to that property. My right to the property creates obligations on others not to trespass onto my property or use my property without my permission. I might also have a claim right to build a house without having others interfere in the construction of this house. My rights are not necessarily unlimited, however, and if I try to build a commercial property in a parcel that is zoned for residential use only, my neighbours and the government can interfere and prevent me from building it.

Consider my right to an education or my right as a citizen of the United States to vote in the presidential elections. These rights are claim rights because they create certain duties on others. For instance, a right to an education creates a duty, on the part of the government, to provide the necessary services so that I can obtain an education. Thus, it creates an obligation on the part of a community or government to provide me with such services. Similarly, a right to vote creates certain duties on the part of the government to provide the necessary infrastructure to permit me to cast my vote. It also creates a duty on others, including the government, not to interfere or obstruct my right to an education or my right to vote.

These rights, however, are not unlimited, and as in the case of property rights, my right to an education and my right to vote have certain limits as to the kinds of duties they can impose on others. For instance, I cannot infringe on other people's rights to guarantee my right. So, even though I have a right to an education, I do not have a right to take my neighbour's car without his permission to make sure that I get to school. I also cannot request that the government take my neighbour's car, on my behalf, so that I can get to school.

The demands for the fulfilment of claim rights must also be just and cannot infringe on the rights of others.

Liberty rights concern freedoms that are more like privileges; they do not produce corresponding obligations or duties for other moral agents. So, if person A has a liberty right to do *x*, then no one, not even the government, has a moral obligation to provide what is necessary for A to do *x*. For instance, you may have a liberty right to walk freely in common areas, but this does not create obligations for others to provide the means for you to walk in common areas. If the closest common areas to you are, ironically, too far for you to walk to, no one is under any obligation to get you to the common area so that you can exercise your liberty right to walk there. Notice that, in the case of an education, if you live too far to walk to school, then the government would have a duty to make sure that you receive the necessary transportation to get to school, because education is a *claim right* and not just a *liberty right*.

We can also think about the source of rights; that is, how did one obtain the right in question? There are three fundamental sources of individual rights: *natural, legal* and *contractual*. Natural rights are conferred upon one without one doing anything at all; that is, they arise as an intrinsic part of one's nature; they are thus inalienable and they transcend the notions of nationalism, citizenship and statutory law. Natural rights for human beings are sometimes called human rights, and they are ascribed to people solely in virtue of their humanity. For instance, human inalienable rights include the rights to life, liberty and the pursuit of happiness.

Legal rights come about through human convention and thus are created by particular governments to serve a variety of different purposes. Legal rights are conferred upon people by national constitutions, amendments to the constitutions and national, state and local laws. Some of these rights can overlap with natural rights, so, for instance, many of the constitutional amendments of the United States are also natural rights. On the other hand, many legal rights are arbitrary and vary from place to place. For instance, in some states you have a right to drive at the age of 16, while in other states the driving age is 17 years of age. In some countries you have the right to drink alcohol at the age of 18, and in the United States you do not have such a right until the age of 21.

Contractual rights are particular rules and regulations that one has established with other parties through specific voluntary consent of all parties involved. Usually, such rights and obligations are beneficial for all parties or at least they appear beneficial at the time the agreement and contract are drawn up. For instance, a contract to lease a rental property would give a lessee the right to live in the property if the lessee pays the rent and fulfils any other contractual obligations as set forth in the agreement.

All of these classifications of rights have an important role in the abortion debate. For instance, if abortion is illegal, then one's right to an abortion is precluded. If abortion is legal, then one has a legal right to an abortion. Such a right may be a claim or liberty right. If it is a liberty right, then if a pregnant woman cannot afford an abortion the state is not necessarily obligated to assist her in getting an abortion. However, if one believes that the right to an abortion is a claim right, then one will hold that the government does have a duty to assist a pregnant woman in obtaining an abortion. It is important to keep in mind that natural rights are fundamental rights and thus they trump legal and contractual rights. In other words, if a legal or contractual right conflicts with one's natural right, then the legal or contractual right must be overridden. For instance, a law that legalizes slavery can never be sustained because it contradicts the natural law that proscribes a rational agent's natural autonomy.

A final important issue is to understand the relationship between rights and moral obligations. Some philosophers hold that rights are fundamental and moral obligations can be assessed through an analysis of rights. According to this view, claim rights and moral obligations will be symmetrical. In other words, if no claim right exists against you, then one has no moral obligations towards the non-claim holder. Moreover, one's moral obligations can only be derived through another's claim rights against one. However, some philosophers disagree and hold that moral obligations are either more fundamental than or just as fundamental as claim rights. Therefore, it is possible that person A has a moral obligation towards person B to perform act x, despite the fact person B has no claim right against person A to perform act x.

An example might help to illustrate this point. Thomson asks us to imagine that a mother gives one of her two children, child A, a box of chocolates. A's sibling, child B, also wants chocolates, but the mother gave one box only to child A. In this case, we may conclude that child A has a claim right to the chocolates, and child B does not have a claim right to the chocolates. Child A's claim right to the chocolates creates a moral duty on child B to refrain from taking the chocolates. In addition, because child B has no claim rights to the chocolates, child A has no moral obligation to share his chocolates with his sibling, child B. Moreover, child A does not act unjustly towards child B if he decides to eat all the chocolates and share none with child B. Thomson says, 'My own view is that it just does not follow from the truth of this that the brother [child B] has any right to any of the chocolates. If the boy [child A] refuses to give his brother any he is greedy, stingy, callous – but not unjust.'[3] Here we can see that justice is symmetrical with rights. However, some might disagree with this outlook and argue that child A has a moral obligation to share his chocolates with his brother (child B), and moreover child A acts morally wrong and unjustly in not doing so. We will discuss this issue further below.

The argument from a woman's right to her body

Before we consider Thomson's argument, let us investigate the abortion defender's argument from a woman's rights to her body. One common line of argumentation is that an abortion is morally permissible because ultimately it is the pregnant woman's body, and a woman should have the right to do with her body as she wishes. First, we should ask ourselves if a person has an absolute right to control his or her body. One apparent and most obvious answer is 'yes'. A person's body is the most intimate and personal belonging one has; it is more than just property. A person's body is part of their identity, and it is a substantial part of who they are. For instance, a person should be able to decide whether they want to have a tattoo on their body or whether they want to undergo plastic surgery on their body. These are personal decisions that do not seem to directly affect anyone else, and the final say of such decisions should be left up to the person whose body it is.

Even if we agree that the authority to make decisions concerning one's body should be left up to the individual person whose body it is, it remains an open question whether third parties can objectively evaluate the decisions. That is, can others objectively judge another's actions concerning the use of their bodies? For example, if a person decides to partake in pornographic films, can we say that, even though they are within their rights to make that decision, we can objectively evaluate the decision as a morally wrong one? If the answer is yes, and I think it is, then it follows that having a right to certain actions does not mean that one is not subject to moral evaluation with respect to that action.

Do we have an absolute right to the use of our bodies in whatever way we want? Does the argument 'it's is my body, therefore, I am free to do whatever I want with it' have much traction? Are there exceptions to the right to use one's body as one desires? First, consider the case in which a person lacks the cognitive ability to make an informed decision about the use of his or her body. The cognitive deficiency may be a result of a disability, drunkenness or youth. Consider a thirteen-year-old young man who would like to get married. He might argue that it is his body and life, and he should be free to do as he pleases with it. However, most would agree that a thirteen-year-old person lacks the necessary experience and knowledge to make such a life-changing decision such as getting married. For this reason, we might argue that the thirteen-year-old is not free to do with his body as he pleases. Second, consider a person whose cognitive faculties are not completely functional. They might have some mental deficiency that prohibits them from making fully informed choices. In these cases, we might limit a person's freedom to use their body as they wish in order to secure their safety and welfare. Finally, there might also be persons who are temporarily psychologically impaired and thus might not be acting as they would act under normal circumstances. We might, legitimately, again, be justifiably permitted to intervene in such people's freedom to use their body as they wish.

In addition to these exceptions, there are other limitations to one's freedom to use one's body as one desires. For instance, I am not free to use my fist to punch a hole in the wall of a hotel room. Using my fist to punch a hole in a hotel wall will not only affect me, it will also affect the hotel owner since it is her wall. In other words, while I have a right to my body and the authority to make decisions about the use of my body, I do not have a right to take or damage other people's property. Therefore, I do not have a right to use my fist to punch a hole in a hotel wall. If I do not have a right to use my body to damage the property of others, then, a fortiori, I do not have a right to use my body in ways that might physically harm others. As a consequence, while I have a right to do what I desire with my body, this liberty is restricted when it interferes with the liberty of others not to be harmed and to do as they freely wish with their bodies. Thus, I do not have a right to punch another person in the face. My right to my body has some seriously stringent limitations, for my rights end where the rights of others begin.

We might even question the right and/or the moral permissibility to do things with my body that might cause psychological harm and suffering to others. For instance, do I have a right to commit suicide? While this is a much more complicated situation, it is reasonable to argue that even though I do not physically harm others when I cause my own death, it might be the case that I might cause others serious psychological trauma or even harm if I were to commit suicide. The important point, for our purpose, is to note that one does not have an absolute or unlimited right to the use of one's body, and, even though one's body is the most intimate possession we have (if we can even call it a possession), it does not follow that we are free to do with it as we wish.

Abortion defenders sometimes argue that a woman is free to detach herself from the foetus because it is her body and she has a right to do with her body as she wishes. This view will emphasize that the intention is not to kill the foetus, but rather for the pregnant woman to free herself of the foetus. The killing of the foetus is an unintentional consequence. If the foetus were to survive an abortion, the woman does not have a right to kill the foetus. Abortion critics will respond that if the foetus is considered a person, then the decision to have an abortion will result in taking the life of a person. Moreover, if a person has a right to life, then the woman's decision to have an abortion will infringe upon the foetus's basic right to life. Thus, while it is true that a woman has a basic prima facie right to her body, it is also true that a foetus has a basic prima facie right to life. Moreover, a right to life trumps a right to use one's body; thus the foetus's right to life outweighs a woman's right to use her body as she wishes. The abortion defender's argument from the right to use one's body seems to be in trouble. Or is it?

Judith Jarvis Thomson's argument

The majority of arguments that conclude abortion is ethically wrong rely on a premise that the foetus is a human person. This premise is important, because if it can be shown that the foetus is a human person, then we must ascribe to it all of the rights one would normally ascribe to an adult human person who is a member of the moral community. Among such rights is the right to life. As a consequence, if the foetus has a right to life, then no one, not even the pregnant woman, can take the life of her foetus. The act of abortion is the intentional taking of the life of her foetus; therefore, abortion is ethically wrong. Moreover, this argument prevents the abortion defender's rebuttal from a woman's right to her body, for this right can never outweigh a person's right to life.

As a consequence, arguments that support the conclusion that abortion is ethically permissible have focused on the issue of whether the foetus ought to be considered a human person and a member of the moral community.[4] Most abortion defenders deny the truth of premise (2) (that the foetus is a person). The controversy seems to surround the question concerning the personhood of the foetus, which entails controversial questions: What does it mean to be a person? When does personhood begin? These questions are difficult to answer and no conception of personhood promises to be uncontroversial, as we have seen in previous chapters.

Thomson's argument in defence of the moral permissibility of abortion, however, adopts another strategy, one quite unexpected and one that, in part, is responsible for making her argument so fascinating. Instead of rejecting premise (2), Thomson denies the truth of premise (1). This strategy does a couple of things. First, it removes from the argument the controversial questions concerning personhood. Her analysis does not require an answer to the personhood question because she is willing, for argument's sake, to grant the abortion critics the truth of premise (2). Second, it shifts the central issue in the abortion discussion from ontology and metaphysics to the realm of individual rights and moral obligations. That is, the questions no longer are: What is a person? When does a foetus become a person? Instead, the questions we need to address are: What are the rights and moral obligations of a pregnant woman vis-à-vis a foetus that is considered a person?

Thomson claims that abortion critics believe that once it is shown that the foetus is a person the argument against the moral permissibility of abortion is home free. She argues that this assumption is not so obvious once we closely examine the arguments. She believes, instead, that the arguments will demonstrate that, even if it can be shown that the foetus is a person from the moment of conception, with all the rights of personhood, abortion remains morally permissible in some cases. Her argument is complex and has many nuanced elements. First, we will examine her general position. Then, we will elaborate her view more thoroughly by examining a series of objections to her argument along with her responses to these objections.

The violinist analogy: Clear cases of unconsented pregnancies are morally permissible

Thomson begins her argument by presenting an analogy as a counterexample to the abortion critics' argument that demonstrates the falsity of premise (1) (i.e. 'Intentionally killing an innocent human person is always morally wrong') and thus that the argument is not sound. This analogy has become well known in abortion discussions as 'the violinist analogy'. It goes as follows:

> You wake in the morning and find yourself back to back in bed with an unconscious violinist. A famous unconscious violinist. He has been found to have a fatal kidney ailment, and the Society of Music Lovers has canvassed all the available medical records and found that you alone have the right blood type to help. They have therefore kidnapped you, and last night the violinist's circulatory system was plugged into yours, so that your kidneys can be used to extract poisons from his blood as well as your own. The director of the hospital now tells you, 'Look, we're sorry the Society of Music Lovers did this to you – we would never have permitted it if we had known. But still, they did it, and the violinist is now plugged into you. To unplug you would be to kill him. But never mind, it's only for nine months. By then he will have recovered from his ailment, and can be safely unplugged from you.' Is it morally incumbent on you to accede to this situation?[5]

Let us reconstruct the abortion critics' argument using the violinist instead of the foetus so that we can clearly see the strength of the analogy:

Premise 1: Intentionally killing an innocent human person is always morally wrong.

Premise 2: The famous violinist is an innocent human person.

Premise 3: Disconnecting yourself from the violinist will kill him.
Conclusion: Therefore, disconnecting yourself from the violinist is morally
              wrong.

This argument is valid and premises 1–3 seem to be true. Premises 2 and 3 are certain and uncontroversial. If the three premises are true and the argument is valid, then it necessarily follows that the conclusion is true, and thus disconnecting yourself from the violinist is morally wrong. Notice that the moral wrongness is grave, because it entails the killing of another innocent person. Moreover, the amount of time that is required of you to stay in bed connected to the violinist is irrelevant. Therefore, according to this argument, even if you had to remain connected to the violinist for the rest of your life, it would be morally wrong for you to disconnect yourself from him. Finally, even if we recognize that you have a right to your body and to control it as you wish, this right does not outweigh the violinist's right to life, and therefore you cannot deny premise 3 and thus the conclusion.

Despite the strength of this argument, our moral intuition finds it very problematic to accept the conclusion. There is something terribly unjust and unfair about requiring you to stay connected to the violinist against your will and without your consent. Instead, we have a strong moral intuition that you do not have a moral duty to remain connected to the violinist for nine months. The fact that you were kidnapped and that you were connected without your consent provides the moral ground for the ethical permissibility of disconnecting yourself from the violinist, even if this causes the death of the innocent violinist, who had no knowledge of the evil plot. But, if we reject the conclusion and the argument is valid, then one of the premises must be false.

Thomson argues that the first premise is false and thus it is not the case that it is always morally wrong to kill an innocent person. Thomson's point is that while it is true that persons have a claim right to life, they do not have a claim right to all things that they need to secure their continued existence. A claim right to life may mean a right to the bare minimum for one's existence or a right not to be killed, but it does not mean a right to all things needed to sustain one's existence. For instance, just because I have a claim right to life does not mean that I have a right to other people's organs to sustain my life, and it does not mean that other people have a moral obligation to sustain my life no matter what the cost to them. Thomson explains:

This [abortion critics'] argument treats the right to life as if it were unproblematic. It is not, and this seems to me to be precisely the source of the mistake.[6] ... But I would stress that I am not arguing that people do not have a right to life – quite to the contrary, it seems to me that the primary control we must place on the acceptability of an account of rights is that it should turn out in that account to be a truth that all persons have a right to life. I am arguing only that having a right to life does not guarantee having a right to be given the use of or a right to be allowed continued use of another's body – even if one needs it for life itself. So the right to life will not serve the opponents of abortion in the very simple and clear way in which they seem to have thought it would.[7]

Having a right to life, then, does not guarantee a right to all things needed to protect and sustain that life, and it does not guarantee a right to the use of another's body without their consent. The question now is whether someone commits an injustice if they deny another the use of their body for the other's continued existence.

Rights and justice

Thomson argues, 'To deprive someone of what he has a right to is to treat him unjustly.'[8] In contrast, to deprive someone of what he has no right to is not to treat him unjustly. For instance, if person A has no claim right against person B's body, then B's denying person A the use of their body, even if it is needed for person A's continued survival, does not commit an injustice against person A. Thomson presents a conception of rights that is imbued with a more nuanced notion of justice, so that having a right to life doesn't simply mean having a right not to be killed but rather having a right not to be killed *unjustly*. Returning to the case of the violinist, Thomson does not deny that he has a right to life and thus he has a right not to be killed unjustly. However, if you decide to unplug yourself from him you do *not* kill him unjustly, and therefore you have not violated his right to life.

Thomson provides several other examples to illustrate the relationship between rights and justice. Consider her example of Henry Fonda:

> If I am very sick unto death, and the only thing that will save my life is the touch of Henry Fonda's cool hand on my fevered brow, then all the same I have no right to be given the touch of Henry Fonda's cool hand on my fevered brow. It would be frightfully nice of him to fly in from the West Coast to provide it. It would be less nice, though no doubt well meant, if my friends flew out to the West Coast and carried Henry Fonda back with them. But I have no right at all against anybody that he should do this for me.[9]

Another example Thomson provides concerns two siblings that receive a box of chocolates that we discussed above. Let us consider another version of this example. Imagine that a box of chocolates is given equally to two siblings.

Therefore, the younger brother has a claim right to half the chocolates. If the older brother refuses to share the chocolates with the younger brother, he is depriving him of his legitimate rights, and therefore we can conclude that he is being *unjust*. However, (as we saw above) if the box of chocolates is given only to the older brother, then the younger brother does not have a claim right to half of the chocolates (or any of the chocolates), and thus if the older brother does not want to share any of the chocolates with him, he does not deprive him of a legitimate right to anything. As a consequence, 'if the brother refuses to give his brother any [chocolates], he is greedy, stingy, callous – but not unjust'.[10]

Thomson distinguishes moral obligations from just actions. According to her, we cannot derive rights from moral obligations. So, for instance, just because John has a moral obligation to help Nancy with her homework, it does not mean that Nancy has a claim right to have John help her. Now, if Nancy does not have a claim right to have John help her with her homework, then we cannot conclude that John has committed an injustice against Nancy if he refuses to help her. Thomson's view has the awkward result that one can act immorally towards another without acting unjustly, with respect to the same action. So, John may have a moral obligation to help Nancy with her homework, and if he refuses, he acts immorally but not unjustly. We will examine this problem further below in the objections.

According to Thomson's argument, then, to show that abortion is unjust, it is not sufficient to demonstrate that the foetus is a person and that an abortion is the killing of a foetus. It also must be demonstrated that an abortion or this specific case of killing a person is a case of *unjust* killing. If we consider a case in which a woman gets pregnant involuntarily, such as in the case of rape, it is clear that a woman has not consented for the foetus to use her body. Therefore, the foetus does not have a right to the woman's body and thus killing it is *not* a case of *unjust* killing. Notice that a woman can kill a foetus insofar as she denies it the use of her body, which she never consented to; she cannot, however, kill the foetus for any arbitrary reason. For instance, imagine that a woman detaches itself from the foetus and the foetus continues to live; she cannot, then, go and kill the foetus. Similarly, in the case of the violinist, imagine that once you have detached yourself from the violinist, he miraculously survives. You do not have a right to then kill the violinist.

The extreme case of self-defence

Thomson examines the extreme case in which a pregnant woman's life is at risk if she were to carry the pregnancy to full term. Some abortion critics view this case as an exception to their anti-abortion stance. They argue that since the mother's life is in danger, and she also has a right to life, she can have an abortion in self-defence. However, more conservative abortion critics claim that, even when the woman's life is in danger, abortion is tantamount to murder, and thus it remains morally wrong. The latter argument depends on a distinction between killing a person and letting a person die. These more extreme abortion critics argue that letting the mother die does not require an agent to act and thus it should not be considered murder. The death of the mother is, ultimately, one that comes about through natural causes. However, killing the foetus does require an agent to act and thus it constitutes murder.

Thomson argues that the extreme anti-abortion view that argues that letting the mother die is morally superior to killing the foetus requires further premises such as the following:

(1) Directly killing an innocent person is always and absolutely impermissible. (2) Directly killing an innocent person is murder and murder is always and absolutely impermissible. (3) One's duty to refrain from killing an innocent person is more morally stringent than one's duty to keep a person from dying. (4) If one's only options are directly killing an innocent person or letting a person die, one must prefer letting the person die, and thus an abortion must not be performed.[11]

Premises (3) and (4) rely on the view that positive immoral actions are morally worse than negative immoral actions. But this is highly controversial. Many philosophers claim that – all other things being equal (such as intentions) – letting someone die and killing someone are equally morally wrong. For instance, imagine that person C hates his partner and wishes her dead. One morning person C realizes that she is drowning in the pool. Person C's desire to see her dead is so great that he decides not to lend a hand and pull her out of the pool. He sits by and watches her drown. Now imagine person D hates his partner and wishes her dead. He throws her in the pool and pushes her head down with his foot. She drowns and dies. Can we say that person C is morally superior to person D? This seems incorrect because person C's decision to let his partner die is just as morally reprehensible as person D's decision to kill his partner.

According to Thomson, premises (1) and (2) have already been shown to be wrong, since, if Thomson's argument is correct, it is permissible to kill another person as long as one does not do so *unjustly*. Returning to the violinist example, if we were to accept premises (1) and (2), then it would be morally impermissible, under all circumstances, for the kidnapped person to detach herself from the violinist. However, according to Thomson, we have already shown that this is not the case, even if your life is not at risk. Now imagine that the doctor comes in and tells the kidnapped person that if she stays attached to the violinist she will die. Thomson claims, 'If anything in the world is true, it is that you do not commit murder, you do not do what is impermissible if you reach around to your back and unplug yourself from the violinist to save your life.'[12]

Another important point that Thomson makes is that it is the woman who 'houses' the foetus; that is, it is the mother's body and not the foetus's; or, as she puts it, 'the mother *owns* the house.'[13] Therefore, even if the mother and the foetus are considered persons, the woman has a superior right over the foetus, who is only a guest in the woman's house. Thomson concludes, 'In sum, a woman surely can defend her life against the threat posed by the unborn child.'[14]

In response to the argument from self-defence, Baruch Brody has raised an interesting objection, suggesting that the argument from self-defence is not as simple as Thomson believes it to be. Consider the paradigm case of killing an attacker[15] where person A (the attacker) intentionally attempts to kill person B (the victim). In such a case, person B would be justified in defending herself and killing person A. However, let us consider another more complicated example. What if person B is dying and needs a specific medicine to survive that only person C has. Person C will give the medicine to B only if he kills person A. Person A is innocent. Does person B have the right to kill person A to save his life? While person A's continued existence is a danger and obstacle to B's survival, B does not have the right to kill A in self-defence.

Brody claims we can understand the distinction between this case and the paradigm case of self-defence by setting forth three conditions: (1) the condition of danger: one person puts in danger the life of another; (2) the condition of attempt: one person intentionally attempts to take the life of another and (3) the condition of guilt: one person attempts to take the life of another and is fully capable to understand his actions. Brody argues that the paradigm case of self-defence has all three conditions while the second case of the medicine only has condition (1). If we compare these cases with the abortion situation, we can conclude that abortion resembles the second case more than the paradigm case of self-defence. While the foetus's continued existence may pose a danger to the continued existence of the pregnant woman, the foetus neither attempts to kill her nor is it guilty of such an attempt.

Objections and responses

Objection 1: Non-rape cases as consented pregnancies

Let us, for argument's sake, conclude that Thomson's violinist analogy has demonstrated that in cases of rape a woman is justified in having an abortion.

In this respect, Thomson's argument serves an important purpose, since, if we reject Thomson's interpretation of a right to life as a right not to be killed *unjustly*, then it would be difficult to justify abortions even in the case of rape. However, most abortions are not a result of rape; instead, they are cases in which women consented to having sexual intercourse. Moreover, anyone who engages in sexual intercourse should know that there is always a chance, no matter how careful one is, for the woman to get pregnant. But, if this is the case, then doesn't consenting to sexual intercourse give explicit or implicit consent to the foetus to use the woman's body? If so, then in non-rape cases an abortion is an unjust killing. On the other hand, if consenting to sexual intercourse does not necessarily give explicit or implicit consent to the foetus to use the woman's body, then an abortion should not be considered a case of unjust killing and thus should not be protected under the right to life. How can we distinguish between cases in which women give consent to a foetus to use their body from cases in which they do not give consent?

Thomson recognizes the concern for cases in which a woman can be held responsible for getting pregnant. If a woman has sexual intercourse, knowing and understanding full well the risk of getting pregnant is high, and she gets pregnant, is she not partly responsible for the creation of this new foetus, and doesn't this translate into a form of consent? Doesn't this kind of responsibility oblige a pregnant woman to allow the foetus to use her body for its survival? If the foetus has a right to the use of a pregnant woman's body, then killing it would be unjust, because it would deprive it of its right to use her body.

Thomson responds to this objection by first noting that the details in these cases make all the difference. However, the simple fact that a woman has consented to sexual intercourse, knowing full well that it is *possible* that she could get pregnant, does not constitute a voluntary invitation or consent for a foetus to use the woman's body for its survival. Thomson presents several interesting analogies that can help us understand her view.

Analogy 1: Imagine that you open your window to get fresh air and as a result a burglar gets into your apartment. Can we argue that since you opened your window, you are partly responsible for the burglar getting into your apartment? Moreover, since you are partly responsible for the burglar getting into your apartment, have you implicitly consented for the burglar to be in your apartment? Can we conclude, then, that, as a result of this implicit consent, the burglar now has a right to live in your apartment? This seems absurd and it demonstrates that non-negligible actions (assuming that the opening of the window is normal in this neighbourhood), on the part of a woman, that result in pregnancy cannot be interpreted as consent for the foetus to use her body for its survival.

Analogy 2: Imagine that your windows have bars to prevent burglars and thus you have taken extraordinary precautions to make sure that no one gets into your apartment without your consent. You open the windows and leave them open thinking that you are well protected from intruders. But suppose that, through no fault of your own, the bars are defective and a burglar does get in. If in analogy 1, we concluded that the apartment owner did not implicitly consent to the burglar coming into the apartment, then, certainly, in this case also we can conclude that the apartment owner did not implicitly consent to the burglar coming into the apartment. Analogy 2 represents a woman who uses contraception responsibly and yet, because of some defect in the contraception, she ends up pregnant. In this case, Thomson believes we are safe to conclude that the woman did not consent and thus having an abortion would not be an unjust killing of the foetus.

Analogy 3: Thomson describes a hypothetical, and somewhat strange, situation in which there are people-seeds floating around in the air. We know that if one of these people-seeds enters one's apartment, and they plant themselves in one's carpet, then a person will grow. To make sure that this does not happen, we buy and install very fine screens in our windows. They guarantee to protect our apartment from these floating people-seeds. However, unbeknownst to us, one of our screens is broken and a people-seed is able to enter and plant itself in our carpet. The question is whether the people-seed person has the right to use our carpet and our apartment for its survival? In this case, Thomson claims that this plant-person does not have a right to use your carpet, and, given that you took reasonable measures to prevent its entry, you also have the right to destroy it without committing an *unjust* act.

Thomson does concede that a high degree of irresponsibility could be interpreted as implicit consent and thus create situations in which an abortion is an act of unjust killing and thus not morally permissible. Moreover, in cases where a woman gives explicit consent, it would be morally wrong to later change her mind. So, for instance, if a woman voluntarily gets pregnant but during her seventh month of pregnancy changes her mind about having a child for a frivolous reason, such as 'to avoid the nuisance of postponing a trip abroad',[16] then in such a case abortion would be morally wrong.

Objection 2: Third-party interference

Thomson observes that there is a morally relevant difference between a woman having an abortion and a doctor or some other third party intervening to assist the woman in having an abortion. It is not clear that even if one were to agree that it is morally permissible for a woman to have an abortion, it follows that it is also morally permissible for a third party to intervene and assist the woman in having an abortion. This point is essential because it is extremely difficult, if not impossible, for a woman to perform her own abortion.

Imagine a case of self-defence in which the life of another person puts your life at risk. However, imagine that the person is innocent and the threat they create to your life is accidental and not malicious. In this case, while you might have some justification for defending your life against the agent who is the cause of the mortal threat, a third party would not have the same justification. From the third party's perspective, there are two innocent persons and one must die, but there is no justification for the third party to choose one over the other. Thus, in cases where the foetus presents a life-threatening risk to the mother, a third party might argue that they cannot perform an abortion, because they have no right to choose the mother over the foetus.

Notice that if we accept the premise that the foetus is a person from the moment of conception, then we require some moral reason why a third party ought to choose to save the mother's life over the foetus's life. Thomson argues that what gives the third party the moral justification to intervene is the fact that it is the mother's body and not the foetus's. She explains it as follows:

> For what we have to keep in mind is that the mother and the unborn child are not like two tenants in a small house which has, by an unfortunate mistake, been rented to both: the mother owns the house. The fact that she does ... casts a bright light in the supposition that third parties can do nothing. Certainly it lets us see that a third party who says, 'I cannot choose between you' is fooling himself if he thinks this is impartiality.[17]

Therefore, it appears that the notion of a woman's body being her body and no one else's is a key part of the moral permissibility of third-party intervention in abortions to save the life of the mother.

Here are some examples of how ownership can not only justify intervention but also require it. Imagine that person A takes a coat which he needs to keep him warm. Person B also needs the coat to keep himself warm. Imagine that the coat belongs to person B. It seems preposterous to claim that one cannot choose to whom the coat ought to be given. It also seems preposterous to claim that the view of not choosing between persons A and B is somehow the most impartial view. It might be the case that one *does not want to choose* or that one *does not want to intervene*, but this does not preclude others from intervening and doing so in a morally permissible way. Certainly, it seems that the appropriate people to intervene are those with the authority and power to secure people's rights. We might argue that not only can a third party intervene but also they *should* intervene.

Thomson also argues that in cases in which a mother's life is not at risk but in which she is required to experience extraordinary sacrifice to accommodate another person who has no right against her, a third party has the moral permissibility to intervene and rectify such injustices. For instance, consider the violinist analogy once again. Imagine that you are the kidnapped person and you are required to stay connected to the violinist for the next nine years of your life. Also, imagine that you cannot unplug yourself from the violinist alone; the only way that you can escape this situation is with the help of a third party. Would it be morally wrong if some third party took the initiative to help you escape from this situation? Doing so might be viewed as not only morally permissible but also morally praiseworthy.

Objection 3: Minimal sacrifice

Let us return to the violinist analogy and change some of the facts. Imagine that when you wake up and find out that you have been kidnapped, you are told that you are only required to stay connected to the violinist for one hour. If you unplug yourself and leave the hospital the violinist will die; however, if you stay for one hour, he will be completely healed and will continue to survive on his own. Moreover, the process will have no negative effect whatsoever on your health.

This presents a different moral dilemma and may change our moral intuitions about the case. It remains true that you did not consent to allow the violinist to use your kidneys for his survival, even if it is only for an hour. The violinist has a right to life; however, such a right does not give him the right to use your organs without your consent to sustain his life. The question is whether you have a moral obligation to stay plugged into the violinist for an hour to save his life or whether you have no such moral obligation?

Thomson's view runs into some difficulty here. First, she argues that it is clear, given that the violinist has no right to use your body, you do not commit an injustice if you decide to unplug yourself from him and let him die. Thomson claims that the amount of sacrifice that is entailed in situations like these is irrelevant to whether or not an action is considered just or unjust. All that matters is whether one is depriving another of some legitimate right that belongs to him or her. Consider this emended version of Thomson's Henry Fonda example:

Take the case of Henry Fonda again. I said earlier that I had no right to the touch of his cool hand on my fevered brow, even though I needed it to save my life. I said that it would be frightfully nice of him to fly from the West Coast to provide me with it, but that I had no right against him that he should do so. But suppose he isn't on the West Coast. Suppose he has only to walk across the room, place a hand briefly on my brow – and lo, my life is saved. Then surely he ought to do it, it would be indecent to refuse. Is it to be said, 'Ah, well, it follows that in this case she has a right to the touch of his hand on her brow, and so it would be an injustice in him to refuse?' So that I have a right to it when it is easy for him to provide it, though no right when it is hard? It's rather a shocking idea that anyone's rights should fade away and disappear as it gets harder to accord them to him.[18]

In the case of the violinist, since he has no right to your body, unplugging yourself from him and killing him does not violate any of his rights, including his right to life. However, Thomson also says, 'It seems to me you *ought* to allow him to use your kidneys for the hour – it would be indecent to refuse.'[19]

The problem seems to be that, according to Thomson, one may *not* perform the action that they *ought* to perform, and thus act immorally or indecently, and yet act in accordance with what is just. For instance, according to Thomson, a person can, with respect to the same action, be 'self-centred', 'callous', 'indecent', refrain from doing what they *ought* to do, and also not be unjust. Can a person be such a moral monster and still be just? This seems problematic for her view. Imagine I am walking down the street, and I see a burning house. I am not related to the owners of the house nor do I know who they are. By the window there is a baby in a crib. I can easily and with no risk to my well-being walk up to the window and reach my hands inside and rescue the baby. However, the child has no right against me; she does not have the right to have me come save her and she (or anyone else) cannot demand this of me. According to Thomson, if I continued on my way, you might think of me as a callous, indecent, selfish, cold, thoughtless, self-centred and uncaring person but not unjust. Should we consider such a person as not having committed an injustice?

I guess it depends on whose conception of justice we are using. Certainly, from an Aristotelian perspective, for instance, this would be impossible, for just actions are the actions of a good and virtuous person and unjust actions those of an unvirtuous and vicious person. Moreover, most conceptions of justice entail a certain degree of goodness, and a basic moral principle of a good person is someone who would prevent a horrible evil if they could with little or no sacrifice to their person. One challenge to Thomson's view, then, is that it seems to equate and reduce justice to the conception of claim rights. Under this view, justice seems to have very little to do with moral duty and goodness; justice seems to be severed from morality. However, this is not our intuition about the relationship among rights, justice and morality. For instance, from the fact that person A does not have claim rights against person B, with respect to the performance of some action, it does not follow that person B does not have a moral obligation towards person A, with respect to that action. And, if person B does have a moral obligation to perform an action and does not do it, some would argue that he has committed an injustice against person A.

Consider once again the case of the siblings and the chocolates. The fact that one sibling does not have a right to the chocolates does not necessarily mean that the other sibling does not have a moral obligation to share some of his chocolates with his brother. Furthermore, if he does not do so, we might conclude that he has committed an immoral and unjust action against his brother. It is conceivable, then, for there to be moral situations in which we could act unjustly towards another person, and yet we would not violate any of the other person's rights.

This objection does not contradict Thomson's view that the sacrifice required of an individual in performing an action is irrelevant to the conception of rights. In other words, one's rights towards another do not depend on the difficulty or sacrifice required to perform the act. Interestingly, however, the required sacrifice does seem to affect one's moral obligations and duties, so that as one's sacrifice diminishes the strength of the moral duty increases. For example, consider once again the moral obligation of saving a baby from a burning house. Imagine that, unlike the previous scenario, where the baby was next to the window, the baby is somewhere inside the house. In this case, trying to save the baby will require risking our life. Thomson is right that in both cases the baby's rights against you do not change; in both cases, the baby has no right to demand you to save her. However, doesn't your moral obligation and ethical duty change? Don't you have a greater moral duty in the case in which there is no risk to your life?

If one believes that acting ethically entails, in part, bringing about a great good or preventing a great evil when possible, and if we can bring about a great good or prevent a great evil with no or little sacrifice, wouldn't we have an ethical duty to do so? In addition, if we understand moral obligations to be a matter of degrees, then it is reasonable to hold that one's ethical and moral obligations might fluctuate inversely in accordance with the degree of sacrifice required from the moral agent. Therefore, in cases where one could bring about a great good or prevent a great evil, with minimal sacrifice, one might be morally obligated to do so, and not doing so would constitute a grave injustice.

Some might argue, however, that even if this view of morality were true, there simply is no such thing as a pregnancy that entails minimal sacrifice. All pregnancies demand maximal sacrifice from the pregnant women. As a consequence, there are no clear cases in which a pregnant woman could bring about a great good or prevent a great evil with minimal sacrifice.

Objection 4: Mother–child relationship is special

An objection that can be raised against Thomson's view is that the violinist's analogy fails to capture the important relationship that exists between a pregnant woman and the foetus. This is a naturally evolving relationship that is based primarily on nurturing. The violinist example is a relationship between two strangers. If this is true, then Thomson's analogy is a false analogy and the argument fails. Thomson responds to this critique by emphasizing that what is essential here is not the biological connection but rather the notion of consent. She says, 'Surely we do not have any such "special relationship" for a person unless we have assumed it, explicitly or implicitly.'[20]

For instance, if a couple plan to have a child, intentionally get pregnant, have the baby, and they take it home, then it is clear through their actions that they have assumed responsibility for that child. They have consented to support the child and the child has rights against the parents as a result. In contrast, however, imagine a couple that do all that is possible not to get pregnant. Despite the reasonable precautions taken, she gets pregnant. In this case, the couple has not assumed responsibility, and they have not consented to the child's use of the mother's body. The biological relationship adds nothing to the notion of responsibility or consent in this case.

Objection 5: Justice and moral obligations do not always require consent

Related to the previous objection is a critique of the notion that justice requires consent.[21] According to Thomson, there are no cases in which I can be found to have a given moral obligation to perform a certain act to which I have not previously consented to. Therefore, all moral obligations must be obligations to which I have previously consented. However, there seem to be clear cases in which people are held responsible for their unintended and unconsented actions.

For instance, consider Francis Beckwith's example of a couple that has protected sexual intercourse, and neither one of them consents to having a child. However, imagine that the woman, despite responsible contraceptive protection, gets pregnant and decides to have the child. The man acted responsibly during sexual intercourse in trying to avoid a pregnancy, and he also has done everything possible to dissuade his partner from having the baby. He has not implicitly or explicitly consented to the pregnancy. If the woman gives birth and has the child, child-support laws will hold the man responsible for the care and support of the child, despite the man's lack of consent.

Beckwith points out that this is not only because the man is the biological father of the child, for this condition is also held by many sperm donors with the children of the sperm recipients but they are not held responsible for the care and support of these children. The crucial factors on which the obligation of the man for the child is maintained are both (i) that the man is the father of the child and (ii) that the man consciously entered into the sexual act with the woman, knowing full well that she could get pregnant. This case shows that consent is not always required for one to enter into legally binding obligations with others.

One might point out that a legal obligation and a moral obligation are two very different things. However, it is also the case that legal obligations are importantly connected to moral obligations. In fact in many cases the former are grounded in the latter. For instance, consider the civil rights laws as an example. Similarly, in the case of the reluctant father, it might be argued that the legal obligation to support his biological child is grounded on the moral obligation he has towards the child.

Objection 6: Good and Minimally Decent Samaritan

Related to the previous two objections is the view that we should be required to go the extra mile for our neighbours or the less fortunate. Moreover, as we have already pointed out on several occasions, there is a difference between legal and moral obligations. Some ethicists and ethical theories argue that our moral obligations go beyond our legal obligations. For instance, some ethical theories argue that one should go above and beyond what is required by the civil laws of the society we live in. Certainly this might be the case under both utilitarian and deontological ethical theories.

Consider, for instance, our acts of charity. Giving *voluntarily* to the poor or those who are less fortunate might at first not appear to be a moral duty, because we are not under any legal obligation to give our money to strangers who have no right to it. However, just because we do not have a legal obligation to help the poor does not mean that we do not have a moral obligation to do so. Many ethicists would argue that what we consider forms of charity are not charities at all but rather morally required duties and, moreover, not performing them would constitute serious immoral and unjust acts.

Peter Singer, for instance, believes that the line that divides what constitutes morally voluntary acts and obligatory moral duties needs to changed dramatically. In his view, most of the acts that people consider morally voluntary, such as giving money to the poor or donating many material goods to the less fortunate, are in fact morally obligatory. Performing these acts of charity does not make me morally superior since they are not above and beyond my duty; however, not performing them does make me morally inferior. Therefore, in the case of abortion, one might argue that a woman ought to sacrifice herself for the sake of the foetus, even if the foetus does not have a claim right on the use of her body for its survival. Moreover, doing so might be above and beyond her legal duty but not her moral duty.

Thomson acknowledges that there are moral systems that might require more and others that might require less of us. She distinguishes between a

Good Samaritan and a Minimally Decent Samaritan. The Good Samaritan is he who gives of himself to others more than the others have a right to demand of him. A Good Samaritan, for instance, might make some sacrifice in order to save the life of another. However, and here is the important point, according to Thomson, if he decides not to make the sacrifice, no matter how minimal it is, he should not be considered unjust.

A Minimally Decent Samaritan represents a much lower standard of sacrifice. For instance, consider the case of Kitty Genovese. She was murdered while thirty-eight people heard her cry for help and no one called the police. A Good Samaritan would have risked his own life to save Kitty. A Minimally Decent Samaritan would have phoned the police. This seems to be the minimum that is expected of a morally decent human being. However, phoning the police is not legally required, which shows that most laws do not even reach the standard of a Minimally Decent Samaritan.

In the case of abortion, the sacrifice that is required of a woman to continue a pregnancy to full term and give birth to a child, whether or not the woman intends to keep the baby or give it up for adoption, always entails a monumental physical and psychological sacrifice. There is no such thing as an easy pregnancy, but there are many that can be extremely taxing on a woman's life. Some pregnancies might require extreme physical and psychological sacrifices. Therefore, the abortion critics' position requires women to behave in accordance with the Good Samaritan standard. However, according to Thomson, no one should be held to such a standard. She writes: 'No person is morally required to make large sacrifices to sustain the life of another who has no right to demand them, and this even where the sacrifices do not include life itself; we are not morally required to be good Samaritans or anyway Very Good Samaritans to one another.'[22]

Objection 7: Saving a foetus versus killing a foetus

Baruch Brody claims that Thomson's argument is flawed because it does not make the proper distinction between the moral obligation of saving someone and killing someone.[23] Brody agrees that one may not have a moral duty to another person to save his or her life by giving him use of one's body. For instance, consider a foetus that is conceived in a laboratory and will die unless it is implanted into a woman's body. This foetus, even if it is considered a person with all of the rights of a full-fledged human adult person, has no right to any woman's body in order to save its life. Brody agrees with this interpretation of Thomson's argument.

However, he goes on to point out that this circumstance is irrelevant to the abortion issue. In the abortion issue, the woman is not required to simply save a foetus, she must kill the foetus. Brody claims that there is a difference between the moral obligation one has *for saving* another person and *for not killing* another person. The latter is much stronger than the former. Therefore, while it may be true that the right of a woman to control their body can override another person's right to be saved, it does not override the right not to be killed.

Is this distinction as clear as Brody claims? The laboratory foetus example seems to imply a weaker moral duty because there is an assumption that many women can fulfil this responsibility and thus why should it be you. But imagine that the only woman that has the right blood type to carry the foetus is you. So, you either carry the foetus or the foetus will die. If you do not volunteer, would you then claim that you have killed the foetus? The saving–killing moral distinction seems to be related to the moral distinction between letting someone die and killing someone. Is there a moral distinction between these two? Many philosophers have argued that there is no moral distinction between letting someone die and killing them. But, if this is the case, then not saving the foetus is morally equivalent to killing it.

Let us consider once again Brody's example of a foetus that is conceived in a laboratory and will die unless it is implanted into a woman's body. Now, let us imagine that you are kidnapped and attached to the foetus without your consent. Brody's intuition is that this makes your duty towards the foetus stronger instead of weaker. However, the fact is that the rights of the foetus towards you do not change at all and this is the point that Brody misses. Thomson does not claim that you have a right to kill the foetus *per se*, but rather that you have a right to detach yourself from the foetus. This is clear because if by some miracle the foetus were to survive after your separation, you do not have the right to kill it.

Summary

In this chapter, we analysed and studied Thomson's violinist analogy and her view that even if the foetus is considered a person with a right to life, it is not always the case that it is morally impermissible to have an abortion. In fact, she argues, if a woman has not given implicit or explicit consent to the use of her body, then she does not commit an injustice against the foetus/person if she decides to detach herself from him or her. According to Thomson, the foetus/person does not have a right to use the pregnant woman's body, and therefore she does not violate the foetus's rights when she has an abortion.

We examined seven objections to Thomson's view: (1) the objection from non-rape cases as consent; (2) the objection from third-party interference;

(3) the objection from minimal sacrifice principle; (4) the objection from the special relationship between the pregnant woman and the foetus; (5) the objection that justice does not always require consent; (6) the objection from Minimally Decent and Good Samaritan principles; and (7) the objection based on the distinction between saving and killing the foetus. In summary, some of these objections seem to create challenges that need to be explored further. First, there are difficulties with the view that all moral obligations have to be voluntary and assume some form of consent. Can't there be situations in which a person has not consented to care for another but is obliged to? Consider the case of the father who never consents to having a child, and yet he is held responsible for the care of the child. If you find a dying infant in a dumpster, are you morally obligated to care for it until you can give the infant to the proper authorities? If an agent can prevent a great evil from occurring, and he needs to sacrifice very little to do so, does the agent have a moral obligation to perform the act, even if the agent has not consented to the situation that brought about the moral obligation? It seems that some people's moral intuitions about such cases will be very different from Thomson's. In these cases, some people will find that an agent has a moral duty to prevent a person from suffering, even if the suffering person has no right against the agent. Moreover, the agent commits a grave injustice if he does not perform the act.

Thomson seems to be aware of this tension; for according to her view, there can be cases in which a person *ought* to perform a certain action even though he or she does not commit an injustice in not performing it. This seems paradoxical. For instance, according to Thomson, it might be the case that Henry Fonda ought to touch the dying person on their forehead if doing so would save his or her life, and it requires minimal sacrifice on the part of Henry Fonda. This *ought* seems to be a moral or virtuous ought and not one that concerns justice. But how can the notion of justice be completely severed from the virtues and from morality? This separation between morality and justice seems puzzling and leads Thomson to say that people can be vicious, cruel and selfish, and also just. Compare this view with Aristotle's idea that justice is the summation of all the virtues and that only a person who is completely virtuous and good can be just.

In conclusion, if any of these objections are successful, it is because of the original assumption that Thomson grants, which is that the foetus at conception (or shortly thereafter) is a person. This assumption strengthens all of these objections. Thus, we might question whether Thomson has granted the abortion critics too much? The violinist analogy might be more cogent if we were to make a less generous assumption at the start. For instance, we might imagine a case in which the personhood status of the violinist is unknown; thus we cannot make a decisive determination on whether it is or is not a person. This could be easily accomplished by tweaking the story so that one cannot see the violinist. Therefore, one can never know whether the whole story is a hoax or real. As a consequence, one can never know whether your sacrifice is really saving a person. Another way of accomplishing the same moral insight is to imagine that the violinist is in a coma and has a 50 per cent chance of recovering from the coma. These hypothetical cases will produce very different moral intuitions (more representative of the reality of the abortion issue) about what one's moral obligation ought to be. However, notice that by doing this we have reclaimed and reintroduced the *personhood* issue once again.

Study questions

1   What are claim rights and liberty rights?

2   Explain the abortion defenders' argument from a woman's absolute right to use her body. Is it a good argument? Why or why not?

3   Explain in what way Thomson's argument provides a paradigmatic change to the abortion issue.

4   Explain Thomson's violinist analogy as an argument for the moral permissibility of abortion.

5   What is the difference between a 'right not to be killed' and 'a right not to be killed unjustly'? Why is this difference so important for Thomson's argument?

6   Considering the violinist example, under what conditions, if any, does the violinist have a right to use your kidney? If the violinist only needs your kidney for five minutes, does he have a right to it? Should you allow him to use it? Explain?

7   Thomson's argument seems relevant to cases of rape, where the woman did not consent to have sex. Does it apply to cases where a woman voluntarily has sex?

8   Briefly explain the seven objections to Thomson's argument. Which of the seven do you think is most effective and why?

5

The Ethics of Killing and Abortion

In this chapter, we study Don Marquis's abortion critics'[1] argument that attempts to answer the question: Why is killing morally wrong?[2] According to Marquis, the traditional abortion defenders' and abortion critics' arguments have not provided an essential explanation for the wrongness of killing. This is apparent since the moral generalizations they produce about what makes killing wrong cannot explain all cases of killing. According to Marquis, what is required is a more thorough and focused enquiry into the essential nature of the wrongness of killing. Once we have discovered the essential nature of why killing an adult human person is morally wrong, then we can enquire into whether killing a foetus is morally wrong. Marquis argues that at the end of this enquiry we will discover that, given the essential nature of why killing is wrong, 'abortion is, except possibly in rare cases, seriously immoral, that it is at the same moral category as killing an innocent adult human being'.[3] Before we examine Marquis's argument, we need to understand the nature of the standoff between the traditional personhood abortion defenders' and abortion critics' arguments. This will elucidate why such arguments have overlooked the essential explanation for the wrongness of killing.

Standoff between personhood arguments for and against abortion

Why can't we make progress on the abortion issue based on the conception of personhood? It is commonly accepted that killing an innocent person is *prima facie* morally wrong. This has been a common deontological moral principle used in many arguments in the ethics of abortion. When we have enquired as to why it is morally wrong to kill an innocent person, our answers have relied on the argument that persons have a basic and fundamental right to life, and when we kill a person, we violate their right to life, and this is morally wrong. The abortion issue, according to Marquis, essentially deals with the moral status of the foetus, and for this reason the goal has been to determine whether the foetus should be categorized as a person or non-person and whether the foetus should be ascribed the right to life.[4]

Abortion critics have tried to connect the *biological* elements of personhood to serve as a sufficient condition for the conception of *moral* personhood. They justify their argument on the following moral principle: 'It is always prima facie seriously wrong to take a human life.'[5] This premise, however, is too broad, because its category of moral personhood permits anything that is living and human such as a human cancer-cell culture. On the other hand, abortion defenders have attempted to connect the *psychological* elements of personhood to serve as a necessary condition for the conception of *moral* personhood. They justify their argument on the following moral principle: 'It is prima facie morally wrong to kill only rational beings.'[6] However, this principle also has problems because it excludes non-rational human beings, such as infants, children and those that are mentally disabled to the extent that they lack rationality. Moreover, we have strong intuitive moral precepts about the wrongness of killing infants and children. Thus, any theory that permits the killing of infants and children must be mistaken. In addition, it also leaves out sentient animals. Therefore, this moral principle is too narrow.

According to Marquis, the traditional abortion critics' position might modify the grounds of its argument to the following moral principle: 'It is always prima facie morally wrong to take the life of a human being.'[7] However, this only introduces new difficulties concerning the ambiguity of the term 'human being' (see Chapters 1 and 2). Do we mean a being with a human genetic code, or do we mean a fully functioning human being (i.e. a being that is conscious, can reason, communicate and make decisions), or do we mean something different? Similarly, the traditional abortion defenders' position might try to introduce another moral principle that will explain why killing infants, children and mentally disabled people is wrong while sustaining the moral permissibility of abortion. For instance, they might argue that it is wrong to kill infants, children and the mentally disabled because they are part of the members of the moral community and foetuses are not. However, since it is questionable whether children who lack the cognitive sophistication of a well-functioning human adult can be considered a full member of the moral community, we are back to the same problem of excluding infants and children. Finally, if the abortion defenders' position modifies the moral principle to 'it is prima facie seriously morally wrong to kill only persons',[8] it runs into the same problems of ambiguity we mentioned above with the term 'human being' (see Diagram 1).

Defining personhood is a difficult task. The abortion critics' position, in trying to include the foetus from the moment of conception, must define personhood broadly, as anything living and human, and this casts the net too wide to include organisms that are obviously not persons. The abortion defenders' position, on the other hand, in order to exclude a foetus must define personhood narrowly, as psychologically active agents who are conscious and rational, and thus they exclude 'infants or young children or severely retarded or even perhaps the severely mentally ill'.[9] Therefore, we seem to be at an irresolvable standoff and the culprit seems to be our focus on the concept of personhood.

According to Marquis, the problem is that the investigations into the abortion issue have relied on *accidental* moral generalization and have not examined the essential moral problem upon which the abortion issue ultimately depends. So, for instance, abortion arguments have dealt with the issue concerning the personhood status of the foetus and have used general moral principles that killing a human being or person is prima facie morally wrong. However, Marquis argues that what needs is to be investigated is the question: *Why is killing a person wrong?* He argues as follows:

There is a way out of this apparent dialectical quandary [between the traditional personhood arguments of the abortion critics and abortion defenders]. The moral generalization of both sides are not quite correct. The generalization holds for the most part, for the usual cases. This suggest that they are all *accidental* generalizations, that the moral claims made by those on both sides of the dispute do not touch on the *essence* of the matter. This use of the distinction between essence and accidental is not meant to invoke obscure metaphysical categories. Rather, it is intended to reflect on the rather atheoretical nature of the abortion discussion. If the generalization a partisan in the abortion dispute adopts were derived from the reason why ending the life of a human being is wrong, then there could not be exceptions to that generalization unless some special case obtains in which there are even more powerful countervailing reasons. Such generalizations would not be merely accidental generalizations; they would point to, or be based upon, the essence of the wrongness of killing, what it is that makes killing wrong. All this suggests that a necessary condition of resolving the abortion controversy is a more theoretical account of the wrongness of killing. After all, if we merely believe, but do not understand, why killing adult human beings such as ourselves is wrong, how could we conceivably show that abortion is either immoral or permissible.[10]

(1) Wrong to kill *human life* (too broad).   (2) Wrong to kill *rational beings* (too narrow).

TOO BROAD

Includes Zygotes
Blastocysts,
Fetuses and
Infants.

Includes cancer
cells.

TOO NARROW

Includes Rational
agents.

Excludes Infants,
children and
unconscious
adults.

DIAGRAM 1 *Defining personhood: (1) human life and (2) rational beings.*

What is required, then, is a more profound, theoretical investigation into the essential nature of what makes killing wrong.

Why is killing wrong?

Marquis begins his analysis of why killing is wrong by analysing the following question: Why is it wrong to kill us? Some answers seem easy to dismiss, such as it is morally wrong to kill us because our absence will harm and cause suffering to our friends and family. While this might be true, this is not what makes killing us essentially wrong. It's true that our death might negatively affect friends and family and cause grave suffering, but this is not the essential explanation for why killing us is wrong. Another possible but unlikely candidate is that killing is wrong because it might harm the killer by making him or her more violent (i.e. 'killing brutalizes the one who kills').[11] Again, while it might be true that committing a murder can harm the agent that commits such an act, it does not explain the essential nature of the wrongness of the act. In fact, it seems preposterous to suggest that what makes killing us wrong is that it harms our killer.

Marquis wants us to reflect on what it is that we value and lose if we are murdered. This natural property can help us discover what makes killing morally wrong. He argues that the natural property that explains the wrongness of killing is that it deprives the victim, in an *absolute* manner, of *all* of his or her future personal experiences. It is not simply the biological changes that occur to my physical being but rather all of the lost value in the activities, experiences and happiness that reside in my future and are unjustifiably taken from me. All of my future plans, hopes and aspirations are taken from me in a definitive and absolute manner. What makes killing someone a terrible crime is the nature of this deprivation; it is absolute and all-encompassing. First, notice that it is not a temporary punishment that deprives a victim of something(s); rather, it is absolute insofar as it definitively and forever deprives a victim of his or her future. Second, it is all-encompassing insofar as it deprives a victim of *all* future experiences and not just some future experiences.

Consider the punishment of incarceration. When someone is in jail, they are essentially deprived of many of their liberties and of a large set of valuable future experiences; the punishment essentially consists of the deprivation of part of a person's future but not a person's entire future. The more valuable the content of the deprivation (i.e. the longer or the broader the deprivation), the greater the punishment. Therefore, to deprive someone of ten years of their future is worse than to deprive them of one year of their future. To incarcerate them in strict quarters, such as in isolation or maximum security, is worse than to incarcerate them in a low or minimum security institution. However, there is nothing worse than to deprive someone of the possibility of any and all experiences for all eternity. This explains why killing another person is considered one of the worst crimes a person can commit.

Killing us is wrong because it deprives us of our future. Killing a person is wrong, therefore, because it deprives him or her of a future-like-ours. Killing any being is wrong if it deprives them of a future of value. We can also say that the wrongness of the killing is proportional to the value of the future of the being. Moreover, it is not important whether the living organism belongs to the human species. What matters is whether the being has a future-like-ours. If it does, then it is just as morally wrong to kill it as it is to kill an adult human person. Let us refer to Marquis's view as the Deprivation Theory. Marquis explains it as follows:

> Therefore, killing someone is wrong, primarily because the killing inflicts (one of) the greatest possible losses on the victim. To describe this as the loss of life can be misleading, however. The change in biological state does not by itself make killing me wrong. The effect of the loss of my biological life is the loss to me of all those activities, projects, experiences, and enjoyment which would otherwise have constituted my future personal life. These activities, projects, experiences, and enjoyments are either valuable for their own sake or are means to something else that is valuable for its own sake. Some parts of my future are not valued by me now, but will come to be valued by me as I grow older and as my values and capabilities

change. When I am killed, I am deprived both of what I now value which would have been part of my future personal life, but also what I would come to value. Therefore, when I die, I am deprived of all of the value of my future. Inflicting this loss on me is ultimately what makes killing wrong. This being the case, it would seem that what makes killing any adult human being prima facie seriously wrong is the loss of his or her future.[12]

Advantages of the deprivation theory

Does the Deprivation Theory provide an essential explanation of what makes killing wrong? Marquis attempts to show that the truth of this theory is supported by the explanatory values it provides for other ethical issues unrelated to abortion. Here are four consequences of the Deprivation Theory that further confirms its plausibility: (1) the theory is impartial and not biased towards human beings; (2) it supports our common sense and intuitive beliefs about non-human animal rights; (3) it is consistent with reasonable views about euthanasia and (4) it makes the killing of infants and children seriously immoral and permits the killing of cancer-cell culture.

First, the deprivation view of why killing is morally wrong is compatible with the view that killing non-human persons is just as morally wrong as killing human persons, if such non-humans can be deprived of a valuable future like ours. Therefore, it is not biased towards *Homo sapiens*; it does not arbitrarily or dogmatically favour the value placed on human life over other organisms, like many other abortion critics' positions do. Instead, it is impartial, insofar as it bases the value of an organism on a morally relevant natural criterion that is not necessarily limited to *Homo sapiens* (i.e. a valuable future or a future-like-ours). In terms of this impartiality, it is more similar to the abortion defenders' views than to traditional abortion critics' views, and Marquis finds this to be a merit of the theory.

A second important point is that the deprivation view opens the theoretical possibility to ascribe fundamental rights to non-human animals. If killing is wrong because it deprives the victim of a valuable future or a future-like-ours, then this would make killing animals with a valuable future morally wrong. It opens the theoretical possibility that killing some animals is seriously immoral and possibly as wrong as killing human beings. This would be especially true if the animals in question can be shown to have a valuable future, one closely resembling the future of human adults. Some might claim that this view seems to be biased and speciesist insofar as a valuable future is being defined as 'a valuable-future-like-ours'. More will be said below on how we ought to define a valuable future.

Third, in the extreme cases where a person lacks any valuable future, this theory is consistent and supportive of euthanasia. Imagine, for instance, a terminally ill person who has only a few days left to live and these days are full of pain and misery. In such cases, killing that person would be morally permissible, because it would not deprive her of a valuable future or of a future-like-ours. This consequence is very different from those of the traditional abortion critics' positions that hold that the killing of a human being is morally wrong in virtue only of their humanity. For instance, consider the premise from a traditional abortion critics's argument: 'Killing an innocent human being is prima facie morally wrong.' If we accept this premise as true, then killing a terminally ill patient would be morally wrong, even if she has no valuable future at all. Marquis finds the Deprivation Theory's consistency with (what he takes to be) common sense views on euthanasia to be a merit of the theory.

Fourth, unlike the abortion defenders' views of personhood, the deprivation argument provides sufficient justification for concluding that it is morally wrong to kill infants, young children and mentally ill people. This, according to Marquis, is a valuable consequence of the theory because it is highly intuitive that killing infants, young children and mentally ill people is morally wrong. Any theory that condones such actions and categorizes them as morally permissible clashes with our most basic moral intuitions and this is problematic. Therefore, adopting Marquis's theory of the wrongness of killing 'makes the wrongness of such actions (killing babies) as obvious as we actually think it is'.[13]

Competing theories in the ethics of killing: Discontinuation and desire theories

To fully defend the future-like-ours account of what makes killing wrong, we need to look at competing theories and see if they can do a better job at explaining the wrongness of killing. Marquis examines two other theories: (1) the desire theory and (2) the discontinuation theory.

Before we take a closer look at these, it is worth noting that Marquis only needs to show that having a valuable future (one like ours) is a *sufficient* condition for concluding that killing someone is wrong. He does not have to show that it is also a *necessary* condition. In other words, if we can show that a being has a future-like-ours, then we can conclude that it is morally wrong to kill it. But notice that it does not follow that if it does not have a future-like-ours, then it would be okay for us to kill it. There can be other reasons why it is still morally wrong to kill a being that lacks a future-like-ours. For instance, it might be argued that it is wrong to unjustifiably kill a being because it has intrinsic value or its continued existence will lead to a greater good. These and other possibilities remain open. In addition, we should also note that the abortion defenders' position has a different standard than the abortion critics' position, because it wants to show that it is permissible to kill a foetus. Therefore, its criterion needs to be a *necessary* condition (and not a sufficient condition) of what makes killing immoral.

Let us begin with the abortion critics' theory based on a desire to live. This theory states that killing a being is wrong only if the being has a desire to live. The central point of desire theory is that it is morally permissible to kill things that do not have a desire to continue living. The reasoning is that if a being does not or cannot have a desire for living, killing it would not deprive it of anything of value. It would be like depriving an elephant from attending college or from owning and driving a car. These are things that an elephant could never desire and thus depriving it of these things does not harm the elephant. Similarly, if a being does not have a desire to live or cannot have such a desire, then it is morally permissible to kill it. As a consequence, killing a being that has a desire for living is what makes killing morally wrong. How would this play out in the abortion debate?

Foetuses do not have the sufficient mental development to have desires to continue living and thus killing foetuses is not morally wrong. There are three serious problems with the desire account. First, it goes contrary to our most clear and self-evident moral intuitions, as well as some of our most basic beliefs about murder and killing. Most people regard it as morally wrong to kill people who sometimes show no desires to live, either because they are sleeping, unconscious or in a coma. It is also a commonly accepted moral principle that it is wrong to kill people who have a desire not to live. These people might be suffering from depression and are suicidal. But if a desire to continue living is a necessary condition for the moral wrongness of killing, then it would be morally permissible to kill people who are sleeping, unconscious, in a coma, depressed or who do not want to continue living. Therefore, it is hard to explain how having a desire to continue living can be a necessary condition for the moral wrongness of killing.

Second, one reason, among others, why people think it is morally wrong to kill someone who has no desires to live or has a desire *not* to live is because this desire may change in the future. Certainly, this is true of people who are sleeping and unconscious. When they wake up, they will most probably have a desire to continue living. But if we allow the possibility that the necessary condition is not an actual desire to live but only a future desire to live, then this will no longer justify abortions, for foetuses also can be ascribed a future desire to live.

Third, the desire to live is based on the perception of a valuable future. It is this good that is the foundation for such a desire in the first place.

Moreover, desires can be manipulated, and it would seem trivial to say that by simply erasing a person's desire to live we have moral permission to kill that person, even though they still have a very valuable and good future ahead of them. The point seems to be that desires can fluctuate quite easily, and they are dependent on a person's perceptions of things; therefore, they are not a metaphysically sound justification for the morality of killing, as a-future-like-ours is.

Let's now turn to the discontinuation theory of killing. This view claims that what is wrong about killing a person is that it terminates one's *actual* or *existing* activities, experiences or projects. Since foetuses do not have actual or existing activities, experiences or projects, killing a foetus would not result in the discontinuation of anything. Therefore, killing foetuses would be morally permissible. Marquis claims that the discontinuing account has several problems. First, it does not refer to the value of the activities, experiences and projects that are discontinued if a being is killed. However, we must assume that the things that are to be discontinued have a great amount of value for the subject of these experiences. If they did not, then it would be difficult to understand why it would be wrong to kill a being and terminate these valueless experiences. Therefore, as is the case of the deprivation theory, the discontinuation theory must make reference to the value of the future experiences. For it is the value of these experiences and depriving the subject of them that makes killing wrong. In this sense, and with reference to the future, the discontinuing theory and the deprivation theory are similar.

What is the difference, then, between the discontinuation theory and the deprivation theory? The former seems to presume that there is a history and past with which the future is connected, hence the idea of *discontinuing*. But what exactly do these past activities, experiences and projects add to the ethics of killing? Marquis argues that the value of the past is irrelevant for determining whether it is morally permissible to kill someone. Whether the past is good, bad or non-existent seems to make no difference and adds no weight to the permissibility of killing a person. (Below we will revisit this response and present several new objections to Marquis's view.) Instead, it seems that, for the discontinuing theory, it is the future value of the individual's experiences that is doing all of the moral lifting. The conclusion, therefore, is that the discontinuation theory does not add anything substantial to the future-like-ours account of killing. Moreover, if the past adds nothing of weight or justification to our moral deliberations on the ethics of killing, it is difficult to see how this theory can support the abortion defenders' position on abortion. In effect, Marquis believes that the discontinuation theory, once it is examined closely, supports the abortion critics' position.

Marquis's deprivation argument for the moral wrongness of abortion

How is Marquis's theory different from other abortion critics' positions? Marquis claims that the same justification that is used for arguing that killing an adult human person is morally wrong can be used for an infant and a foetus. The argument is that killing an adult human person is prima facie morally wrong because it deprives him or her of a valuable future. Similarly, killing an infant or a foetus is also morally wrong because doing so will deprive them of a valuable future. Moreover, the future of the infant and of the foetus is a-future-like-ours, and thus it is just as valuable (if not more valuable) as the future of an adult person. As a consequence, the act of killing a foetus is just as wrong as the act of killing an adult human person. Given the deprivation theory, can it be argued that killing a foetus is morally worse than killing an adult, since it has a longer expected lifespan? We will consider this and other possible consequences of the deprivation theory below.

An important point that Marquis makes concerning the Deprivation Theory is that it 'does not rely on the invalid inference that, since it is wrong to kill persons, it is wrong to kill potential persons also. "The category that is morally central to this analysis is the category of having a valuable future like ours; it is not the category of personhood."'[14] The argument does not need to claim that a foetus is a person and does not require that we clarify what a person is. This, in itself, makes Marquis's argument unique, bringing a new perspective and framework from which we can view the abortion issue.

Argument from the wrongness of killing or the deprivation argument

1   What makes killing a person prima facie morally wrong is that it deprives the victim of a future-like-ours.

2   A foetus has a future-like-ours.

3   Abortion is the killing of a foetus.

4   An abortion deprives a foetus of a future-like-ours (from 2 and 3).

5   Therefore, abortions are prima facie morally wrong.

The argument shows that abortions are prima facie morally wrong. The prima facie means that, unless there are some extraordinary circumstances that could morally justify an exception, abortions are morally wrong. The exceptions would have to be cases in which, if an abortion was not performed, then some equal or greater evil than the foetus's deprivation of a-future-like-ours would occur. This standard is very high and such cases would be rare, such as when the pregnant woman's life is in serious danger if she continues her pregnancy to full term.

Finally, it should be noted that the future-like-ours can be ascribed to the foetus during any time of its gestation period that it is considered an individual, which could mean once the possibility of twinning has occurred or fourteen days after conception.[15] It should also be noted that Marquis's deprivation argument permits abortions in cases in which a foetus is malformed or defective to such an extent that it would preclude it from having a future-like-ours, unless, of course, there is some other reason for why killing it would be wrong.

Objections and replies

Objection 1: Value entails consciousness

Let's address several possible objections to Marquis's derivation argument. First, the idea that a future has value entails that there is some subject or agent capable of valuing his or her own future experiences *as* valuable. A foetus cannot value its future, and so its future has no value, at least for the foetus. Therefore, killing it would not deprive it of any future value. How could the abortion critic respond to this objection?

Desire is a concept that is ontologically dependent on a subject, for a desire cannot exist if there is no agent to experience the desire. However, the concept of value is not dependent on the agent in the same way, and it seems reasonable to say that a being can have a future of value even though that being cannot recognize or know it. The difference between desire and value, then, is that, in the case of desire, if an agent is cognitively undeveloped, it cannot have this desire in the present, even though it might have such desire sometime in the future. However, in the case of value, a cognitively undeveloped agent can have a future value *in the present*, even though it cannot recognize it or be conscious of it until sometime in the future. Therefore, it follows that the metaphysical claim 'foetus A's future at t2 has value at t1' might be true even though the epistemological claim 'foetus A knows at t1 its future value at t2' is false. The truth of the former does not depend on the truth of the latter, although the truth of the latter does depend on the truth of the former.

Objection 2: A desire for continued existence

Second, Marquis addresses Michael Tooley's argument that to ascribe a right to life to an agent, the agent must first have the ability to desire its continued existence. Foetuses and children cannot have a desire for their continued existence, thus they cannot be ascribed the right to life. As a result, killing a foetus or a young child does not violate their rights, and thus it is morally permissible. We have addressed Marquis's rebuttal to such an argument from desire above. We noted that having a desire and having a future-value-like-ours are concepts that lead to very different conclusions about the wrongness of killing. Tooley's argument centres on the notion of a right to life, and the essence of his argument is to determine the properties that give something a right to life. Marquis, on the other hand, focuses on what makes killing wrong. These two lines of enquiry will result in different standards and criteria, but they are not necessarily mutually exclusive. One could hold that Tooley is right about the right to life, and Marquis is also right about the wrongness of killing. The disagreement only arises if we also hold that a right to life is a necessary condition for the wrongness of killing. But this is not at all an obvious point.

Objection 3: Moral wrongness requires victimization

Third, Marquis addresses Paul Bassen's view of victimization.[16] Bassen argues that to be a victim, sentience is required. One cannot harm or hurt another subject that lacks sentience and mentation (mental life). As long as a foetus is not sentient, and thus cannot suffer, the foetus cannot be harmed and therefore cannot be a victim of any action. Therefore, killing a foetus does not victimize it, and therefore it is not morally wrong. Bassen's view seems to consider the perception and feeling of harm and suffering as necessary conditions for moral wrongness. Certainly many cases of moral wrongness entail harm and suffering, and we might even argue that there is a proportional relationship between the degree of moral wrongness of an act and the degree of suffering and pain the act causes, although this relationship does not always hold. There are two different problems with Bassen's view: first, that moral wrongness requires victimization; and second, that victimization requires sentience. Let us address the first problem.

Does moral wrongness require victimization? Imagine that you are teaching a course and that you have a certain bias towards a student. It is not that you dislike him; instead, it is that you like him very much. At the end of the semester, when you are adding up the final grades, you decide to bump up his grade from a C to a B. This act is morally wrong for it is unjust and dishonest, but there does not seem to be any direct victim in this case that endures direct suffering from your morally wrong action. Consider another case. Imagine a relatively honest person who, on one occasion, cheats on an exam. Imagine that he is never discovered, and he never does it again. Moreover, this dishonest act produces no negative long-term damage to his character or person. We might argue that no one has been hurt or harmed in this situation. Nevertheless, we might still hold that this individual's act of cheating on an exam was morally wrong. These counterexamples illustrate that it is possible to commit a morally wrong action without harm or injury and thus without victimization.

Second, Bassen seems to presume that victimization requires that the victim be sentient, because to be a victim requires one to be harmed and suffer some injury. But it seems that Bassen is interpreting the concept of harm too narrowly to coincide with feelings. Do we need to experience negative feelings to be a victim of someone else's wrongdoing? Consider cases in which the victim is unaware of the harm. In these cases, the agent's being sentient makes no difference. For instance, imagine a man who has an affair and their partner never discovers the affair. Wouldn't we agree that the partner is a victim of betrayal and deception, and thus has been morally harmed by their partner's morally wrong action? I believe so, and, if this is the case, then this would be an example of a situation in which someone is harmed and is a victim of a moral doing without them experiencing any sensations of harm or suffering. Thus, it does not follow that just because the foetus is unaware of the harm and cannot feel or suffer the act of being killed that it is not a victim of an immoral action.

Objective 4: How do we determine the future value of a person?

Marquis's deprivation account argues that what makes killing morally wrong is that it deprives the victim of a valuable future-like-ours. If this is the case, then it would also seem reasonable to say that the degree of wrongness of killing will fluctuate with the degree of value deprived of the victim in question. However, it is not clear, if and how, we can determine the value of an agent's future. There are two possible formulas for determining the value of someone's future. First, by the person's expected lifespan. Second, by the quality of a future-like-ours and thus by the particular decisions, projects and activities of each person with a future-like-ours.

Let us consider these possibilities in more detail. If we accept the first formula (a), then killing a younger person will always be more morally reprehensible than killing an older person. We certainly have some basic moral intuitions that support this view, since, for instance, we would probably lament the death of an eight-year-old child more than the death of a ninety-year-old person. Therefore, the moral sensibility that tells us that killing a younger person is morally worse than killing an older person is supported by the thesis that the value of a person's future is determined by the expected length of time of the future-like-ours of the person. This also would permit us to calculate the seriousness of the deprivation that a killing has caused. The basic idea is that a younger person is harmed more than an older person, insofar as they are deprived of a longer future-like-ours. Thus, killing a younger person is always morally worse than killing an older person.

Nevertheless, we also have very strong moral intuitions that this way of viewing the ethics of killing is highly problematic. First, while we may lament the death of a younger person more than the death of an older person, when it comes to the *wrongness* of killing, we have strong moral intuitions that the murder of a younger person and the murder of an older person are equally morally wrong. In other words, a commonly accepted moral principle is that to murder another person is seriously immoral, and the gravity of the *wrongness* is not dependent on the age of the person murdered or on the expected length of a future-like-ours. But if this intuition is correct, and murdering a younger person is morally equivalent to murdering and older person, then it cannot be the case that what makes killing wrong is the deprivation of a person's future.

Let us consider the second formula. If we accept the second formula (b) for interpreting the value of a future-like-ours, then the value of a person's future life is determined not by the quantity of a future-like-ours but by the quality of a future-like-ours, and thus the value of a future-like-ours depends on the particular decisions, projects and activities of each person with a future-like-ours. There are some moral intuitions to defend this interpretation. For instance, consider the killing of a twenty-year-old person who has lived a life of crime. He has murdered and raped many victims. Currently, he is serving a life sentence in prison. After serving one year in prison, he is murdered by another inmate. Now consider a fifty-year-old person, who is a mother of four children, an oncologist and surgeon. She has dedicated her life to saving the lives of others, and she plans on continuing her work on medical research for curing and treating cancer patients. One might argue that, in terms of only the good consequences that we should expect from these two agents, the future value of the fifty-year-old mother, oncologist and surgeon is greater than the future value of the twenty-year-old criminal. If you agree with this assessment, then it seems that the value of a person's future life is determined not by the quantity of a future-like-ours but by the quality of a future-like-ours. Thus, it appears that the future value is directly dependent on the kinds of decisions an agent has made, as well as the kinds of decisions and actions the agent is expected to make in the future.

But this formula also has problems. First, if the degree of wrongness of killing is dependent on the degree of the future value of an agent, and the latter is based on the qualitative aspect of the future in question, the wrongness of murder would vary on a case-to-case basis. Moreover, it would seem difficult to develop the formula to calculate the different values pertaining to the particular cases of killing. How do we determine with objective certainty the future value of agents? Second, we continue to have strong intuitions that, while we might lament the death of the oncologists more than that of the criminal simply based on future good consequences we expect from the former and the evil consequences we expect from the latter, the murder and killing of both persons still seem to be *equally* morally wrong. However, if this is the case, then the wrongness of killing (i.e. what makes killing *wrong*) cannot be based on the deprivation of a future-life-like-ours.

Objection 5: Considering the past too: Ronald Dworkin's frustration view

Marquis's Deprivation Argument focuses entirely on the future value of an agent. By doing so, we arrive at some paradoxical and counterintuitive conclusions. For instance, according to the deprivation view, we ought to deplore more the killing of a two-week foetus than a four-year-old child. Or, we ought to lament more the killing of an early foetus than an adolescent girl. But this seems to go contrary to our moral intuitions about how we in fact feel about these cases of killing. The fact is that we would tend to lament much more the killing of a teenager or young adult than an early foetus. Why?

People grieve and lament the killing of young adult(s) not only because of the loss of their future but also because of the investment they have already made (in the past) towards their future. This is why we tend to feel more regret for the killing of a teenager than for an infant or early foetus. In *Life's Dominion*, Ronald Dworkin explains the value that our past investments add to our life. He writes:

The 'Simple loss' view we have been considering is inadequate because it focuses only on *future possibilities* [my emphasis], on what will or will not happen in the future. It ignores the crucial truth that waste of life is often greater and more tragic because of what has already happened in the past. The death of an adolescent girl is worse than the death of an infant girl because the adolescent's frustrates the investments she and others have already made in her life – the ambitions and expectations she constructed, the plans and projects she made, the love and interest and emotional involvement she formed for and with others, and they and with her.[17]

Marquis's Deprivation Theory entirely ignores this past investment and thus cannot account for the value that is lost as a result of the loss of such an investment in one's life. Therefore, the answer to what makes killing wrong cannot be simply the deprivation of a future-life-like-ours.

It seems that we need a more comprehensive theory about dying and killing that will capture two of our most basic intuitions that seem to contradict each other: (1) we lament more the death of a younger person, say a twelve-year-old child, than the death of a much older person, say a ninety-year-old adult; and (2) we also have the opposite intuition in that we lament more the death of an older person, say a twelve-year-old child, than the death of a much younger person, say a newly born infant. Fortunately, Ronald Dworkin's 'frustration' view about the intrinsic value of human life captures well these contradictory moral intuitions. Dworkin explains:

> I shall use 'frustration' (though the word has other associations) to describe this more complex measure of the waste of life because I can think of no better word to suggest the combination of past and future considerations that figure in our assessment of a tragic death. Most of us hold to something like the following set of instinctive assumptions about death and tragedy. We believe, as I said, that a successful human life has a certain and natural course. It starts in mere biological development-conception, fetal development, and infancy- but it then extends into childhood, adolescence, and adult life in ways that are determined not just by biological formation but by social and individual training and choice, and that culminate in satisfying relationships and achievements of different kinds. It ends after a normal lifespan, in a natural death. It is a waste of the natural and human creative investments that make up the story of a normal life when this normal progression is frustrated by premature death or in other ways. But how bad this is-how great the frustration-depends on the stage of life in which it occurs, because the frustration is greater if it takes place after rather than before the person has made a significant personal investment in his own life, and less if it occurs after any investment has been substantially fulfilled, or as substantially fulfilled as in anyway likely.[18]

So, the basic idea is that we value highly the investment people make in their lives in order to fulfil their aspirations, desires and life goals. The more investment one makes into one's life, the more value one adds to one's life. This explains why we probably would view the death of a twenty-two-year-old college graduate as more tragic than the death of a foetus. Moreover, as one fulfils one's aspirations, desires and life goals, one's life gradually loses its value. This would explain why we feel that the death of an infant is much more tragic than the death of a ninety-year-old adult.

Objection 6: Killing persons is equally morally wrong, regardless of their past investment and future value-like-ours

The views espoused above on the wrongness of killing as dependent on the victim's future (or on the victim's past investment in his or her own life) seem to go contrary to some of our most basic intuitions about *murder*. We do not tend to believe that the murder of a person who has a less valuable future is less morally wrong than the murder of a person who has a more valuable future (no matter what formula we use to calculate the future value of a person). Moreover, the same could be said with respect to past investment in one's own life. Most of us would probably not be inclined to believe that the murder of a three-year-old is not as morally wrong as the murder of a twenty-year-old. Instead, we tend to view murder as equally morally wrong and unacceptable, regardless of the determined value of an agent's future or of the agents' past investment in their own lives. But if the wrongness of killing (how wrong killing is) is not dependent on a future-like-ours, then Marquis's view that the essential nature of what makes killing wrong is that it deprives a person of a future-like-ours must be mistaken.

Gerald H. Paske has presented a similar critique by pointing out that Marquis's conception of a future-like-ours is neither a necessary nor a sufficient condition for the wrongness of killing. Paske argues that 'Marquis's own position presupposes the concept of personhood'.[19] To show that depriving someone of a valuable future is not a necessary condition for the wrongness of killing he provides the following example. Imagine an eighty-nine-year-old man who is about to die. In fact, we know with certainty that his life will terminate in just sixty seconds. If someone were to take a gun and shoot this person just one second before he was about to die, would we hold that this killing is wrong? If it is morally wrong, it cannot be that it is wrong because the killer deprived the person of a future-like-ours; it must be instead that it is wrong for some other reason. I would argue that this example of an unjustified killing of an innocent person is a case of homicide, and it is seriously immoral, despite the fact that the victim did not have a future-like-ours.[20]

Paske also demonstrates that a future-like-ours is not a sufficient condition for the moral wrongness of killing. Paske asks us to imagine a kitten who has been injected with a newly developed genetic modifier that will in a few months change the kitten's genetic structure to one like ours. The kitten, therefore, will have a future-like-ours once this serum has taken effect. However, imagine that we have an antidote that can neutralize the effect of the genetic serum. If we used it before the kitten made the transformation to personhood (thus, it is not yet a person), would we consider it murder? Paske believes our moral intuitions tell us that, even though the kitten has a future-like-ours, we would not consider it murder or morally wrong. However, if we used the antidote after the kitten had transformed into a person, we would be more inclined to classify this as morally wrong (or, at least, as seriously morally questionable). What this creative hypothetical situation reveals is that what drives our moral intuitions about the wrongness of killing is not that the victim is deprived of a future-like-ours (since this is neither necessary nor sufficient) but rather that they are a person (or, possibly, that they have some other property such as intrinsic value or moral standing). If these objections resonate with you as reasonable, then we can conclude that the personhood issue and the status of the foetus remains an essential part of the abortion debate.

Objection 7: Conflating badness of death with the wrongness of killing

What is attractive about Marquis's Deprivation Theory? Why think that this theory could provide the essential nature of the wrongness of killing? It is undeniable that what makes dying such a bad thing is that it deprives us absolutely and permanently from all future experiences. As Dworkin puts it, it frustrates all our plans, aspirations and future experiences. This is a terrible thing, probably the worst thing that could happen to someone. Marquis is right about this. Moreover, if death comes prematurely, before we are permitted to fulfil any of our plans and ambitions in life, this would be considered not just a bad event but a tragedy. However, there is a difference between the badness of death and the wrongness of killing. If we clarify this distinction, many of the puzzling counterexamples and paradoxical problems that arise as a result of Marquis's view disappear.[21]

First, there are many possible causes that can lead to one's death. Being unjustly killed or murdered is only one way that one might die. One could also die by getting run over, falling from a cliff, getting into a car accident, developing a deadly disease or illness etc. The tragedy of one's dying is similar irrespective of the cause. So, whether an adolescent boy dies as a victim of a murder or from an illness, his death will be a great tragedy. The tragedy of his death is a result of the deprivation of his future life (a future-like-ours), as well as the natural and creative investments that he has already made into his own life. These factors are what make dying such a horrible event. However, it is not what makes killing wrong. The case of an adolescent who is murdered by another person is not just tragic (like, for instance, the deaths of other adolescents who die as a result of illnesses or an accident), it is also characterized by a moral wrongness that has occurred. In this case, another person made a decision to act violently and maliciously against another human being, causing them the most harm and injury possible: taking their life.

Second, by distinguishing the badness of dying from the wrongness of killing, we can understand why killing a twenty-year-old person and a ninety-year-old person are equally morally wrong and yet the deaths are not equally bad or tragic. The *badness* or tragedy of the deaths of a twenty-year-old person and a ninety-year-person are a result of the deprivation of the future-like-ours, but the *wrongness* of their deaths is not determined by the future-like-ours. Instead, the wrongness is attributed to the killer's decision to commit murder and violate another's person's right to life. Therefore, in this case, we can conclude that the badness of the death of the twenty-one-year old is much worse than the badness of the death of the ninety-year-old and also hold that the wrongness of killing is the same for both cases.

So, what is it that makes killing wrong? The wrongness of killing another person is not the tragic result of the loss of the person's life. This is what makes dying, in general, such a bad thing. The wrongness of killing is the violation of a person's rights; it is the intentional, unjust, unfair, unjustified, violent and malicious interference into a person's affairs, in a way that directly causes that person's most unfortunate and destructive life event: the loss of their lives. A critic of the deprivation view, therefore, might submit that Marquis has conflated the badness of death with the wrongness of killing. The moral wrongness of killing, then, can be attributed to the killer's decision to commit a violent crime, a terrible, unjustified, unwarranted and malicious transgression against another innocent[22] human being.

Summary

In this chapter, we studied Don Marquis's view that what makes abortion morally wrong is that it deprives a foetus of a future-like-ours. First, we engaged Marquis's arguments for how and why the traditional personhood arguments come to an irresolvable standoff. Next, we analysed Marquis's argument for a shift in perspective on how to deal with the abortion issue while circumventing the personhood issue altogether. We studied Marquis's argument that the essential property that makes killing wrong is that it deprives the victim of a future-like-ours. Applying this to the abortion argument, we noted that the justification of what makes an abortion morally wrong is the same as the justification for what makes killing an adult person morally wrong: it deprives them both of a future-like-ours.

Next, we examined seven objections to Marquis's view and replies to these objections. The first objection claimed that for something to have value it requires consciousness. The second objection tries to connect the value of a human person with the desire for a continued existence. In both cases Marquis provides rebuttals claiming that the value of a being is independent of its actual mental life. He argues that the latter is not a necessary condition for the former. The third objection claims that moral wrongness requires victimization and that victimization requires the ability to be harmed or injured. Moreover, injury and harm require some degree of sentience. Since a foetus is not a sentient being, it cannot be harmed and thus it cannot be a victim. If the foetus cannot be a victim, then killing it is not morally wrong. In response, it was argued that injury and harm do not always require sentience, since one can be harmed and never know it. Thus, being harmed does not always require victimization as defined through sentience. A moral wrong can occur even if there is no sentient being that is harmed.

If the moral wrongness of killing is based on the deprivation of victims' future value, then it would seem reasonable to conclude that the wrongness of killing will fluctuate depending on the future value of the person murdered. The fourth objection questions the notion of a future value: How can we determine the future value of a person? There are two possibilities: first, the future value of a person's life might depend on the length of time that a person is reasonably expected to live. Second, the future value of a person's life might depend on the quality of life the person is expected to live. We went on to show that problems arise with both of these possibilities. Therefore, it is difficult to understand exactly how we are to calculate the future value of a person's life.

The fifth objection shows that the badness of dying and the wrongness of being killed cannot be determined only by the loss of one's future. Here we invoked Dworkin's frustration theory: the conception that the intrinsic value of a person's life is partly determined by the natural and creative investment a person has made in his or her own life. Thus, the deprivation view of what makes killing wrong, which only looks to the future, is, at a minimum, an incomplete theory.

Next, we raised Gerald H. Paske's objection that demonstrates that depriving one of a future-like-ours is neither a sufficient nor a necessary condition for the wrongness of killing. Instead, Paske argues that Marquis's view ultimately presupposes the notion that he originally set out to avoid, namely, the notion of personhood. According to Paske, our basic instinctive moral intuitions tell us that unjustifiably killing an innocent person is always equally morally wrong, no matter how different the value of the person's future.

Finally, we introduce the possible underlying problem with Marquis's view which is that he has conflated the badness of dying with the wrongness of killing. Making this distinction clarifies many difficulties and objections that arise as a result of the deprivation view. For instance, we are able to explain why it is equally morally wrong to kill a ninety-year-old person who is just about to die and a twenty-year-old person who is only starting to live, while also noting that the deaths are not equally tragic or bad. We can agree with our common sense intuitions that the tragic nature of these deaths are very different. We can say that the latter death is severely tragic and the former is not as tragic, and yet we can also maintain that the killings are equally morally wrong. We then argued that what makes killing wrong is not the loss of a future-like-ours but rather the unjust, intentional and malicious violation of a person's right to life.

Study questions

1 Explain the standoff between the traditional abortion defender and abortion critic personhood arguments? What is the central problem?

2 What is the essential property that makes killing an adult human being morally wrong, according to Marquis?

3 What are some of the advantages of the Deprivation Theory, as it relates to other important ethical topics such as animal rights and euthanasia?

4 Does a future value of a person require consciousness?

5 Does a future value of a person require a desire for continued existence?

6 Does moral wrongness require victimization?

7 How do we determine the future value of a person? What are some difficulties with accomplishing this?

8 Is killing a person equally morally wrong, regardless of the value of a person's future-like-ours?

9 Does the value of a person consist in more than their future? What about their past?

10 What is the difference between the badness of dying and the wrongness of killing? How does this distinction affect the Deprivation Theory?

6

A Virtue Ethics Approach to Abortion

Most of the arguments we have studied so far use a consequentialist or a deontological ethical framework. Deontology claims that moral agents have a prima facie duty to perform or refrain from performing certain actions irrespective of the expected consequences of the action. Some actions, such as keeping promises, are right in and of themselves. Consequentialism, on the other hand, claims that a moral agent's obligations are to the expected consequences of an action and not to the action itself. There are no actions that are right or wrong in and of themselves; instead, actions are made right or wrong by the effects they produce.

Some of the arguments we examined in previous chapters focused on the moral status of the foetus (e.g. Warren, Baker, Schwarz and Noonan), and they argue that, given the foetus's moral standing or lack of moral standing, either it is prima facie morally wrong or morally permissible to kill the foetus. These are good examples of typical deontological arguments in which an agent's moral obligations (or lack of moral obligations) towards the foetus are central to the arguments. Some arguments of abortion defenders also use strands of consequentialist or utilitarian ethical theories. Lynn Rudder Baker's view, for instance, requires that we assess the facts and circumstances of each particular case individually in making a moral decision about the moral status of abortion. In doing so, we must consider and weigh the possible positive and negative outcomes and consequences of each particular action to make the best moral decision. This is a good example of a consequentialist model of ethical evaluation.

There are also some philosophers who believe that determining the personhood status of the foetus cannot be accomplished. Moral deliberations of these more sceptical views depend heavily on weighing the consequences of the various alternative actions. Consider, for instance, Dan Moller's theory of moral risk. He suggests that even if our first level of moral deliberation concludes that an abortion is morally permissible, since there is some chance that we could be non-negligibly mistaken about such abstract and abstruse reasoning, we ought to consider what are the consequences of having an abortion and making a mistake about the non-personhood status of the foetus. Moreover, his moral risk theory also requires that we weigh the consequences if the pregnant woman were not to go through with the abortion. His position on abortion, therefore, is fundamentally derived from and founded on consequentialist ethical thinking.

We also studied philosophers who argued that we should consider a completely different approach than focusing on the morals status of the foetus. Don Marquis, for instance, argues that we ought first to determine what makes killing wrong. He argues that we should not assume that killing is self-evidently wrong. We should not simply say 'killing is wrong because it just is'. Instead, we should look for the ultimate justification for the wrongness of killing. In doing so, he turns to the consequences of killing. What makes killing wrong, according to Marquis, is that it deprives the victim of a valuable future. Therefore, killing is wrong because of the terrible consequence of depriving the victim of a valuable future (i.e. a future-like-ours). But if this correct, then killing a foetus is just as wrong as killing an adult person, since killing a foetus deprives it of a valuable future-like-ours. The justification for the wrongness of killing and for the immorality of abortion is based on the consequences that the victim suffers, namely, the loss of his or her valuable future experiences. What all these views have in common is that they focus on the act of having an abortion and try to determine its moral status. Hence, deontological and consequentialist ethical theories are *act-centred*.

In this chapter, we introduce a new ethical framework to evaluate the abortion issue, namely, *virtue ethics*. Virtue ethics deviates significantly from the nature of the moral justifications offered through deontological and consequentialist theories. Virtue ethics focuses more on the person instead of the act. Its main concern is on *how to* become a good person? What constitutes a good life? Therefore, we could say that virtue ethical theory is *agent-centred*. Before we apply virtue ethics to the issue of abortion, a basic introductory understanding of virtue ethics is required. Therefore, we begin with a brief introduction to Aristotle's virtue ethics.

Neo-Aristotelian virtue ethics

In the *Nicomachean Ethics*,[1] the Greek philosopher Aristotle (384–322 bc) provides a practical guide on how to live an excellent human life.

Our lives are made up of the feelings we have, the decisions we make and the actions we perform (or do not perform) on a daily basis. Aristotle provides a holistic theory about human nature and how we can sculpture and mould our character, appetites, passions, dispositions, habits, practical reasoning and rational intentions to produce the right feelings, decisions and actions that will lead us to a good life. We will study seven main ideas that will provide a basic foundation to Aristotle's virtue ethics: (1) What is virtue? (2) *eudaimonia* or happiness and the human good; (3) Aristotle's concept of a human being; (4) the role of pain and pleasure in virtue theory; (5) virtues of the intellect: the special place of practical reasoning for deliberative action; (6) virtues of character: bravery, temperance, generosity, magnanimity, beneficence, compassion etc. and (7) the virtue of justice. Before we begin our discussion on these central ideas of virtue ethics, we should be clear about the purpose of Aristotle's *Nicomachean Ethics*.

The purpose of the Nicomachean Ethics

Aristotle did not view the *Nicomachean Ethics* as a theoretical study but rather as a practical investigation to produce practical results for people's lives. What he wanted was to establish a guide on how to live a flourishing and happy life in a way that would make one a *good* person rather than an evil person. For Aristotle, the flourishing happy life and the good person go hand-in-hand. At the beginning of Book II, he makes clear his objective and goal:

> Our present discussion does not aim, as our others do, at study; for the purpose of our examination is not to know what virtue is, but *to become good* [my emphasis], since otherwise the inquiry would be of no benefit to us. And so we must examine the right ways of acting; for us as we have said, the actions also control the sorts of states we acquire.[2]

How do we become good? First, we should be aware that Aristotle is not interested in just any kind of good or the right action for any particular goal. He is *not* interested in how to become a good piano player or a good football player or a good student or a good doctor; he is also not interested in the idea of the good itself. Instead, he is interested in how we can become *good human beings*.

What is virtue?

Virtue comes from the Greek word *arête* and it means *excellence*. To act virtuously means to act excellently. Excellence, however, is a relative concept because its meaning will change depending on the context and with respect to its intended reference. For instance, an excellent golf ball will have very different properties than an excellent basketball. Consider, for instance, the activities associated with becoming an excellent marathon runner and the activities associated with becoming an excellent weightlifter. Two persons engaged in these two different activities with a desire to do them well will require very different training regiments and diets. Consider the differences that are required for an excellent shoemaker and an excellent warrior. The former requires no special physical strength, however the latter requires a lot of physical strength and endurance. From these simple examples, it is evident that to understand Aristotle's conception of virtue, we also need to understand the reference to which Aristotle intends the notion of virtue or excellence to be associated with.

Aristotle is interested in trying to determine what constitutes excellent human behaviour over an entire lifetime. In other words, he is interested in what constitutes an excellent human life and what one needs to do to live such a life. His interests are not simply about knowing what are the right feelings and actions, but also about knowing how one can come to acquire the right feelings and do the right actions in a consistent, reliable and enduring way. Aristotle wants to investigate how to become excellent and live a virtuous human life. He says, 'It is clear that the virtue we must exam is human virtue, since we are also seeking the human good and human happiness.'³ To understand Aristotle's notion of human excellence or human virtue we need to examine the concepts of *eudaimonia* and the human good.

Eudaimonia *and the human good*

For Aristotle, *why* we do what we do is as important as what we do. The intentions and motivations of human actions are an important part of Aristotle's virtue ethics. Moreover, a central line of enquiry in his *Nicomachean Ethics* is the ultimate universal motivations of human actions. What is the ultimate end that we all desire? Why do we go to school? Why do we study so hard? Why do we search for a partner whom we love and who will love us? What is the purpose and motivation for all of these things? It seems to Aristotle that all of these human objectives, goals and ends are merely means to another more ultimate end. If something is simply a means to an end, that is, if we only desire something because it can help us achieve something further and not because it is something we want for its own sake, then it cannot be what Aristotle calls a 'complete end'. The human good must be found in a complete end, because this is something that we seek for its own sake and not merely as a means to something else.

The only thing, according to Aristotle, that has this characteristic is *human happiness* (i.e. Gk. *Eudaimonia*). Our actions always seem to be motivated to achieve happiness, and, moreover, we desire happiness for its own sake. It would seem foolish to ask someone, 'Why do you want to be happy?' He or she might respond with, 'I just do.' And this response will be reasonable since it does not appear that one would need any further justification for the desire to be happy. Instead, it seems that all the things we do are for the sake of happiness. Aristotle concludes, 'Happiness, then, is apparently something complete and self-sufficient, since it is the end of the things achievable in action.'[4]

Eudaimonia, the Greek word for happiness, has a broader connotation than the English word 'happiness'. This can cause some misunderstandings. *Eudaimonia* should not be interpreted as momentary or temporary states of euphoria or as simple emotions of elation. Instead, Aristotle has something much more profound in mind. *Eudaimonia* should be interpreted as broadly as possible to mean a good human life that entails all of one's years of living. The goodness of good people lies essentially in the acts that they perform over an entire lifetime; and the happiness or *eudaimonia* of these active people is not something distinct that arises as a result of the actions they perform, but rather it is something that is part of the actions themselves. Aristotle points out that 'what is just pleases the lover of justice, and in general what accords with virtue pleases the lover of virtue. ... Hence these people's lives do not need pleasure to be added [to virtuous activity] as some sort of extra decoration; rather, it has its pleasure within itself'.[5] Thus, happiness is the good that we all strive for, and it is coextensive with the good in our lives, which is achieved through good deeds over a lifetime.

What is a human being?

How do we become good human beings? How do we achieve *eudaimonia*? To answer these questions, we need to enquire into the nature of our humanity. What is a human being? The meaning and definition of a human being can be given by discovering what are the essential properties of a human being. To discover the essential properties of human beings, Aristotle claims we have to observe the proper natural function of human beings; that is, what is that special function that only human beings do and do well. Some background in Aristotelian metaphysics is necessary here. Aristotle believes that things in nature have a proper natural function (i.e. a *telos*); they are meant to work in certain ways, as is the case with human artefacts that are created for a given purpose. For instance, imagine a knife that is created to cut meat. This knife will have certain characteristics that are relevant to its intended proper function or its *telos*. Therefore, the knife will be large, sharp, have a comfortable handle and its blade will be especially made to cut flesh. These characteristics make it a good steak knife. Now, whether or not it is an excellent steak knife can only be determined in reference to its intended proper function. It will be an excellent knife if and only if it cuts meat well. It will not be an excellent steak knife if and only if it does not cut meat well. Aristotle explains it as follows:

> For just as the good, i.e., [doing] well, for flautist, a sculptor, and every craftsman, and, in general, for whatever has a function and [characteristic] action, seems to depend on its function, the same seems to be true for a human being, if a human being has some function.[6]

Aristotle observes that many of our human organs and parts, such as our eyes, lungs and heart, have natural proper functions too. For instance, the proper natural function of the eye is to see. Therefore, an excellent eye sees well and a defective eye does not see so well. Just as these parts have a natural function, the human being in its totality also has a proper natural function. If we can determine the proper natural function of human beings, then we can derive what constitutes a virtuous or excellent life in reference to that function.

Aristotle acknowledges that human beings are animals and that they have many things in common with other animals, such as their reproductive, nutritive and sentient functions. However, he also says that human beings have a mental life that transcends that of other animals, and, moreover, that this rational function of human beings is the essential function that makes human beings special. The ability to reason is what sets human beings apart from other animals, and thus it is this capacity that makes us unique (in an essential way). If we put reasoning and the life of action together, we get the special proper natural function of human beings: 'We have found, then, that the human function is activity of the soul in accord with reason or requiring reason.'[7] If human beings' proper natural function is to act in accordance with reason, then we should be able to assess and evaluate the excellence or virtue of a person by measuring how well their actions are directed and in accordance with reason.

Pain and pleasure

Before we go any further to explain what good reasoning is and what it means to act in accordance with reason, we need to understand the role that pain and pleasure play in Aristotle's virtue ethics. He acknowledges that, as human animals, pains and pleasures play a significant role in determining our feelings and actions.[8] He writes:

For virtue of character is about pleasures and pains. For pleasures causes us to do base actions, and pain causes us to abstain from fine ones. ... Further, virtues are concerned with actions and feelings; but every feeling and every action implies pleasures and pains; hence, for this reason too, virtue is about pleasures and pains.[9]

Human beings have a strong instinctual desire to feel pleasure and avoid pain, and many of our actions are motivated not by reason but by the expected amount of pleasure and pain we believe we will receive or avoid, respectively, as a consequence of performing them.

Aristotle realizes that our appetites and passions for pleasure and pain are extremely powerful motivating forces that strongly influence our feelings and actions. Moreover, he also realizes that the right actions that will lead us to a flourishing and good life do not always coincide with what is most pleasurable and least painful. Sometimes the right action requires that we risk suffering pain that is not naturally desirable and in accordance with our basic, animal desires. In short, Aristotle is aware that there will be times in which our rational desires will conflict with our animal and instinctive desires of pleasure and pain. This is why the two virtues of *temperance* (controlling our desire for pleasure) and *bravery* (controlling our fears for pains and suffering) are two of the central moral virtues in Aristotle's ethics. (See below.)

Human being's greatest obstacle in performing the right action is not always bad practical reasoning or our inability to know what the right action is, but rather our inability to control our strong desires, appetites and passions required to perform the right action. To offset this conflict between practical reasoning and our appetites, Aristotle claims that if a person has received the right ethical education and has been instructed well from an early age, then he or she receives pleasure from doing the right thing, and will suffer pain when they do the wrong action. In this way, some degree of pleasures and pains will nicely correlate with the right and wrong actions. In addition, doing the right thing and being a good person will lead one to a pleasurable and happy life. Aristotle explains: 'That is why we need to have had the appropriate upbringing – right from early youth, as Plato says – to make us find enjoyment or pain in the right things; for this is the correct education.'[10]

Therefore, there seems to be three tasks in living virtuously: (1) an epistemological normative task: knowing what the right action is in a given circumstance; (2) an educative axiological task: learning to value and desire the right ends, so that one feels pleasure when doing the right action and pain when doing the wrong action and (3) a moral task: having sufficient character to perform the action that we know is ethically right. The first two are intimately connected and thus will be discussed together.

Intellectual Virtue

How do we determine morally right actions? First, we need to distinguish between the metaphysical question 'What makes a right action right?' and the epistemological question 'How can we know what is the right action?' These two questions are not always clearly distinguished. For instance, it has been proposed by some that according to virtue ethics the right action is the act that 'an agent with a virtuous character would do in the circumstance'.[11] This seems to suggest that what makes the action right is that a virtuous person would perform the action. For instance, Justin Oakley says, 'What *makes* the action right is that it is what a person with a virtuous character would do here.'[12] However, this view seems to conflate the epistemological and metaphysical criteria. We can identify what are the right actions and learn about the deliberative process of how to discern right actions by observing how virtuous persons go about making moral decisions; however, it is not their decisions that make the actions right. Instead, it is their clear thinking, practical wisdom and virtuous character that allow them to identify the *true* right action in particular circumstances.

But if it is not the virtuous person's choosing the action that makes the action right, then what is the metaphysical criterion? What is it that makes the right action right? According to Aristotle, the right action is always the action that, in the particular circumstances, will best advance one's life towards the ultimate goal of *eudaimonia* or a flourishing life. Aristotle says, 'Prudence [practical wisdom] is a state grasping the *truth* [my emphasis], involving reason, concerned with action about things that are good or bad for a human being.'[13] Hence, a right action is right if and only if it is one of a set of plausible acts (or close to it) that will lead the agent (and others involved), given the particular circumstances and context, to *eudaimonia* (i.e. to what is good *for* a human being). This relationship between virtuous action and our proper end is an essential one, or, as Alasdair MacIntyre calls it an 'internal one' instead of an external one. MacIntyre explains:

> We need to remember however that although Aristotle treats the acquisition and exercise of virtues as means to an end, the relationship between means to an end is internal and not external. I call a means internal to a given end when the end cannot be adequately characterized independently of a characterization of the means. So it is with the virtuous and the *telos* which is the good life for man on Aristotle's account.[14]

As a result, the right action is independent of a virtuous person identifying it as the right action, since a virtuous person may *think* that a particular action is one of the best possible actions that will advance her life towards *eudaimonia* and yet she may be mistaken. This is why it is possible that a virtuous person can make mistakes and identify a wrong action as right.

Notice that this rational ability that Aristotle calls *phronesis* or practical wisdom requires two different tasks. First, it requires the axiological task that the person correctly identify what is the end or goal they are striving for. In other words, they need to have a well-formed value system that will direct them to recognize *eudaimonia*; this requires that they understand in what a flourishing life truly consists of. If a person aspires or wishes for the wrong ends, then no matter how well he uses his practical reasoning, he will not be virtuous. Aristotle claims we might consider such a person 'clever', since he is very good at identifying the best means to arrive at his desired end. However, to be a virtuous person, one's ends or aspirations must be good and one must recognize them as good. To be virtuous, therefore, an agent must be able to correctly identify *a good end or goal* towards which the agent is striving for. This knowledge is mostly gained through some form of education in which the more experienced and wiser people of a society teach the younger and less experienced the correct notion of a flourishing life.

Second, practical wisdom also requires the epistemological task of knowing what are the best actions that serve as the best means to arrive at the good goals that one aspires to. This entails good, reflective, rational deliberation on the part of an agent; it is this that constitutes the essential nature of what Aristotle refers to as practical reasoning or deliberation. An important point to note about right actions within a virtue ethics framework is that there is no such thing as '*the* right action'. There is only a set of closely associated right actions. Moreover, as one deviates from this cluster of approximate set of right actions one deviates from what is good, since these actions are what most effectively will lead one to the good end. We must remember that Aristotle claims that ethics is an inexact discipline that works with rough approximations rather than precise calculations. Its method is not deductive like mathematics; instead, it is more like the establishing of hypotheses that are later confirmed through our lived experiences. The right action is the best alternative within a set of particular circumstances that will lead a virtuous agent to her desired good end. Practical reasoning, then, is an *enquiring and rational calculation* about the right actions within particular circumstances. Aristotle notes, 'For it is not merely the state in accord with the correct reason, but the state *involving* the correct reason, that is [intellectual] virtue.'[15] How we learn to identify these actions is through our close observations of people who already have a noted reputation for achieving flourishing and good lives. Ethical knowledge is based on experience, one's teachers and practice. This is why Aristotle believed it is important to have good role models and ethical teachers from a young age. Moreover, the best way to acquire good ethical reasoning is to watch and learn from how people who are already virtuous do it. However, this is not the only way. There is one central moral principle that ought to guide practical reasoning, namely, the *principle of the mean.*

The principle of the mean

The principle of the mean states that virtuous actions lie somewhere between the two extremes of a given kind of behaviour. Vice, on the other hand, lies somewhere close to the extremes. For instance, when confronted with a situation in which we face a certain danger we can respond in a variety of ways. However, our attitude seems to fall within a spectrum of possibilities, from running away to confronting it recklessly. The first extreme represents the vice of cowardliness and the other extreme represents the vice of rashness; both are wrong. The virtuous attitude and behaviour is one that lies somewhere in between these two extremes. But where exactly is the mean?

Aristotle's virtue ethics does not provide a formula for determining specific ethical behaviour, and the mean is dependent on the particular facts and circumstances of the situation, and it is relative to the individual and his or her particular traits, skills and other personal characteristics. Some have criticized Aristotle's view for its lack of specificity and its indeterminacy when it comes to making the right ethical decision, but one could also argue that this flexibility is where virtue ethics' strength lies. The mean is guided more by human practical reasoning than anything else, and using practical reasoning as a guide permits the deliberative process to take into consideration a wide range of circumstances as we weigh, measure and assess all of the options available to us in dealing with a particular issue, at a particular time and within a particular context.

Making ethical decisions is a complicated matter and there are individual nuances in every particular case that might be unique and morally relevant. The virtue of the intellect, *phronesis* or practical reasoning, is the ability to think through these situations, to assess the agents involved, how they are involved, what are their legitimate interests, what are the consequences of the various options etc. The goal is to make a judicious decision about how to act, in the particular situation, given the context and all of the information available to one at the time, in a way that will best advance one's life towards *eudaimonia*. It is this form of rational deliberation towards the good life, guided by good teachers and experiences, that helps provide the intellectual practical skills to make good ethical decisions.

The mean for Aristotle is not the same as the midpoint between two extremes. Instead, we should assess and take into consideration where our natural instincts and appetites are strongest, and to which of the extremes and with what force they tend to move us. Once we have evaluated these factors, we should use the information to determine our behaviour; in general, we ought to select behaviour that will resist our natural inclinations and move us in the opposite direction of our instincts, appetites and passions. For instance, consider once again the case above in which we are confronted with a dangerous situation. In these cases, we might have a natural instinctive desire for self-preservation and to avoid pain, and thus we might have a natural desire to move towards the extreme of acting cowardly. This natural aversion to pain and strong instinct to avoid situations that could cause us harm and injury might be an obstacle to perform the morally right action in dangerous situations. Therefore, moral courage or the virtue of bravery should choose a target closer to acting rashly than cowardly. Thus, we should intend for our actions to come closer to rashness than cowardliness.

Cowardliness_____**Mean**_____Rashness
Too little (Natural tendency towards cowardliness)   **Moral Courage or Bravery**   Too Much

Consider another example. Aristotle claims that a person who never experiences any bodily pleasures whatsoever illustrates the extreme behaviour of *insensibility*. On the other hand, an individual who indulges in all bodily pleasures at all times exhibits the other extreme behaviour of *intemperance*. The individual who can control his or her behaviour to act in accordance with the mean between these two extremes exhibits the virtue of *temperance*. But where exactly is the mean? We should begin by asking ourselves: Where do our natural and instinctive tendencies lie? In other words, towards what extreme do our natural appetites move us? Aristotle claims that we have a strong natural desire to experience bodily pleasures, and therefore our instincts and appetites will move us towards the vice of intemperance. Therefore, we ought to strive towards the extreme of insensibility. For instance, imagine we are offered an all-you-can-eat pass to a new restaurant of our favourite food. We have a natural tendency towards pleasure, indulgence and gluttony. Thus, we naturally have a strong desire for the one extreme (to eat too much). Therefore, to offset this natural inherent strong desire towards one extreme and vice, the mean or temperance ought to be closer to the extreme of insensibility.

Insensibility_____**Mean-Temperance**_____Intemperance
Too little (Natural tendency towards intemperance)   Too Much

Aristotle also notes that each individual will be born with certain natural virtuous states that do not require the agent to intentionally practise, develop and perfect. Sometimes there are individuals who are born temperate or brave, and hence it requires very little effort on their part to acquire these ethical moral virtuous states. He calls these 'natural virtues'. Two things are important with respect to natural virtues: first, natural virtues are not necessarily moral virtuous; they must be performed in the right psychological state to be considered morally virtuous. If acting bravely comes to one naturally, and it is not performed deliberately and within the control of practical reason, then this act is not morally virtuous, even though the act resembles externally a morally courageous act. Second, given that we each have our own and different natural inclinations towards the virtues, we need to take into account our own personal and innate traits and characteristics when assessing the mean or the virtuousness of an action in a particular circumstance.

As we can appreciate from the above account of Aristotle's virtue ethics, it inherently entails a rational and objective *contextuality* that includes the agent's personal traits and the particular circumstances of the person making the decision. In addition, it also entails an analysis of the decision-making process and an understanding of the agent's psychological state of mind when they perform the action (i.e. it is important not only *what* one does but also *how* and *why* one does it).

Moral Virtues

Once we have developed our intellectual ability and our practical reasoning to consistently and approximately identify what is excellent behaviour in particular situations, we will have acquired the intellectual virtue of practical reasoning. In other words, according to Aristotle, we will have perfected our practical reasoning, which involves the rational aspect of humanity that is most essentially human. However, this by itself will not guarantee that we will perform the virtuous action. Why? Aristotle realizes that one reason why people do bad things is because they lack sufficient character to follow through with the right action. It is not that they do not know or understand what the right action is, but rather that they cannot perform it because they are too scared to do so, or because they give in to their appetites or desires for bodily pleasures. We sometimes refer to this as 'weakness of the will' or 'lack of will power'. This is why Aristotle claims, 'What we have said, then, makes it clear that we cannot be fully good without prudence, or prudence without virtue of character.'[16] There is, therefore, a sort of symbiotic, synergistic relationship between intellectual virtue and moral virtues of character. You need the former to acquire the latter, but you also need the latter to practise the former.

Consider most actions people commit that are deemed morally wrong and that are, in most cases, regretted in the future. For instance, imagine someone who cheats on an exam. Students commit this action because they perceive studying to be a painful experience that they would prefer to avoid.

They are motivated by taking the easy way out and trying to accomplish what requires great sacrifice without having to suffer through the hours of studying. Consider someone who has an affair and betrays the trust of their partner. In most cases, these people know that what they are doing is morally wrong, and they are not motivated by the desire to harm their partner, but rather by bodily desires which they lack the moral character to control. Similarly, in many cases, our strong feelings to avoid pain and injury prevent us from doing the right thing or what is virtuous. Human beings are frightened of many things. For instance, we are nervous about what other people might think of us or that other people might injure or harm us in some way. These feelings can cause us to hesitate and not do what we know to be the right thing.

Aristotle believes that the solution is to develop certain dispositions, attitudes and habits that will harmonize with practical reasoning and the decisions that lead to a good life. It is not sufficient to know what is temperance, bravery, generosity etc.; we also have *to be* temperate, brave and generous. We might also add that in addition to being temperate, brave and generous, we also need *to want* to be temperate, brave and generous. Temperance is the character trait that disposes us to consistently and habitually act in ways that avoid and resist in engaging in activities that provide excessive bodily pleasures. To want to act and to act moderately in all cases when confronted with the temptations of bodily pleasures is to have acquired the virtue of temperance. To want to act and to act bravely in all cases when confronted with threats of injury and pain is to have acquired the virtue of bravery. These two virtues will provide an individual with the character to perform the right action and to follow the direction and path of practical reasoning, even in situations in which we are tempted by pleasure or pain not to do the right action. But how do we acquire these character traits?

Aristotle claims that the moral virtues are acquired through practising them and having them become part of you. Once you perform these virtuous actions, over and over, they will be forged into your person, until they become identical with who you are; hence, they make you the person you are. Your character is your character traits and your virtues. Therefore, *to act* temperate and act bravely is *to be* temperate and brave. Another way of understanding the relationship between your character and the virtues is to think of the development of character as taming your appetites and desires. Little by little you modify your natural appetites to cohere with practical reasoning. In this way, your natural desires will coincide with what is right, and hence doing the right thing will produce a natural happiness about doing the right thing. Aristotle explains it as follows:

The active exercise of appetites are large and intense, they actually expel rational calculation. That is why appetites must be moderate and few, and never contrary to reason. This is the condition we call obedient and temperate. And just as the child's life must follow the instructions of his guide, so too the appetitive part must follow reason. Hence the temperate person's appetitive part must agree with reason; for both [this appetitive part and reason] aim at the fine, and the temperate person's appetites are for the right things, in the ways, at the right times, which is just what reason also prescribes.[17]

Even though we can separate the virtues into the intellectual virtue and the moral virtues, and we can further speak about various different kinds of moral virtues, Aristotle wants to argue that the virtues have a structural unity grounded in the intellectual virtue, at least for those who are fully virtuous. Thus, it is not the case that you can simply have one or two virtues and not the others. He writes:

> For, [it is argued], since the same person is not naturally best suited for all the virtues, someone will already have one virtue before he gets another. This is indeed possible in the case of natural virtues. It is not possible, however, in the case of the [full] virtues that someone must have to be called good without qualification; for one has all of the virtues if and only if one has prudence, which is a single state.[18]

The virtue of justice

For Aristotle justice is 'complete virtue in relation to another'.[19] This means several things. First, unlike the virtues of prudence, temperance and bravery that consist of improving one's intellect and character, justice is the virtue that considers the treatment of *others*. Justice, therefore, concerns how we ought to treat other individuals such as friends, neighbours, colleagues, strangers. There are two fundamental aspects of justice when it concerns treatment of others: fairness and lawfulness. We ought to have a sense of fairness when we interact with others and in being fair with others we act justly. We also ought to be respectful of the laws and abide by them, and in being law abiding citizens, we are also just.

Second, to be just we have to have already acquired the intellectual virtue of practical reason and the moral virtues, especially temperance and bravery. In other words, the virtue of justice requires *complete virtue*. It is not difficult to see why this is the case. It would be challenging for someone who is intemperate and indulges in bodily pleasure to act fairly and lawfully in a consistent manner. Eventually, an intemperate person will find himself in a situation in which he will have to choose between satisfying his appetites and desires or doing what is morally right. In such a case, if he lacks self-control, he will be likely to choose bodily pleasure over what is morally right.

Consider a person who commits adultery and betrays his or her partner. Such a person is not fair or just, and the reason for the injustice is a result of the person's lack of the virtue of temperance and not necessarily a deliberate intent to harm the other. To be just, therefore, requires that one be in a state of virtue. It is impossible to be just if one is a coward or intemperate or imprudent. Aristotle says, 'And that is why justice often seems to be supreme among all of the virtues, and "neither the evening star or the morning star is so marvelous", and the proverb says, "And in justice all virtue is summed up." Moreover, justice is complete virtue to highest degree because it is the complete exercise of complete virtue.'[20]

Finally, we should point out the difference between *special* and *general* injustices. General injustice concerns unfair and lawful actions that are caused by some lack of virtue of character as described above. For instance, the example of the cheating partner is an example of general injustice because the root of the morally wrong action of the injustice is a weakness in the character trait of the person. On the other hand, special cases of injustice are cases in which a person acts unlawfully or unfairly, and the root cause of the unjust action is an unfair gain or profit for the individual. Aristotle refers to it as an act of 'overreaching'. Good examples of this are actions that are motivated by excessive greed and ambition. Notice that in these cases of injustices, certain moral virtues can accentuate the injustice, since a greedy person who is temperate and brave can commit more of an injustice than a greedy person who is intemperate and a coward.

Virtue Theory and Abortion

In 'Virtue Theory and Abortion', Rosalind Hursthouse applies virtue ethics to the issue of abortion. This is one of the first and only essays that attempts such an enterprise. In doing so, she highlights the many misconceptions about virtue ethics, including the erroneous idea that the only thing that can truly be applied is the virtue of justice. With this in mind, she says:

> But these are caricatures; they fail to appreciate the way in which virtue theory quite transforms the discussion of abortion by dismissing the two familiar dominating considerations [rights and the moral status of the fetus] as, in a way, fundamentally irrelevant.[21]

According to Hursthouse, then, the main focus of the abortion debate, which is the rights of the woman and the moral status of the foetus (i.e. the personhood status and the right to life of the foetus), not only loses its central place in the debate, it becomes irrelevant in determining whether abortion is morally wrong or morally permissible.

Rights from a virtue ethics perspective

Right-based arguments for the moral permissibility of abortion argue that a woman has a right to control her body. A woman's autonomy and privacy include her reproductive choices such as whether she wants or does not want to carry a pregnancy to full term. Of course, the well-known rebuttal to this line of argumentation is that if the foetus is a person with a right to life, a foetus's right to life will always outweigh a woman's right to control her body. A pregnant woman's autonomy over her reproductive choice cannot override the right to life of another person.

Judith Jarvis Thomson's prominent pro-choice rights-based abortion argument is a direct response to this rebuttal. Thomson's argument is based on the violinist analogy (see Chapter 4) and claims that even if the foetus is considered a person with the right to life, it has no claim rights against the pregnant woman, if the woman never consented for the foetus to use her body. As a result, Thomson argues that the pregnant woman does not do an injustice if she decides to terminate the pregnancy and deny the foetus the use of her body for its survival. In this case, there is no injustice because the pregnant woman does not violate any of the foetus's rights.

Hursthouse argues that from a virtue ethics perspective the questions of rights are morally irrelevant. As a consequence, all of the above arguments based on rights, including Thomson's, do not get us any closer to determining whether abortion is morally right or wrong. If Hursthouse is correct, then this is a substantial and revolutionary claim. Hursthouse says:

> Supposing only that women have such a moral right, *nothing* follows from this supposition about the morality of abortion, according to virtue theory, once it is noted (quite generally, not with particular reference to abortion) that in exercising a moral right I can do something cruel, or callous, or selfish, light-minded, self-righteous, stupid, inconsiderate, disloyal, dishonest – that is, act viciously. ... So whether women have a moral right to terminate their pregnancies is irrelevant within virtue theory, for it is irrelevant to the question 'in having an abortion in this circumstances, would the agent be acting virtuously or viciously or neither?'[22]

Recall that according to virtue ethics moral goodness is determined by living an excellent life that leads to *eudaimonia* or to a flourishing life. Developing certain character traits and acting in accordance with them (and with the mean) is the method by which we can achieve this life. But the notion of rights and whether I have a right to perform an action will not be very helpful in selecting the virtuous action or in determining the mean. Take the simple example of eating healthy. We might have a right of eat as much as we wish but this does not mean that eating too much is not a vice.

Consider Thomson's example of a child who owns a box of the chocolates and refuses to share any of these with his brother. In this case, Thomson argues that if the brother who owns the chocolates decides not to share with his brother, he commits no injustice. However, from a virtue ethics perspective, we could argue that not sharing with his brother might be the manifestation of several possible vices, such as greediness, stinginess, self-centredness, selfishness, inconsiderateness. Moreover, the correct action is not dictated by the right of either of the brothers but rather by the action that will lead the brother with the chocolates to being a good person and advance his path to a good and flourishing life. Aristotle describes it as follows:

> Actions in accord with virtue are fine, and aim at the fine. Hence the generous person will also aim at the fine in his giving, and will give correctly; for he will give to the right people, the right amount, at the right time, and all the other things that are implied by correct giving. Moreover, he will do this with pleasure, or at any rate without pain; for action in accord with virtue is pleasant or at any rate painless, and least of all is it painful.[23]

The virtue of generosity or giving correctly is the mean between wastefulness and selfishness. Our giving (how much, when and to whom) should be guided by what we determine to be the proper mean between these extremes, after we take into consideration and carefully reflect on the circumstances of the particular situation. We should also note that being generous is never a sacrifice that entails suffering for the virtuous person. For, if it is painful to give correctly, then even if we give as a virtuous person gives, we are not virtuous in our giving for we lack the right attitude and feeling towards our giving. Let us now turn to the moral status of the foetus.

The moral status of the foetus from a virtue ethics perspective

Some of the most prevalent and prominent arguments for the moral wrongness of abortion are based on the moral status of the foetus. Many abortion critics argue that the foetus is a person and thus killing the foetus is equivalent to homicide. Others argue that it is morally wrong to kill the foetus based on the foetus's potentiality to become a person. Yet, others have argued that it is morally wrong to kill the foetus because of the high probability that a foetus will eventually become a person. Still others have avoided the personhood issue and instead have focused on the moral standing of the foetus.[24] How do these arguments that rely on the moral status of the foetus affect the moral question of abortion from a virtue ethics perspective? According to Hursthouse, the moral status of the foetus is irrelevant to whether an abortion is morally permissible or morally wrong. Hursthouse says: 'And this entails the following, rather startling, conclusion: That the status of the fetus – that issue over which so much ink has been spilt – is, according to virtue theory, simply not relevant to the rightness or wrongness of abortion.'[25]

Hursthouse points out several reasons for this. First, the question of the personhood status of the foetus is a complicated metaphysical question that might never be completely settled. Thus, it would be absurd to think that we have to suspend our ethical judgement on abortion until such questions are answered. Second, even if it is resolved, its solution will most probably entail complex and technical philosophical theories that should not be part of the virtue ethics practised by non-philosophers. According to Hursthouse, the information that should be relevant is 'the familiar biological facts', meaning the basic facts that any rational adult human being should know, such as that 'pregnancy occurs as the result of sexual intercourse, that it lasts nine months, during which time the fetus grows and develops, that standardly it terminates in the birth of a living baby, and that this is how we all came to be'.[26]

Finally, Hursthouse points out that virtue requires that we have the right attitude towards a situation. To have the right attitude, we must have correct knowledge of the facts involved. We cannot have the right attitude if it is based on false information. This means that if the moral status of the foetus is relevant to our moral evaluation of the abortion from a virtue ethics perspective, then we would need to know the truth about the status of the foetus. But determining the moral status of the foetus with certainty is impossible, therefore we would not be able to morally evaluate the abortion issue. If Hursthouse is correct, we might conclude that a virtue ethics framework radically shifts the ethical paradigm for moral assessment of the abortion issue. However, we still need to get clearer about how to morally assess the abortion issue from a virtue ethics perspective.

Assessing the moral status of abortion from a virtue ethics perspective

If neither rights nor the moral status of the foetus is relevant in determining whether abortion is morally right or wrong, then how does virtue ethics go about evaluating the moral status of abortion? Hursthouse claims we need to begin with the common and basic biological and sociological facts surrounding the abortion issue and available to all adult human beings. Here, we need to consider not only the biological mechanics of how reproduction works but also our conceptions of offspring, parenting, motherhood, fatherhood, family and so on. Next, we need to assess what are the right disposition and attitudes we ought to have towards these facts and concepts. Hursthouse puts it as follows: 'How do these facts figure in the practical reasoning, actions and passions, thoughts and reactions, of the virtuous and the nonvirtuous? What is the mark of having the right attitude to these facts and what manifests having the wrong attitude to them?'[27]

Attitude matters

According to Hursthouse, once we bring these facts to the table, we ought to reflectively evaluate the importance and significance of an abortion. According to Hursthouse, a correct attitude towards abortion is one that considers it a grave and serious issue that is related to the importance of parenting, the commencement of a new life, children, family etc. Moreover, as has been shown above, virtue ethics is highly contextual and thus all of the facts concerning the particular case should influence our disposition and attitude towards the case. First, let us consider what ought to be the right attitude towards the loss of human life.

A right attitude towards the loss of human life is one that understands how family, parenting and children can lead one to a full and flourishing life (*eudaimonia*). A wrong attitude is one that underestimates the importance and significance of an abortion. Hursthouse notes: 'Anyone who genuinely believes that an abortion is comparable to a haircut or an appendectomy is mistaken.'[28] Here, virtue ethics comes into a point of conflict with other act-centred theories. First, an act-centred theory will argue that people's thoughts or attitudes should not be given any moral weight at all. After all, we cannot help what we think and our thoughts do not hurt anyone, as long as we do not act on them. Thus, so what if we think that an abortion is like a haircut, and so what if our attitudes about our friend's miscarriage is lighthearted. Why are these thoughts morally wrong?

This point of disagreement highlights the stark difference between agent-centred virtue ethics and act-centred ethical theories. According to the former, being good and acting rightly entail one's intentions, dispositions, habits and so on, and it is simply impossible to be virtuous if one lacks the right attitude or is in the wrong state of mind. As a consequence, a person who doesn't understand the importance of human life and is not rightly disposed to the loss of human life cannot act rightly. Hursthouse puts it as follows: 'But the character traits that virtue theory emphasizes are not simply dispositions to intentional actions, but a seamless disposition to certain actions and passions, thoughts and reactions.'[29]

According to Hursthouse there is a virtuous and vicious attitude towards abortion. The virtuous attitude is one that understands the prima facie good derived from family life, parenting, motherhood, fatherhood, childbearing, love, friendship and related life events. Someone's inability to understand the intrinsic worth of these things and how they contribute to a flourishing and good life lacks the intellectual virtue to grasp the proper ends and goals of a good life. Hursthouse explains it as follows:

> If we are to go on to talk about good human lives, in the context of abortion, we have to bring in our thoughts about the value of love and abortion, and our proper emotional development through a natural life cycle. The familiar facts support the view that parenthood in general, and motherhood and childbearing in particular, are intrinsically worthwhile, are among the things that can be correctly thought to be partially constitutive of a flourishing human life.[30]

A second important difference between virtue ethics and act-centred theories is that, unlike the latter where impartiality is emphasized to a fault,[31] virtue ethics seriously considers the various relationships as important information in one's ethical deliberations. Our relationships with family, friends, loved ones and members of our community are morally relevant and their distinctions are also morally relevant when it comes to making certain decisions. For instance, Aristotle would argue that our attitudes, obligations and feelings towards family members should be different than our attitudes, obligations and feelings towards non-family members or strangers. We might have special obligations to family members, in virtue of them being part of our family, that we do not have to non-family members. In addition, we ought to treat good friends differently than persons who are not good friends, because we have special obligations towards the former that we do not have towards the latter.

Context and attitude modification

The intellectual virtue entailed in the theory of virtue ethics requires that in our moral deliberation we consider the particular facts associated with each particular case. Aristotle's conception of the mean and how it is determined require that we consider and weigh the agent's particular circumstances as well as the circumstances influencing and affecting the situation the agent is in. In addition, good, practical and rational calculations also require that we carefully consider the context surrounding the moral event (time, place, people etc.), and these facts ought to properly influence and affect our moral decisions. In the case of abortion, Hursthouse takes into consideration this form of practical reasoning and contextuality in various ways. She argues that several factors ought to influence any moral decision on abortion: (a) the foetus's developmental stage, (b) the pregnant women's particular situation and (c) the idea of being in a moral dilemma facing only two possible inevitable evils.

The foetus's developmental stages

The robust contextual nature of virtue ethics easily permits us to argue that our attitude towards the seriousness of abortion ought to change as the foetus develops and grows and becomes more fully human. Two factors should influence our attitude: first the foetus's biological growth, sophistication and its proximity to becoming conscious and sentient; second, the longer the foetus is with the pregnant woman the more the pregnant woman becomes aware of its existence, and thus the more the woman may become emotionally attached to the foetus. Hursthouse argues:

> To say that a the cutting off of a human life is always a matter of some seriousness, at any stage, is not to deny the relevance of gradual fetal development. ... Abortion for shallow reasons in the later stages is much more shocking than abortion for the same reasons in the early stages in a way that matches the fact that deep grief over miscarriage in the later stages is more appropriate than it is over miscarriages in the earlier stages.[32]

Pregnant woman's particular situation

We can maintain that the loss of human life is a tragic and awful thing while also maintaining that in some situations a pregnant woman does not act viciously by having an abortion. Hursthouse presents a host of different possible scenarios that, she believes, according to virtue ethics ought to be morally relevant in our moral analysis of the question of abortion. For instance, consider a woman who has several children and unintentionally gets pregnant. Imagine that she is older and is ready to be a grandmother. Or imagine a case in which a woman whose health is extremely fragile discovers that she is pregnant and the pregnancy threatens her life. Or we might imagine a man and a woman who have very fulfilling lives dedicated to a worthwhile cause. Their lives and worthwhile causes preclude them from having children. What if the woman unintentionally gets pregnant? In all of these cases, it is possible that a woman chooses to have an abortion and yet does not manifest the wrong attitudes towards human life and death, family relationships, parenting etc. That is, these women are not necessarily callous, cowardly, self-indulgent, irresponsible or light-minded about the issue of abortion. In fact they may understand and agree that motherhood, in many cases, is intrinsically worthwhile and can lead to a good, fulfilling and flourishing life (*eudaimonia*), while maintaining that in their particular circumstances this is simply not the case. Recall that from a virtue ethics perspective our feelings and decisions should lead to actions that advance our well-being towards a good and flourishing life (*eudaimonia*). As a result, the question as to how these facts relate to a good life must be carefully assessed.

Virtuousness within and an inevitable evil

Hursthouse points out that there may be circumstances in which the particular act falls within what is virtuous and yet the act may still be something evil and thus regrettable. In these cases, the agent may appropriately feel guilt or remorse for having an abortion. She explains it as follows:

> However, even when the decision to have an abortion is the right decision – one that does not itself fall under a vice-related term and thereby one that the perfectly virtuous could recommend – it does not follow that there is no sense in which having an abortion is wrong, or guilt inappropriate. For, by virtue of the fact that a human life has been cut short, some evil has probably been brought about, and that circumstances make the decision to bring some evil the right decision will be a ground for guilt if getting into those circumstances in the first place itself manifested a flaw in character.[33]

Hursthouse brings up two issues. First is the issue concerning a virtuous action that is regrettable. Second is a virtuous action that is regrettable and you share some of the responsibility for being in the position that you are in. Let us consider the first case. Imagine a woman who is raped and as a result gets pregnant. She is not responsible for the circumstances she finds herself in, since she was forced into sexual intercourse that led to her getting pregnant. Imagine that she is in very fragile health conditions and carrying pregnancy to full term will put her life at risk. Even so, she recognizes the importance of human life and the seriousness of the action of aborting her pregnancy. In this case, having an abortion would not be considered vicious and her decision might be consistent with a virtuous attitude and a virtuous life, and yet the woman might still feel that there is something terribly wrong in killing the foetus.

Consider a second case in which a woman gets pregnant as a result of consensual sexual intercourse. Imagine that the pregnancy is a result of both the woman's and man's irresponsible attitude and behaviour towards sex.

The pregnancy could have been prevented if they would have used some precaution. This case might demonstrate that the man and woman lack some of the virtues that might have prevented them from being in this situation in the first place. Hursthouse says:

> What 'gets one into those circumstances' in the case of abortion is, except in the case of rape, one's sexual activity and one's choices, or the lack of them, about one's sexual partner and about contraception. The virtuous woman (which here of course does not mean simply 'chaste woman' but ' woman with the virtues') has such character traits as strength, independence, resoluteness, decisiveness, self-confidence, responsibility, serious-mindedness, and self-determination-and no one, I think, could deny that many women become pregnant in circumstances in which they cannot welcome or cannot face the thought of having *this* child precisely because they lack one or some of these character traits. So even in the cases where the decision to have an abortion is the right one, it can still be the reflection of a moral failing-not because the decision itself is weak or cowardly or irresolute or irresponsible or light minded, but because lack of the requisite opposite of these failings landed one in the circumstances in the first place. Hence the common universalized claim that guilt and remorse are never appropriate emotions about abortion are denied. They may be appropriate, and appropriately inculcated, even when the decision was the right one.[34]

So, even in cases where abortion might still be a morally acceptable decision for a woman, it might entail an evil action that she will feel guilt and remorse for committing. It is also possible that even if she was partly responsible for her pregnancy, she demonstrates the right attitude towards her decision of having an abortion. That is, she understands the gravity of the situation and the importance of family, parenting and human life. She illustrates this correct attitude by feeling a sense of regret in having to perform an abortion.

Objection and replies

We will consider here two objections to the virtue ethics approach. First, there is a general objection to virtue ethics concerning the lack of specificity and guidance in determining the right action. Some philosophers will point out that the notions of 'a flourishing life' and 'acting in accordance with reason' are so vague that they could justify a wide variety of actions as virtuous. In fact, one might even argue that the theory opens itself up to a certain degree of subjectivity, leaving ethics more to preference than to some objective criterion. In response, a defender of virtue ethics might concede that there is a certain truth to the indeterminate nature of the virtue ethics approach. However, this need not be a disadvantage of the theory. Instead, it could be interpreted as an advantage insofar as the flexibility inherent in the theory allows it to more properly and accurately account for the relevant facts of each particular case. While this makes deliberation more difficult and possibly opens the door to more ways in which one can make mistakes, it also provides an opportunity for a more thorough consideration of the particular facts of each given case.

Second, there is a specific objection to Hursthouse's theory concerning her claim that the rights of a pregnant woman and the moral status of a foetus are completely irrelevant from a virtue ethics perspective. While it is true that these issues do not have the same degree of evidential weight and influence as they do in act-centered ethical theories, they nevertheless are an important part of the contextual facts that a virtue ethicists should consider when deliberating an abortion decision. Therefore, they are not completely irrelevant. For Hursthouse to say that they are irrelevant seems to go too far. It might be better to say that their function and influence within virtue theory are relegated to the function of mere facts about the contexts of the situation and are not the pivital factors upon which a moral decision hinges (as is the case in act-centered theories).

Summary

In this chapter, we have analysed the abortion issue from a virtue ethics perspective, First, we examine the central ideas of neo-Aristotelian virtue ethics. Aristotle claims that the ultimate end of human beings is happiness or a flourishing life, i.e. *eudaimonia*. In pursuing this ultimate end, human beings must use their rational abilities to become excellent deliberators and decision-makers. We can learn this by observing other virtuous individuals. This decision making skill is Aristotle's central intellectual virtue known as the virtue of *prudence*. It entails the ability to both know and select the right goals and also to determine the right decisions in any particular situation as the best means for arriving at one's goals. Aristotle claims that a virtuous life, therefore, is a life in accordance with reason. This also entails an ability to select the mean between extremes in our decision-making. Moreover, Aristotle also notes that in addition to the intellectual virtue, we also need to develop the right character traits, dispositions, habits and attitudes to be virtuous. These he calls the *moral* virtues. Thus, for Aristotle it is not only one's actions that count; one also needs to have the right attitude and state of mind while performing the action for the action to be virtuous. According to Aristotle, the virtuous person will receive pleasure from doing the right thing.

Hursthouse applies the virtue ethics framework to the abortion issue and argues that doing so substantially changes one's approach and analysis of the issue. This change is so significant that we can count it as a paradigm shift in which the usual elements of the abortion arguments, such as the rights of a pregnant woman, the rights of a foetus and personhood status of the foetus, become irrelevant in our ethical deliberation. According to Hursthouse, then, rights and the personhood status are not relevant issues that help determine how to act virtuously. Instead, what is important is one's attitude towards abortion and related concepts such as family, life, death, motherhood and parenting. Being virtuous means having the right character traits, such as bravery, temperance, independence, resoluteness, decisiveness, self-confidence, responsibility, serious-mindedness and self-determination. It also means having the right attitude to the abortion issue: taking it seriously, appreciating the value of family, parenting, motherhood and fatherhood etc. Because virtue ethics is essentially a contextual theory, the relevant facts of each particular case will make a difference in deciding what is the virtuous action in that particular case. Therefore, every ethical case of abortion will be different and it is possible, according to Hursthouse, that the decision to have an abortion be the right one and yet that the woman feels regret and even guilt in doing so.

Study questions

1 How are act-centred and agent-centred ethical theories different?
2 What is virtue and what is *eudaimonia*?
3 What are the intellectual and moral virtues?
4 What makes a right action right in virtue ethics?
5 How do we know (or learn) to determine the right action in virtue ethics?
6 What are the epistemological, educative and morals tasks for living a virtuous life?
7 Why are rights and the moral status of the foetus irrelevant within a virtue ethics framework?
8 How would one assess the morality of abortion from a virtue ethics perspective?

9   According to Hursthouse, what is the right attitude towards abortion? What is the wrong attitude?

10 What are some important contextual factors that Hursthouse believes should play a role in an agent's rational moral calculations in evaluating the morality of abortion?

7

Feminism and Abortion

It is difficult to grapple with such a broad topic as feminism and abortion. One way to begin is with a basic definition of feminism. However, this, too, is a complicated strategy for there are many views and interpretations of feminism. For our purposes, we can briefly sketch out a broad interpretation of feminism that could serve as an appropriate introduction to feminist perspectives on the ethics of abortion. First, we can make a distinction between political feminist movements and feminist ideas, claims and beliefs. The former refers to activists groups that seek to promote and advance women's rights. The latter refers to theoretical ideas and views held by people who support women's rights. While feminist political movements and feminist ideas are intimately connected, since they mutually affect and influence one another, it is possible to separate the two, at least for practical purposes. For our discussion on the ethics of abortion, we are more interested in feminist ideas, claims and beliefs than in feminist political movements.

Second, feminist ideas can be further divided into normative and descriptive. Normative feminist ideas are concerned with the legal and political rights women ought to have in society, as well as with the respect, dignity and autonomy that women deserve. The descriptive ideas are concerned with the actual political, legal and societal status of women in society and the actual respect, dignity and autonomy with which women are treated in society.[1] A central normative idea of feminism is that, in any society, women ought to have legal and political rights equal to those of men. This ideal is the most basic and rudimentary requirement for any feminist view. Its implementation would remove any overt injustice, oppression, subjugation and exploitation that result from a society's public legal and political system. One example of the advancement of gender equality in the public realm is the women's suffrage movement of the nineteenth and twentieth centuries. Before 1920, women were not permitted to vote in national elections in the United States. It was only with the passage of the 19th Amendment of the United States Constitution on 18 August 1920 that women were given the right to vote. Similarly, an important contemporary topic in women's reproductive health is the current laws and policies associated with limiting women's reproductive choices. Today, as a result of the Supreme Court case *Roe v. Wade* (1973), women have an unrestricted liberty to terminate a pregnancy during the early stages of foetal development. However, the future of women's rights in this regard remains uncertain.

Feminism

Most feminists today would not consider the fight for equality in the public realm as sufficient to define the central ideas of feminism because much of the oppression, prejudice, discrimination, subordination and domination of women that exist in contemporary society happen at the covert, private, social and cultural layers of society and not in the public, political and legal arenas. Moreover, many of the latter are the result of the former. We need normative feminist ideas, therefore, that will reach into the historical patriarchal structures that permeate all of society: the institution of marriage, parenting and child care; corporate culture, economic practices and policies, including hiring and promoting and income distribution practices; work environments and employer–employee relations; educational systems and curricula in elementary, middle and high schools; mass media; religious institutions; healthcare institutions and policies; and other important organizations and institutions that constitute the fabric of our society and culture in which we live our everyday lives.

A central tenet of feminism is that women should be respected and treated equal to men in all domains of society. This means that women's interests and talents ought to be given equal consideration, weight, worth, value and compensation. Moreover, women's rights, opportunities and social positions ought to be equal to those of men. Therefore, there should be gender equality in the workplace, in the family, in healthcare and in all areas of culture and society. The lack of such gender equality creates oppressive, exploitative and disadvantageous environments for women. It leads to the undervaluing of the true worth of women and their talents, and this leads to an oppressive, sexist state in which men dominate women. In addition, in order to ameliorate the oppression of women in society we also need to incorporate the basic presumption of intersectionality. We ought be aware of and understand that the concerns of women must be dealt with in a complex social system in which there are many more diverse social divisions and power inequalities than simply gender (e.g. social status differences, economic differences, racial differences, LGBT differences, ethnic differences). Feminist solutions to inequalities must be considered and negotiated within the actual complex social structure that includes all of these other divisions, differences and inequalities. Only in this more comprehensive way can we represent accurately the realities of women's issues and only then can we provide meaningful and effective solutions to them.

Feminist ethics

In addition, ethics itself must be revisited from a feminist perspective and with feminist ideals. Some feminists, such as Karen Warren, have clearly delineated a set of necessary conditions, or as Warren calls them 'boundary conditions' for a feminist ethics. Warren explains:

> These boundary conditions clarify some of the minimal conditions of a feminist ethic without suggesting that feminist ethics has some ahistorical essence. They are like the boundaries of a quilt or collage. They delimit the territory of the piece without dictating what the interior, the design, the actual pattern of the piece looks like. Because the actual pattern of the quilt emerges from the multiplicity of voices of women in a cross-cultural context, the design will change over time. It is not something static.[2]

The quilt-collage analogy captures well the idea that feminism can have various colours, shapes, designs and patterns, while at the same time have some common aspects that create the solidarity to count them as feminist views. Warren discusses eight boundary conditions of feminist ethics.

First, nothing that is part of the quilt of feminism can incorporate *the logic of domination*. This means that no view that inherently holds a view of superiority and subjugation can be counted as feminist. Therefore, an authentic feminist view must reject all forms of sexism, racism, classism etc. Second, an authentic feminist ethics must be *contextualist*, and the voices of women must take centre place. Third, a feminist ethics must explicitly repudiate the idea that there is only one voice. Fourth, a feminist ethics must consider ethics and ethical principles as essentially evolving and changing over time. Fifth, the notion of inclusiveness, especially of oppressed women, should be a central criterion in determining the correctness of feminist ethical claims. Warren argues:

> Because a feminist ethic is contexualist, structurally pluralistic, and 'in-process,' one way to evaluate the claims of a feminist ethic is in terms of

their *inclusiveness*: those claims (voices, patterns of voices) are morally and epistemologically favored (preferred, better, less partial, less biased) which are more inclusive of the felt experiences and perspectives of oppressed persons.[3]

Sixth, a feminist ethics rejects the idea of a *perspectiveless* perspective or of an objectively neutral position. It concedes the inherent bias of human thought but also argues that there are better and worse biases. A feminist ethics ought to hold that it is always better to be biased towards the oppressed voices of society, because this perspective is more inclusive. Seventh, a feminist ethics will give a central place to values – such as care, love and friendship – that have been traditionally marginalized in Western ethical thought. Finally, a feminist ethics requires that we reexamine the traditional conception of what it means to be a human person and how we understand persons as moral agents. We should no longer think of moral agents as isolated and abstract individuals but rather as beings that are essentially historical and connected in a network of relationships.

While these representative ideas of the meaning of feminism and feminist ethics may seem reasonable and, possibly, even achievable at face value, they require profound changes in our society's perception (or misperceptions) of women, sexuality and gender roles. However, these kinds of profound cultural changes are not ones that are easy to make, because they are not connected to salient and open inequalities, such as denial of the right to vote. Instead, gender inequalities are grounded in deeply rooted, male-dominated world views that have been ingrained and embedded into our culture over hundreds or even thousands of years, and they have been gradually associated with moral concepts such as 'family values', 'religious values' and 'decency'. Disentangling these ideas is not a simple matter. Making gender cultural inequality meaningful within a historically male-dominated culture is like trying to tell a current sports team that their goal in today's game is to lose instead of win. It requires revolutionary critical and philosophical thought that can allow us to step outside the culturally dominated standard ways of thinking. It requires, as Virginia Held writes, 'to turn thought on its head'. She explains:

> If feminists can succeed not only in making visible but also in keeping within awareness the aspects of 'mankind' that have been so obscured and misrepresented by taking the 'human' to be the masculine, virtually all existing thought may be turned on its head.[4]

Feminist ethics, therefore, is more than simply authentic gender equality; it involves substantially changing the way we think about morality and moral decision-making. Feminist ethics has the objective of creating a more just society in which the logic of domination, where one group subjugates another, no longer exists. However, with respect to abortion, there are different patterns, shapes and colours that form the quilt of feminist ethics.

Feminists disagree, for instance, as to whether the 'feminine voice' in ethical decision-making is essentially different than the masculine voice and how that difference plays out in the abortion issue. Carol Gilligan, in *In a Different Voice: Psychological Development and Women's Theory*, argues that feminine moral standards are essentially different than masculine moral standards, and they should not be treated as inferior but rather as equally morally binding and with the same moral authority as the masculine moral standards. Given that the history of ethics has been written almost exclusively from a masculine perspective, it is challenging to welcome a radically new set of moral criteria by which we can judge ethically right and wrong actions. In 'Abortion and the "Feminine Voice"' Celia Wolfe-Devine morally evaluates the abortion issue through a feminine voice and defends the view that adopting the feminine moral perspective will lead to the conclusion that abortion is morally wrong.[5]

All feminists agree that a woman's interests and rights ought to be considered and treated as equal to those of men. While this may seem as a reasonable request and one easy to comply with in theory, in practice, however, when it is predominantly men who legislate, adjudicate and execute the laws and policies, it is difficult, if not impossible, to be genuinely inclusive of and advocate for women's interests and rights. Some feminist philosophers have tried, however, to do just this. They have argued that the traditional abortion defenders' and abortion critics' arguments have ignored the rights, interests and desires of the pregnant woman and have exclusively focused on the rights of the foetus. Within this framework, a woman's rights only come into play after it has been shown that a foetus is not a person. The feminist position has responded by reintroducing the autonomy of the pregnant woman as an essential and central component of any abortion argument, even if the foetus is considered a person (see, for instance, Judith Jarvis Thomson). Within this framework, the abortion issue is a human rights issue and, in this case, it is the pregnant woman's rights that need to be defended vis-à-vis the rights of the foetus.

However, some feminist philosophers do not feel that these arguments accurately account for and do justice to the minority and subordinated status of women as an oppressed group within a male-dominated sexist society. In 'Abortion and Feminism', Sally Markowitz argues that 'this defense [Thomson's and others like it] may fall short of the feminist mark'.[6] She continues, 'Then I shall offer another defense, one derived not from the right to autonomy, but from an awareness of women's oppression and a commitment to a more egalitarian society.'[7] Here, as an introduction to feminism and abortion, we will examine Wolfe-Devine's and Markowitz's arguments as two different patterns in the quilt of feminism.

Abortion and the 'feminine voice'

In a male-dominated society, it is men who establish the rules, and it is men who provide the standards and paradigms for what is 'the right way of doing things'. In ethics, it is no different. What is a flourishing life according to Aristotle, what is happiness according to John Stuart Mill, what is the Categorical Imperative according to Immanuel Kant and what are the supreme virtues according to Thomas Aquinas are perfect examples of what we mean by providing male-dominated standards and paradigms for ethical theories. What society considers to be prima facie commonly accepted universal moral principles are really nothing but prima facie commonly accepted universal *male* moral principles, since their authorship is exclusively from the male perspective.

Carol Gilligan, in *In a Different Voice*, presents a critique of Lawrence Kohlberg's stages of moral development. In his study, Kohlberg argued that the results of his data showed that men reached a higher level of moral development than women. Gilligan responded in her work by noting that Kohlberg's study was fundamentally flawed, because its model was severely limited in its range and hierarchy of commonly accepted moral principles and standards. In addition, she also argued that the model was biased in favour of the male way of reasoning about moral issues. Thus, it is not that men's moral reasoning is superior to that of women's, but rather that men and women reason differently about moral issues. These differences are incommensurable, and they lead to different morally correct decisions. This new feminist voice in moral reasoning is called the *Ethics of Care*. Even though these ideas were presented in 1982 and much has certainly changed since then, the conceptual theory behind the critique of a male-dominated world, establishing standards that are biased towards women, remains relevantly valid.

Feminist and masculine voices

Celia Wolfe-Devine argues that if we consider carefully the abortion issue from the perspective of the ethics of care, we will notice that many feminists have been adopting a masculine voice in their efforts to defend a woman's right to an abortion. She writes:

> What I wish to argue in this paper is that: (1) abortion is, by their own accounts, clearly a masculine response to the problems posed by and unwanted pregnancy, and is thus highly problematic for those who seek to articulate and defend the 'feminine voice' as the proper mode of moral response, and that (2) on the contrary the 'feminine voice' as it has been

articulated generates a strong presumption against abortion as a way of responding to an unwanted pregnancy.[8]

The central premise of the ethics of care is that women reason differently about moral issues; moreover, this way of thinking leads to different moral solutions than those of men. Before we begin to elaborate some of these differences, we need to consider some introductory assumptions to get a more accurate picture of the theory we are espousing here. First, the feminine voice or women's way of thinking about moral issues is not inferior to the masculine voice or men's way of thinking about moral issues. Second, while some feminist philosophers who advocate this view also argue that these different modes of thinking are a result of biological differences, some believe that they are more a result of cultural and educational differences. The nature–nurture debate is an interesting debate and one that is ongoing; however, for our purposes, it is not important to determine the ultimate cause or origin of these different ways of thinking; what is important is that we accept them as morally equal ways of thinking. Third, since the nature–nurture debate is not easily resolvable and there are good reasons to believe that nurture is a strong influence on our moral thinking, we do not have to assume that the feminine voice is necessarily associated exclusively with women and the masculine voice exclusively with men. If we accept the possibility that these moral ways of reasoning can be acquired through nurture and education, it is also possible that men acquire a feminine voice and women a masculine voice. Fourth, we do not have to consider these ways of reasoning about morality as discrete; instead, we can think of them as forming a continuum in which persons can participate or acquire these attitudes in different degrees.

What kinds of rational modes of thinking about morality are different in men and women? This will expose the existing biases in what some consider to be 'standard' moral reasoning. First, women tend to value more than men the feeling of empathy, personal relationships and social relationships. Men, on the other hand, tend to value more than women the abstract notion of fairness, general rules and principles and the notion of individuality. According to Gilligan, these different fundamental value systems are a result of the fact that from an early age women and men are raised differently, and their relationships with their parents are also different. Women are raised within a closer and more intimate relationship with their mothers. Men are expected to separate from their mothers at an early age. Thus, the sense of closeness, intimacy and their feelings about attachment and separation are very different. Boys tend to play in larger groups, where rules and principles are essential, and girls tend to play in smaller groups, where the emphasis is much more on personal relationships among the members of the group. These different roles that girls and boys are forced into from a young age create different social environments that result in the development of prioritizing different values that work best within their social contexts. Wolfe-Devine describes the difference as follows:

The feminine voice in ethics attends to the particular other, thinks in terms of responsibilities to care for others, sensitive to our interconnectedness, and strives to preserve relationships. It contrast with the masculine voice, which speaks in terms of justice and rights, stresses consistency and principles, and emphasizes the autonomy of the individual and impartiality in one's dealings with others.[9]

She also notes that the historical conception of the essence of human nature has been notably provided exclusively from and through a male perspective. From the mind–body distinction, going back to the works of Plato and Rene Descartes, we see an overemphasis on reason to the exclusion of the emotions, the body and our connection with nature. Some feminists, such as Alison Jaggar, Rosemary Radford Reuther, Elizabeth Dodson Gray and Genevieve Lloyd, have critiqued this substance dualism, in which the mind and the body are considered to be two completely different substances, as an implicit and, perhaps, unintentional affirmation of the inferiority of women. According to substance dualism, the human mind can be conceived as separate and transcending of all material nature. Moreover, the mind and reason are also seen as superior to the body, nature and the material world. This view which dominated some aspects of philosophical thought created a schism between human beings and nature.

Wolfe-Devine presents an excellent example of this critique in the work of Carolyn Merchant's *The Death of Nature: Women, Ecology and the Scientific Revolution*. Merchant traces the root of the environmental crisis and our disconnect with nature to the Modern Cartesian philosophy and the mechanical view of the world as a result of Newtonian science and the scientific revolution in general. This world view also clashes with the feminist voice which sees the world as interconnected (and not disconnected) and human beings also as an interconnected part of the whole. This feminist, holistic perspective brings feminism in line with ecologists and a new group called 'ecofeminist'. As Stephanie Leland writes:

Ecology is universally defined as the study of the balance and interrelationship of all life on earth. The Motivating force behind feminism is the expression of the feminine principle. As the essential impulse of the feminine principle is the striving towards balance and interrelationship, it follows that feminism and ecology are inextricably connected.[10]

The feminine and masculine conceptions of society also differ greatly. While many of the same traits continue to drive the different perspectives, when applied to normative societal frameworks, the consequences are quite significant. For instance, the masculine voice views our relationship with others in society as individuals with self-interests, interacting and negotiating under a social contract to obtain the best result for oneself. This competitive, individualistic, rule-driven paradigm contrasts with the feminine voice that views society as an interdependent network of relationships and a community in which communication works best to resolve problems for the entire group. The masculine voice views the problems of others as primarily only the problems of that one person. The feminine voice views the problem of others as societal problems. The masculine voice values hierarchy, power and domination, whereas the feminine voice values egalitarianism, non-violence and cooperation. Some more extreme feminists view the masculine voice as one of male domination that uses violence and all of its power in society to maintain a patriarchy system and to keep women subjugated. In summary, Wolfe-Devine describes the feminine and masculine voices as follows:

> The feminine voice in ethics attends to the particular other, thinks in terms of responsibilities to care for others, is sensitive to our interconnectedness, and strives to preserve relationships. It contrasts with the masculine voice, which speaks in terms of justice and rights, stresses consistency and principles, and emphasizes the autonomy of the individual and impartiality in one's dealing with others.[11]

Feminist argument for the moral wrongness of abortion

Wolfe-Devine argues that if we analyse the abortion issue we will derive very different results depending on whether we use the masculine or feminine voice. She claims that if we emphasize the traditional masculine model of moral ideals and way of thinking, such as abstract general principles of fairness, hierarchical structures, individualism, rights, separation, violence, denomination and controlling attitude, we will infer conclusions in favour of an abortion defender's position. On the other hand, if we emphasize the feminine care perspective model of moral ideals and ways of thinking – such as the principle of care, egalitarianism, a web of relations with members of society, preserving relationships, the interconnectedness of nature, non-violence or pacifism, cooperation, and empathy and nurturing attitude – we will infer conclusions in favour of an abortion critic's positions. (See below for a list of the masculine and feminine model attributes and attitudes.)

MASCULINE VOICE	**FEMININE VOICE**
Ethics of Justice	*Ethics of Care*
(1) Principles of fairness	(1) Principle of care egalitarianism
(2) Hierarchical structures	(2) A web of relations
(3) Individualism	(3) Interconnectedness of nature
(4) Rights	(4) Altruism
(5) Separation	(5) Preserving relationships
(6) Violence	(6) Non-violence or pacifism
(7) Denomination	(7) Cooperation
(8) Control	(8) Empathy and nurturing

Therefore, according to Wolfe-Devine, whether one adopts the feminine or masculine voice in one's analysis of the abortion issue will make a significant difference in the conclusions one will arrive at. She writes:

A person who had characteristically masculine traits, attitudes and values as defined above would very naturally choose abortion, and justify it ethically in the same way in which most feminist do. Conversely, a person who manifests feminine traits, attitudes and values would not make such a choice, or justify it in that way.[12]

The reason why an abortion is supported by the masculine voice is it manifests many of the masculine voice attributes. First, most arguments for the moral permissibility of abortion assume the foetus and the woman to be two individuals. Moreover, according to masculine perspective the abortion issue hinges on the rights of these individuals. Second, the act of abortion, as a solution to an unwanted pregnancy, entails a violent separation of the foetus from the woman. Third, it also manifests the properties of control and domination, in which the woman overpowers the foetus. On the other hand, Wolfe-Devine points out, 'If empathy, nurturance, and taking responsibility for caring for others are characteristic of the feminine voice, then abortion does not appear to be a feminine response to an unwanted pregnancy.'[13]

If she is right, then we have certain inconsistencies within some of the feminist positions. Some feminists would like to maintain a different paradigm of moral reasoning and standards from the ones adopted by the masculine voice and also maintain an abortion defender's position that seems to be supported by the moral precepts of the masculine voice. However, these two positions are inconsistent since, as we have already seen above, adopting a feminist voice seems to logically support the abortion critic's position and not the abortion defender's position. Wolfe-Devine concludes: 'Those feminists who are seeking to articulate the feminine voice in ethics also face a *prima facie* inconsistency between ethics of care and abortion.'[14]

Objections

It is important to begin by recognizing the scope of Wolfe-Devine's argument. She does not try to demonstrate that abortion is morally wrong, per se. Instead, her argument is limited to two conclusions: (1) feminism and the abortion defender's position are logically inconsistent and (2) abortion is morally wrong from a feminist perspective. Is her argument successful?

First, feminists might call into question the assumption that all ethical issues can be resolved nice and neatly within one and only one frame of reference: either a masculine or a feminine perspective. In reality, life is much messier than this. Feminists, therefore, could argue that while the overarching values one uses in moral decision-making might be feminist in orientation, there are cases in which dispositions and attitudes that traditionally are associated with the masculine voice are justified within the more comprehensive feminine framework. For instance, there may be a time in which our love, compassion and care for our child may require responses such as separation, individualism and punishment. If this were possible, then (1) would not be necessarily true, and, at least theoretically, it would be possible to reconcile a feminist perspective with an abortion defender's position.

Second, feminists might call into question the notion that a feminist perspective must *always* adopt an ethics of care regardless of the issue at hand. Such a view seems rigid and restrictive. Why can't a feminist predominantly favour the ethics of care dispositions and nevertheless, when thought to be appropriate, adopt dispositions coherent with masculine perspective? Moreover, feminists might point out that an ethical approach that values *only* the attributes associated with the feminine voice is naïve and incomplete. Such a view would have to exclude essentially valid ethical objectives such as fairness and rights. In addition, it seems over excessive to think that the notions of hierarchy, control and even violence can never be justified within a feminist perspective. Again, if this is conceivable then it seems that (1) must be false.

What about (2)? Some feminists might object by arguing that limiting women's right to an abortion is a form of male domination and violence against women. Thus, it is not the case that the abortion defender's position is inconsistent with the feminist voice. These feminists argue that protecting women's reproductive rights is coherent with empathy, and it advances the objective of *egalitarianism*, which is a feminist goal. Wolfe-Devine responds to this objection by first claiming that it is not the case that men are the main opponents to abortion. She notes that many women are against abortion and thus the notion of male domination is not relevant. However, abortion-defending feminists might point out that whether women support or do not support the right to an abortion does not affect the argument in the way Wolfe-Devine thinks. The question is whether prohibiting the right to an abortion creates social-political structures for the exacerbation of the existing oppressive state of women. Moreover, the question is not one of personal support for or against abortion but rather one of political power. It is difficult to deny that men control the halls of Congress at the state and federal levels, as well as the judiciary benches of the US courts. Thus, the issue of male dominance and a sexist society is a very real and fair issue to raise. If, then, women are oppressed and the abortion defenders' overarching attitude is primarily one of compassion and caring for women, especially poor women, as well as a desire for the elimination of a status of domination and exploitation to be replaced by one egalitarianism, then it seems conceivable that one could be a feminist and consistently maintain the position that an abortion is morally permissible.

Abortion and feminism: Advancing towards a sexually egalitarian society

Sally Markowitz argues that the central theme in any feminist argument of abortion must include the status of women, as a group, in society. If women are an oppressed group, as they are in the United States, then the nature and severity of their oppression and a commitment to a more egalitarian society should play a central role in the discussion of the abortion issue. It is not enough to simply consider the issue of the autonomy of women, from a 'gender neutral' perspective, vis-à-vis the rights of the foetus. While these arguments have their own merits, they are not essentially feminist arguments. Feminism must consider gender and gender issues as an important and relevant factor in determining rights, especially when these considerations are about women that live in a sexist society.

The abortion issue is essentially a women's issue, because it is women, and only the women, who can get pregnant, carry the pregnancy to term, give birth and, in many cases, nurture and raise the newborn child. As Alison Jagger points out: since the responsibilities rest only with the woman, only the woman ought to have a say in the abortion decision. Markowitz wants to take this principle a step further by suggesting that we focus on the social realities of women and include these as part of the feminist argument in support of a woman's right to an abortion. In essence, Markowitz's view introduces a dimension of the abortion issue that connects 'the relationship between reproductive practices and the liberation (or oppression) of women'.[15]

Feminist argument for the moral permissibility of abortion

Markowitz begins with a simple question: 'When, if ever, can people be required to sacrifice for the sake of others?'[16] In answering this question, Markowitz wants to make certain that we include the contextual realities of the people in question. In doing so, she formulates what she calls 'The Impermissible Sacrifice Principle', which states: '*When one social group in a society is systematically oppressed by another, it is impermissible to require the oppressed group to make sacrifices that will exacerbate or perpetuate this oppression.*'[17] Notice that this principle does not preclude oppressed groups from making sacrifices in general; instead, it only limits the group from making sacrifices with respect to issues that will make the existing oppression worse. Notice also that this principle applies not only to women but to any and all oppressed groups.

The Impermissible Sacrifice Principle on its own is not sufficient to make a successful feminist argument for a woman's right to an abortion. Two more claims are required: first, that women are oppressed; second, that a law prohibiting abortion would exacerbate this oppression. Markowitz writes, 'So the Impermissible Sacrifice Principle must be supplemented by what I shall call the Feminist Proviso: *Women are, as a group, sexually oppressed by men; and this oppression can neither be completely understood in terms of, nor otherwise reduced to, oppressions of other sorts.*'[18] Women's experience of oppression in the United States can vary widely depending on the particular circumstances of each woman. Thus, as Warren's quilt analogy showed, their voices, experiences and sufferings of oppression will be very different for every woman. Nevertheless, the experience of sexism and male domination in American society need not be monolithic for it to exist. Moreover, the variety of experience can worsen, even if they are different, by anti-abortion policy. The question, then, is whether it is permissible to pass policy that will require an oppressed group to make significant sacrifices that will only make their oppression even worse. The answer seems to be that such policy seems socially unjust and immoral.

According to Markowitz, then, the combination of the Impermissible Sacrifice Principle and the Feminist Proviso provides the necessary ingredients to support an evidentially strong abortion defender's position on abortion. Markowitz concludes: 'The Impermissible Sacrifice Principle and the Feminist Proviso together, then justify abortion on demand for women *because they live in a sexist society.*'[19] According to Markowitz, this argument is more coherent with feminist ethics, and it produces a stronger argument than abortion defenders' arguments that are based only on human autonomy.

Feminist argument versus the autonomy argument

According to Markowitz, the feminist argument for the moral permissibility of abortion has certain advantages over the autonomy argument. First, she claims that if the issue is only about autonomy, then continuing an unwanted pregnancy is really about the liberty of a woman (as an individual) to achieve her aspirations and desires. These might be related to financial goals or career goals. If this is the case then it seems possible, at least in theory, that these losses can be compensated in some way. However, if the issue is not just about individual liberty but about being oppressed as a group, then individual compensation will not help since it presupposes a prior state of egalitarianism. Markowitz says, 'Indeed, even talk of compensation may be misguided, since it implies a prior state when things were as they should be; compensation seeks to restore the balance after a temporary upset. But in a sexist society, there is no original balance; women's oppression is status quo.'[20]

Second, the autonomy argument seems to break down when it can be proven that the woman acted irresponsibly in sexual intercourse. In these cases, the abortion critics' position can argue that if a woman's actions were irresponsible and contributed to her getting pregnant, then this can be interpreted as a form of consent to allowing the foetus to use her body for its survival. In these cases, the abortion critic can argue that a pregnant woman has forfeited her right to an abortion. On the other hand, the abortion-defending feminist argument begins by noting the double standard that exists in a sexist society in which men can have irresponsible sex with no consequences but women cannot. Second, the feminist argument rejects the notion of a woman having 'irresponsible' sex in a sexist society. In other words, it calls into question the very possibility of a woman having irresponsible sex in a sexist society, since this would first require that women have full control of their sexual actions. However, Markowitz argues, 'For in a sexist society many women simply do not believe they can control the conditions under which they have sex. And, sad to say, often they are right.'[21]

Third, under the autonomy defence of abortion, there is no justification for the government to provide resources to help poor women in obtaining access to an abortion. The autonomy defence only requires that the government not interfere with a woman's liberty to have an abortion, but it does not require the government to assist women in the abortion process. However, from a feminist approach, we begin by conceding that women are in an oppressive state within society, and thus they are being harmed by the structures of society; and, moreover, the lack of access to an abortion perpetuates this oppression and harm, therefore, the state is obligated to ameliorate women's conditions. Part of this process entails assisting pregnant women to have easy access to an abortion, especially poor women. Markowitz writes, 'The defense I suggest, however, is clearly committed to providing all women with access to abortions, since to allow abortions only for those who can afford them forces poor women, who are doubly oppressed, to make special sacrifices. An egalitarian society must liberate all women, not just the rich ones.'[22]

Finally, the autonomy abortion-defending arguments have the unfortunate side effect of calling into question a women's character, and seriously denigrating those that decide to have an abortion. It argues that a woman has a right to an abortion, but it also permits a pregnant woman who decides to terminate her pregnancy to be seen as selfish and callous. Even Judith Jarvis Thomson claims that it is possible for someone to have a right to an abortion and thus commits no injustice in having one, and yet we might correctly judge her to be cruel, selfish and callous for having the abortion. However, when the argument is framed from a feminist perspective, the focus is on women as a group and the issue becomes a political one 'which essentially concerns the interests of and power relations between men and women. Thus, what women and men can expect to gain or lose from an abortion policy becomes the point rather than the subject of *ad hominem* arguments'.[23]

Objections

The most glaring objection to Markowitz's argument is to consider foetuses as an oppressed group. If foetuses are considered as an oppressed group, then the abortion critic can argue that their systematic destruction through the practice of abortions is a much more brutal form of oppression than anti-abortion policies are on the liberties of women. More importantly, this objection seems to land Markowitz right back to the position she tried to avoid in the first place, one that frames the issue of abortion as an issue between women's rights vis-à-vis foetuses'. Markowitz has several responses to this objection. First, she questions whether foetuses are really the kind of beings that can suffer oppression. Foetuses are not social beings and they cannot develop relationships within in a community of persons. Therefore, it seems implausible to consider them as oppressed in the same way women and other minority groups are oppressed. Second, Markowitz is adamant that feminists cannot revert back to this position but that they must frame the issue differently. She explains it as follows:

> So we should not see the choice as between liberating women and saving fetuses, but between two ways of respecting the fetus's right to life. The first requires women to sacrifice while men benefit. The second requires deep social changes that will ensure that men no longer gain and women lose through our practices of sexuality, reproduction, and parenthood. To point out

how men gain from women's compulsory pregnancy is to steal the misplaced moral thunder from those male authorities-fathers, husbands, judges, congressmen, priests, philosophers-who, exhorting women to do their moral duty, present themselves as the benevolent, disinterested protectors of fetuses against women's selfishness. Let feminist insist that the condition for refraining from having abortions is a sexually egalitarian society.[24]

Summary

In this chapter we have defined feminism as a set of ideas that advocate that women should be respected and treated equal to men in all domains of society. In addition, feminists claim that women's interests and talents ought to be given equal consideration, weight, worth, value and compensation. We have also carefully analysed feminist ethics through Karen Warren's set of 'boundary conditions' and her quilt analogy. The boundary conditions include: rejecting the *logic of domination*; accepting *contexualism*; accepting a plurality of voices; viewing ethics as essentially evolving; using inclusiveness as an evaluative criterion for ethical decision-making; rejecting the notion of an objectively neutral position; giving a central place to values such as love and care, which have been traditionally marginalized in Western ethical thought; and finally, reexamining the conception of personhood as an essentially historical and relational being.

Given this understanding of feminism and feminist ethics, we then embarked on a philosophical analysis of two feminist arguments deriving different conclusions. We first analysed Celia Wolfe-Devine's argument for the moral wrongness of abortion in 'Abortion and the "Feminine Voice"'. First, she argues that the feminine voice and the abortion defenders' positions are irreconcilably inconsistent. She claims that the abortion defenders' view is consistent with the masculine ethics and is based on applying abstract conceptions of justice that emphasize the attitudes of fairness, hierarchical structures, individualism, rights, separation, violence, denomination and control. Second, she argues that if we emphasize the feminine care perspective model of moral ideals and ways of thinking – such as the principle of care, egalitarianism, a web of relations with members of society, preserving relationships, the interconnectedness of nature, non-violence or pacifism, cooperation, and empathy and nurturing attitude – we will infer conclusions in favour of the abortion critics' position.

Next, we examine Sally Markowitz's argument for the moral permissibility of abortion in 'Abortion and Feminism'. She argues that arguments based solely on women's rights do not accurately account for and do justice to the minority and subordinated status of women as an oppressed group within a male-dominated sexist society. She presents a feminist argument based on two guiding principles: 'The Impermissible Sacrifice Principle' and the Feminist Proviso. The Impermissible Sacrifice Principle states that *'when one social group is a society is systematically oppressed by another, it is impermissible to require the oppressed group to make sacrifices that will exacerbate or perpetuate this oppression'.*[25] The Feminist Proviso states the following: 'So the Impermissible Sacrifice Principle must be supplemented by what I shall call the *Women are, as a group, sexually oppressed by men; and this oppression can neither be completely understood in terms of, nor otherwise reduced to, oppressions of other sorts.'*[26] Based on these two principles she concludes that it is morally impermissible to pass anti-abortion policies because doing so will exacerbate women's oppression which goes contrary to the Impermissible Sacrifice Principle.

Study questions

1 What are some central feminist ideas?

2 What are some of the goals and objectives of feminism?

3 What are the 'boundary conditions' of a feminist ethics?

4 What are the differences between the 'feminine voice' and the 'masculine voice'? How do these affect the abortion issue?

5 Explain Celia Wolfe-Devine's feminist argument in support of the abortion critics' position. Do you agree with this argument? Why or why not?

6 Explain Sally Markowitz's feminist argument in support of the abortion defenders' position. Do you agree with this argument? Why or why not?

8

Prenatal Screening and Human Genetic Ethical Issues

In this chapter, we will consider ethical issues concerning prenatal testing, stem cell research and cloning. Prenatal screening has become a routine, standard procedure for pregnant women. There are obvious benefits to prenatal testing because it gives pregnant women an opportunity to discover early on in their pregnancy if the foetus has a genetic disorder, a disability or a serious illness of some sort. However, some argue that prenatal testing and screening is more about eliminating defective foetuses and disabled people than about giving women more informed decision-making autonomy. In fact, some argue that the way prenatal screening is performed today limits rather than expands women's autonomy. Is prenatal screening encouraging abortions? Is it discriminating against the disabled?

Human embryonic stem cell (hESC) research has given the medical profession enormous hope that it will be able to provide cures to many forms of genetically caused diseases as well as degenerative diseases, such as Parkinson's, heart failure and diabetes. However, to perform certain kinds of embryonic stem cell research, human embryos must be destroyed. If human embryos are individual human beings, can we ever be morally justified in destroying them for the purpose of research and the well-being of others?

In most cases, the mention of cloning is received with great anxiety and suspicion. The visceral response of some people when they hear the word 'cloning' is to imagine some fanciful evil conspiracy such as the creation of a superhuman race to take over the world. Thus, cloning is viewed with ambivalence and as an inimical medical technology that is motivated more by human beings' unmitigated desire to control everything and 'play god' than by the desire to produce wonderful medical benefits for human beings' welfare in the future. Let us begin, then, by trying to remain open-minded and weighing the evidence and arguments in favour and against cloning. Cloning entails the reproduction of identical cells. There are various forms of cloning. The most ethically controversial form of cloning is the cloning of human persons. Is it ethical to intentionally create identical human persons through artificial means?

Prenatal screening

The most common form of prenatal screening is ultrasound. Other prevalent prenatal tests for 'at-risk women' (usually pregnant women over the age of thirty-five) include amniocentesis (performed between 16 and 20 weeks of pregnancy) and chorionic villus sampling (CVS) (performed between 10 and 13 weeks of pregnancy). Amniocentesis and CVS are used to determine genetic disorders or chromosomal abnormalities that may result in Down syndrome. These tests seem, at first, like a wonderful idea because they provide pregnant women with important information about the health status of their developing foetus. However, not everyone agrees with the seemingly innocuous nature of prenatal testing. Adrienne Asch argues that such tests are biased against the disabled, curtail women's freedom, implicitly encourage selective abortions when abnormalities are discovered and are based on misguided assumptions about the notion of disability and what it means to live with a disability. She argues as follows:

> Like other women-centered critiques of prenatal testing, this article assumes a pro-choice perspective but suggests that unreflective uses of [prenatal] testing could diminish, rather than expand, women's choices. Like critiques stemming from concerns about the continued acceptance of human differences within the society and the family, this critique challenges the view of disability that lies behind social endorsement of such testing and the conviction that women will, or should, end their pregnancies if they discover that the fetus has a disabling trait.[1]

To appreciate Asch's argument, let us begin by making some important distinctions. First, there is the empirical question as to whether women do in fact feel pressure to end the life of the foetus if they discover that it has a chronic illness or a genetic abnormality. It seems fair to say that such pressure could exist and could come from family, society, culture or even from within the health profession itself. It might also be fair to say that some women may not feel such pressure. Perhaps they have strong convictions about the sanctity of life, and thus aborting the foetus is simply never an option for them.

The question of whether certain particular women actually feel pressured to have an abortion is not the important question here; instead, the question is whether there exist certain biased views, attitudes and conceptual frameworks within the medical profession that either directly or indirectly promote, endorse and encourage abortions when a foetus is discovered to have some disability. Therefore, the fact as to whether a particular woman feels pressured or not is not relevant to the current ethical issue; instead, the issue is whether there exist attitudes within the health profession about disabilities and prenatal testing that promote such pressures. Asch argues that there is such a bias in the medical profession and in society at large.

Disabilities and abortions

The heart of Asch's argument is that there are unfounded assumptions about disabilities and chronic illnesses that are prevalent within the medical profession and public health that endorse the method of abortion as the most reasonable option for a pregnant woman when her foetus is diagnosed with a genetic disorder or a chronic illness. Why is this? First, there is the commonly accepted idea that the purpose of medicine and public health is to cure and prevent diseases, preserve health and eliminate disabilities. Prenatal testing can warn a parent if their child will be born with chronic illnesses, abnormalities or genetic defects. However, in most cases, this warning does not give parents many options since the diseases, illnesses and genetic defects are not curable. The information is not helpful in promoting the health of the foetus, since there is little that can be done to help the foetus. The only way to 'prevent' disabilities in these cases is if the woman decides to abort the foetus. However, Asch points out that this method of 'preventing disabilities' is not really eliminating them; instead, it is eliminating persons that have them, and these are two very different matters.

> What differentiates prenatal testing followed by abortion from other forms of disability prevention and medical treatment is that prenatal testing followed by abortion is intended not to prevent the disability or illness of a born or future human being but to prevent the birth of a human being who will have one of the undesired characteristics.[2]

Second, there is an underlying assumption that people with disabilities are destined to live a less-than-fulfilling life. According to this view, the disability disrupts a person's life permanently. However, Asch distinguishes chronic illnesses and disabilities from acute illnesses and sudden injuries. The latter can lead to disruptive disabilities, because they arbitrarily interject themselves, in some cases without any forewarning, in a person's life, which might have been a perfectly normal existence until that acute illness or injury occurred. Moreover, they can also cause significant changes in a person's quality of life, resulting in psychological trauma for the patient and the family. However, people with congenital chronic diseases and disabilities do not undergo similar disruptions, and thus they do not suffer any of the anxieties or trauma associated with such change in one's living conditions. In fact, Asch points out that most people with congenital chronic illnesses and defects consider their state as 'normal and healthy' since they have no direct experience of living any other way. She writes:

> Most people with conditions such as spina bifida, achondroplasia, Down syndrome, and many other mobility and sensory impairments perceive themselves as healthy, not sick, and describe their conditions as givens in their lives – the equipment with which they meet the world. The same is true for people with chronic conditions such as cystic fibrosis, diabetes, hemophilia, and muscular dystrophy.[3]

Finally, the medical profession, public health and bioethics point out that people with disabilities will struggle in society. The data demonstrates that they will have more problems finding jobs, and, as a result, they will endure higher unemployment, lower income and a poorer quality of life than the non-disabled. The data also shows that there are wide gaps in education between the disabled and non-disabled. Education, employment and low income are causally interconnected, and it creates a vicious circle of poverty and marginalization, resulting in a poor quality of life for disabled people.

Two points need to be articulated clearer about these statistics. First, notice that they do not entail a value judgement about disabilities or living with disabilities, and thus we cannot simply conclude that, given these statistics, it is bad to be disabled. Nevertheless, this conclusion is almost too obvious for anyone to miss. The clear inference from the data is that living with a disability is guaranteed to lead to a miserable, uneducated life of unemployment, poverty and marginalization. No one wants this kind of future for their own children. Therefore, if one is pregnant with a disabled child, these statistics would certainly provide one with some altruistic rationale for selecting the decision of aborting the pregnancy. Therefore, the implicit argument here is that if you discover that your foetus suffers from some disability, the choice to carry the foetus to term and not have an abortion is, in essence, condemning your child to an inevitable life of poverty and misery.

Asch points out, however, that these statistics do not support what appears to be the obvious conclusion, namely, that these disabilities are the *cause* of the poor state of living of the disabled. The presumption is that the physical disability is the main culprit for these wide gaps of living standards between the disabled and non-disabled. But this is false. Asch argues that while the statistic may be correct, the causes for these social ills are not the disabilities themselves but rather the discrimination that exists in our culture and society against the disabled. She argues that there is no reason to connect the physical disabilities with the social minority status and social marginalization that the disabled people in American society experience. There is also no good argument to claim that the existence of all disabilities will necessarily lead to an inability to work, study or become a successful and contributing member of society. The obstacles for the disabled are not the disabilities themselves but rather the external social impediments that make living with disabilities so problematic. These impediments are external factors caused by discriminatory attitudes from members of society and they can be changed. This adverse discrimination against the disabled has been readily addressed in the Americans with Disabilities Act of 1990:

The Congress finds that: (1) physical or mental disabilities in no way diminish a person's right to fully participate in all aspects of society, yet many people with physical or mental disabilities have been precluded from doing so because of discrimination; others who have a record of a disability or are regarded as having a disability also have been subjected to discrimination; (2) historically, society has tended to isolate and segregate individuals with disabilities, and, despite some improvements, such forms of discrimination against individuals with disabilities continue to be a serious and pervasive social problem; (3) discrimination against individuals with disabilities persists in such critical areas as employment, housing, public accommodations, education, transportation, communication, recreation, institutionalization, health services, voting, and access to public services; (4) unlike individuals who have experienced discrimination on the basis of race, color, sex, national origin, religion, or age, individuals who have experienced discrimination on the basis of disability have often had no legal recourse to redress such discrimination; (5) individuals with disabilities continually encounter various forms of discrimination, including outright intentional exclusion, the discriminatory effects of architectural, transportation, and communication barriers, overprotective rules and policies, failure to make modifications to existing facilities and practices, exclusionary qualification standards and criteria, segregation, and relegation to lesser services, programs, activities, benefits, jobs, or other opportunities; (6) census data, national polls, and other studies have documented that people with disabilities, as a group, occupy an inferior status in our society, and are severely disadvantaged socially, vocationally, economically, and educationally; (7) the Nation's proper goals regarding individuals with disabilities are to assure equality of opportunity, full participation, independent living, and economic self-sufficiency for such individuals; and (8) the continuing existence of unfair and unnecessary discrimination and prejudice denies people with disabilities the opportunity to compete on an equal basis and to pursue those opportunities for which our free society is justifiably famous, and costs the United States billions of dollars in unnecessary expenses resulting from dependency and nonproductivity.

Asch argues that what is required is not to prevent the birth of disabled people but to improve society's acceptance and accommodation of disabled people. This will also relieve much of the stress and anxiety of the families of the disabled.

Let us conclude by making two important distinctions concerning Asch's view. First, she is not arguing that it is morally wrong to have an abortion if one discovers that the foetus has a serious disability. Second, she is not arguing that we should eliminate prenatal testing altogether or that there is something inherently morally wrong with prenatal testing. Instead, her argument is that women ought to receive better counselling when they undergo prenatal testing. They ought to be given a more accurate picture of what it means to live with a disability. She explains it as follows:

> To provide ethical and responsible clinical care for anyone concerned about reproduction, professionals themselves must know far more than they now do about life with disability; they must convey more information, and different information, than they now typically provide. ... Whether the clinician is a genetics professor or (as increasingly the case) an obstetrician promoting prenatal diagnosis as a routine care for pregnant women, the tone, timing, and content of the counseling process cry out for drastic overhaul.[4]

For instance, she suggests that if a woman is told that her foetus has a particular disability, then that woman ought to be given the opportunity to visit with people and families with children and adults with the disability in question. This will provide a more informed diagnosis and will provide more comprehensive information for pregnant women so that they can make more informed decisions.

Human embryonic stem cell research

The moral controversy over the use of hESCs for the purposes of research is relatively new. It began in 1998, when James Thomson, a biologist at the University of Wisconsin–Madison, isolated the first embryonic stem cell. Since then the controversy has intensified, with fierce opposition from abortion critics who believe that human life begins at conception, and with staunch support from the scientific community that believe that hESC research will successfully help cure many forms of disabling illnesses, relieve human suffering and enhance human nature.

The importance of stem cells

Why are stem cells so important? Our bodies are made up of trillions of cells. However, there are only about 200 different kinds of cells. These specialized cell groups form the body's systems and organs, such as the digestive track, the heart, the nerves, the lungs, the brain, the liver. The cells that make up these systems and human organs are essentially different from each other. For instance, the nerves cells are more elongated to help them in their specialized function of transmitting information from the mind to the rest of the body. The digestive cells are especially formed to help them perform their function of absorbing water more efficiently. For our purposes, the important thing to note is that specialized cells that are programmed to perform a specialized function in the human body are limited for any type of gene therapy because they are severely restricted in their use.

However, the 200 different types of cells in a human body originate from one and the same cell, the zygote. The zygote and the first cells after the first few cell divisions are called *totipotent* cells. These cells have the potential to become any of the 200 different types of cells in the human body, and they also have the potential to become extraembryonic cells or the placenta. The next stage of potentiality is the *pluripotent* cells or embryonic stem cells. These cells also have the potential to become any type of the 200 specialized cells within the human body but they cannot become extraembryonic cells. As a consequence, these cells of a living human blastocyst (approximately four or five days old) are very valuable for gene therapy, because they can become any of the different 200 types of cells in the human body. When the cells are at this stage of potentiality, they are called undifferentiated cells. Once they have become specialized cells, they are called differentiated cells.

Finally, there are also *multipotent* stem cells and these lie somewhere in between the specialized and pluripotent cells. Multipotent stem cells have the potential to convert to one or more types of specialized cells. For instance, skin multipotent stem cells can regenerate more skin cells. The body maintains a constant supply of skin stem cells because skin cells are continuously dying and a new supply needs to be continuously regenerated. This cell regeneration process is continuously occurring in the human body. For instance, 96 million cells die every minute, but fortunately 96 million cells divide to create new cells.

Sources of stem cells

Before we move on to discuss the ethical debate surrounding hESCs, we need to distinguish among different possible sources of stem cells and their moral relevance. First, stem cells may be obtained from adult persons. In 2006, Shinya Yamanaka and a team of researchers at Nara Institute of Science and Technology were able to create pluripotent stem cells from adult mature cells; that is, they produced undifferentiated cells from differentiated cells. These stem cells are called Induced Pluripotent Stem Cells (iPS). In 2012, Yamanaka and Sir John Gurdon were awarded the Nobel Prize in Physiology or Medicine for this scientific advancement. Second, pluripotent stem cells can be derived from the blood of umbilical cords. Third, pluripotent stem cells can be derived from foetal tissue. Fourth, pluripotent stem cells can be derived from living embryos. The last option has medical advantages over the rest. John Harris points out: 'For the moment, there is general consensus that embryos are the best source of stem cells for therapeutic purposes, but this may, of course, change as the science develops.'[5] However, it is also the most ethically contentious and it is the one that we will focus on in this section.

Human stem cells derived from living human embryos

Human embryonic stem cells derived from living embryos also have various possible sources and the differences are morally relevant. First, the source can be from preexisting embryos that are left over from Artificial Reproductive Technologies, such as In Vitro Fertilization (IVF). IVF is a regularly used method of artificial reproduction for couples that have fertility difficulties. Part of this process is to create several embryos with the understanding and objective of having only one of the embryos develop into a foetus and a person. In many cases, therefore, not all of the embryos are used and thus some will be left over. A couple has several alternatives on what to do with the left-over embryos: (1) they can freeze the embryos for later use, (2) they can dispose of the embryo by destroying it, (3) they can donate the embryo to another couple or (4) they can donate the embryo for scientific stem cell research. Second, it is also possible that we create embryos for the sole purpose of using them for stem cell research. This source is much more morally contentious than the first. In this section, we will address two moral questions: Is it ethically permissible to use, for the purpose of stem cell research, preexisting living human embryos left over from IVF that are destined to be destroyed? Is it ethically permissible to create living human embryos for the purpose of stem cell research, if we know that these embryos will be destroyed as part of the research?

We have already noted why pluripotent stem cells are so vital for research, but we have not discussed the concrete benefits of embryonic research and the moral relevance of this benefit. Most people would agree that pain, suffering and disease are evils that exist in the world. Moreover, they would probably also agree that we should refrain from performing actions that could cause such evils, unless, of course, we could somehow morally justify them. Finally, I think most would also agree that alleviating pain, suffering and diseases is a good thing, and that we have a moral duty in performing actions that would have such consequences, unless they entail an extraordinary sacrifice, harm or injury to someone else, or a greater evil of some sort. These moral precepts are part of what creates the moral dilemma in stem cell research. The beneficial therapies that could result from stem cell research would alleviate an enormous amount of human suffering, pain and misery from the world. For instance, consider Harris' description of the terrible disease of Parkinson's and how hESC research is expected to help:

> It is difficult to estimate how many people might benefit from products of stem cell research should it be permitted and prove fruitful. Most sources agree that the most proximate is of HESC therapy would be for Parkinson's disease. Parkinson's disease is a common neurological disease, the prevalence of which increases with age. The overall prevalence (per 100 population in persons 65 years of age and older) is 1.8. Parkinson's disease has a disastrous effect on the quality of life. ... Untold human misery and suffering could be prevented if Parkinson's disease became tractable.[6]

However, to carry on such research the destruction of embryos is necessary. For many who believe that human life begins at conception, embryos are living human beings. Sacrificing the life of innocent human beings for the sake of improving the life of other human beings is unjust and immoral and should never be morally accepted. It violates basic human rights, and therefore the means cannot be justified by the end.

Human stem cell research on IVF stem cells

Let us consider the question of hESC research limiting our source of stem cells to those that are left over from IVF practices. Many of the research guidelines requirements issued by medical and research advisory boards, such as The National Bioethics Advisory Commission (NBAC) and the National Academy of Science (NAS), approve of hESC research with the condition the embryos that will be destroyed are shown and treated with respect. Some philosophers have argued that using and destroying embryos for the purpose of research, even if their death is inevitable, is inconsistent with showing them respect.[7] However, other philosophers have argued that destroying embryos for the purpose of hESC research and demonstrating profound respect towards them are not mutually exclusive.[8] In fact, Bertha Alvarez Manninen argues that given the choice between throwing away embryos and using them for research, the latter option demonstrates more respect than the former, and, moreover, that the former demonstrates disrespect towards the embryos. She argues, 'Indeed, merely discarding surplus embryos disrespects *both* the embryos and the people suffering from disease.'[9] Let us take a closer look at these arguments.

There are two central arguments that attempt to show that killing embryos while simultaneously respecting them is impossible: first, killing and respecting are attitudes and actions that are conceptually contradictory and second respecting something entails never treating it as simply a means to an end but always as an end in itself. The first argument seems almost self-evident, since an attitude of respecting another being entails the notion of treating the other as it deserves to be treated. This includes being mindful of the other's interests, desires and rights, and trying not to undermine any of these. Killing another person deprives them of their fundamental right to life and of their fundamental desires and interests to continue to exist.

However, Manninen points out that this is not always the case and there can be exceptions to this general moral maxim. For instance, consider the case of a person who has a loved one who is terminally ill, is in severe pain and agony and has no quality of life left to live. Imagine that this person desires to die but she cannot do it alone. Would it be disrespectful or respectful for the loved one to assist her in such cases of voluntary active euthanasia? If a person is terminally ill and is suffering tremendous amounts of pain, another might show respect by assisting them in their wish to end their life. Notice that we do not need to resolve the issue of whether the action is morally permissible or morally wrong; all that we need to demonstrate is that the action is respectful and not disrespectful. An action that is performed towards another person out of love, compassion and in accord with the person's wishes seems to be highly respectful of the person. As Manninen argues: 'A physician who euthanizes patients out of respect for their autonomy and because of his or her desire not to cause them needless suffering clearly does not manifest the same attitude as a serial killer.'[10] This case, therefore, demonstrates that it is conceptually possible to show respect and kill a human person.

The second argument uses Kant's formulation of the categorical imperative to demonstrate that it is morally impermissible to use human embryos for the purposes of medical research, because doing so uses them only as a means to an end and not as an end itself. The argument claims that human embryos that are selected for research have no possibility of surviving, and as a consequence they are sacrificed for the purpose of advancing medical research. This degrades the respect owed to human dignity, and it resorts to treating human beings as things and not as persons. Moreover, unlike in the case of active euthanasia the human embryo is not suffering and shows no signs that it does not want to continue living.

Does Kant's Categorical Imperative work for defending the human embryos? According to Manninen, this argument conflates categories of being, since Kant's Categorical Imperative is meant to apply to conscious, rational and autonomous persons and not to human embryos. She writes:

There is one major flaw with these attempts to apply Kant's formula of humanity to embryos: Kant restricts his second categorical imperative to *persons*, individuals with rational abilities who can create ends for themselves and follow the moral law; he does not apply it to human beings *qua* members of the species *Homo sapiens*. Kant divides the world into two different types of beings: persons (rational beings that must be treated as ends in themselves) and things (nonrational beings that are valuable insofar as they serve as means for the ends of rational beings). Embryos, given their lack of conscious life, and hence of rationality and the capacity for moral agency, fall into the latter category within a traditional Kantian framework.[11]

However, even if embryos do not have consciousness, rationality and autonomy, this does not mean that we cannot speak about what is in the best interest for human embryos. It is true that we cannot disrespect them by making them suffer or by inflicting pain on them; these are simply states that an embryo cannot participate in. However, is it not possible that we do what is contrary to the human embryos' best interest and thus disrespect them in so doing?

Manninen points out that 'the NAS guidelines explicitly state that embryo donors must first determine whether they want their embryos destroyed or donated, and it is only if they choose to destroy them that they should be given the option of donating them for research rather than simply discarding them'.[12] Given this option, Manninen argues that the ethically right decision is to give the embryo up for hESC research. Manninen appeals to John Robertson's *Principle of Waste Avoidance* to support her argument:

This widely shared principle states that it is right to benefit people if we can, wrong to harm them and that faced with the opportunity to use resources for a beneficial purpose when the alternative is that those resources are wasted, we have powerful moral reasons to avoid waste and to do good instead. ... It must logically, be better to do something good than to do nothing good; it must be better to make good use of something than to allow it to be wasted.[13]

According to the Principle of Waste Avoidance, even if we grant that the embryo, as a living human organism with the potential to develop into a human person, has an important moral status, it might be argued that if we have to choose between killing an embryo or sacrificing it for medical research, we ought to do the latter.

In the future, technological advances in stem cell research might make it possible to extract pluripotent cells from embryos without destroying the embryos. This might revolutionize the ethical issues surrounding stem cell research. However, the issue of surplus embryos from IVF will remain an ethical problem for fundamental abortion critics. Moreover, if pluripotent cells cannot be distinguished from totipotent cells, then we will have new questions about the status of such a cell. If it is a totipotent cell, then in reality it is another zygote and thus it would have the same status as the embryo.

Consistency argument in favour of embryonic stem cell research

Let us now consider the more controversial case: Is it ethically permissible to create living human embryos for the purpose of stem cell research if we know that these embryos will be destroyed as part of the research? John Harris argues that, in principle, the embryonic stem cell research ought to be morally permissible. Moreover, we can use his argument to support the position that morally contentious view above. His argument is based on the idea that we should maintain moral principles consistently throughout our moral reasoning. For instance, if a professor considers it ethically permissible for one student to use her notes during an exam, then (all else being equal) the professor should also find it ethically permissible to allow another student to use his notes during the exam. Following this line of thought, Harris argues that our moral outlook and treatment of embryos in embryonic stem cell research ought to be consistent with our outlook and treatment of embryos in natural reproduction and artificial reproductive technologies. Let's consider natural reproduction first.

During natural reproduction, we know that a woman will have several miscarriages before one embryo attaches to the uterus and begins to develop and results in a live birth. If this is the case, then everyone who decides to have children will inevitably have to sacrifice the lives of several embryos to do so. Harris explains:

> We now know that for every successful pregnancy that results in a live birth many, perhaps as many as five, early embryos will be lost or 'miscarry' ... How are we to think of the decision to attempt to have a child in the light of these facts? ... Thus, the sacrifice of embryos seems to be an inescapable and inevitable part of the process of procreation. ... For everyone who knows the facts, it is a conscious, knowing, and therefore deliberate sacrifice; and for everyone, regardless of 'guilty' knowledge. It is part of the true description of what they do in having or attempting to have children.[14]

The argument, then, is that natural reproduction entails the sacrifice of embryos. Therefore, when a couple considers having a child they know that doing so will mean the destruction and death of several living embryos. Is it morally wrong for them, knowing what is at stake, to have children? One might think that this sacrifice is nature's doing and that the couple is not responsible for the death of the embryos in the process of natural reproduction. Moreover, they might point out that they certainly do not do it intentionally, and moreover if they could prevent the death of the embryos they would. However, this is only partly true and does not excuse them from the responsibility of bringing about the death of the human living embryos.

It is true that the causal relationship between the goal of reproduction and the death of human embryos is not their deliberate intention or making; however, once they are aware of this fact, they cannot excuse their intentionality or responsibility in the death of one or more embryos. For instance, if we believe that a given event, A, is a reprehensibly evil (e.g. the death of a human being) and also know that a certain act, B, itself not necessarily evil, will bring about the reprehensible event A, then it seems that we ought to refrain from performing act B if we can do so. If we do perform act B voluntarily, we are responsible for bringing about the reprehensible evil event A, since we knew the causal relationship existed prior to our committing B. According to the consistency principle, if we find it morally acceptable to sacrifice embryos for the purpose of natural reproduction, then we also ought to find it morally permissible to sacrifice embryos for the purpose of hESC research. Harris explains his argument as follows:

> I am saying, rather, that, if something happens in nature *and* we find it acceptable in nature given all the circumstance of the case, then if the circumstances are relevantly similar it will for the same reasons by morally permissible to achieve the same results as a consequences of deliberate

human choice. I am saying that we do as a matter of fact and of sound moral judgment accept the sacrifice of embryos in natural reproduction, because, although we might rather not have to sacrifice embryos to achieve a live healthy birth, we judge it to be defensible to continue natural reproduction in the light of the balance between the moral costs and the benefits. And if we make this calculation in the case of normal sexual reproduction we should, for the same reasons, make a similar judgment in the case of the sacrifice of embryos in stem cell research.[15]

Let us now consider IVF. As noted above, IVF requires that many embryos be produced of which some will eventually be destroyed. If we were to take a conservative abortion critic's view and argue that a foetus from the moment of conception is a human person, we are never morally justified in killing it. In this case, almost all abortions are immoral and IVF is also immoral. On the other hand, if we morally justify IVF and the creation and subsequent sacrifice of living human embryos because it is a necessary means to a greater good, namely to bring a child into the world, then, to maintain ethical consistency, we should also morally justify hESC research on human embryos produced solely for this purpose. After all, these embryos also have a noble purpose namely to alleviate tremendous amounts of human suffering. Therefore, if we are consistent with respect to our views on natural reproduction and IVF, then we should hold that hESC research on human embryos produced solely for this purpose is morally permissible. Here is the consistency argument in premise-conclusion format.

ARGUMENT FOR THE ETHICAL PERMISSIBILITY OF hESC RESEARCH

1 We know that, in natural sexual reproduction and in IVF, for every successful pregnancy that results in a live birth, some early embryos will be lost.

2 Knowing this fact means that when a heterosexual couple decides to have a family and procreate, whether naturally or through IVF, they also know that they will have to sacrifice the lives of several living human embryos before they can have a child.

3 Natural reproduction and IVF are morally acceptable, because the sacrifice of embryos is for the greater good, namely, procreation.

4 We should use moral principles consistently in cases where there are no morally relevant differences.

5   The sacrifice of human embryos produced solely for the purpose of stem cell research is also morally justified, because it is undertaken for a greater good, namely, saving lives, preventing suffering and improving the health of people.

6   The case of hESC research on embryos produced solely for this purpose is morally consistent with the cases of natural reproduction and IVF.

7   Therefore, if natural reproduction and IVF are morally permissible, then hESC research on embryos produced solely for this purpose is also ethically permissible.

Cloning

Cloning is the process of creating genetically identical molecules, cells or organisms. In 1997, Sir Ian Wilmut and Keith Campbell cloned the first non-human organism, Dolly the sheep, through a process called somatic cell nuclear transfer. The process entails removing the nucleus from an adult cell and removing a nucleus from an egg cell, then transferring the adult cell's nucleus into the egg cell. Since then scientists have cloned many other non-human mammals. These medical advances have opened the door to many possibilities, only limited by our imaginations.

For instance, we can imagine cloning human organs such as hearts, livers, kidneys. This could offer incredible health benefits for patients that need a transplant of any of these organs. We can also imagine cloning nonperson human beings or human beings that lack consciousness and sentience. These human organisms would have all of the biological make-up of a normal human being except for the parts of the brain responsible for consciousness and thought. These human nonperson organisms could be used for spare parts. We could also imagine the cloning of human persons. In this case, the clone persons would have all of the rights ascribed to any adult human person. The moral questions surrounding each of these forms of cloning are very different. For instance, molecular and cell cloning are not morally controversial and can offer many health benefits. Cloning nonperson human beings is controversial but certainly not as controversial as cloning a human person. The most contentious form of cloning is the cloning of human persons, and it is this that we will address in this section.

Is it immoral to clone persons?

Is it morally wrong to clone human persons? Michael Tooley will defend the view that there is nothing, in principle, morally wrong with cloning human persons. Let us begin by clarifying Tooley's position and explaining what he means by 'in principle'. When we consider the ethical status of some medical procedure, we have to consider the procedure itself and the practical conditions and consequences surrounding the procedure. In the case of cloning, for instance, Tooley argues that the procedure has not yet been perfected. For instance, in the case of Dolly the sheep the scientist started with 434 sheep oocytes and only 29 embryos survived. Out of these twenty-nine embryos that were implanted in surrogate mothers all of them died except one.

Even though technology has improved in the past twenty-five years, and cloning non-human animals has become more efficient, it remains a perilous medical procedure in various respects. First, cloning human persons might result in many miscarriages, and this process will pose serious physical and emotional harm on women who undergo the procedure. As a result, cloning should be morally forbidden and banned. Notice, however, that the reasons given here are extrinsic reasons; the argument is not that there is something morally wrong with cloning itself, it is rather that scientists have not yet perfected the method of cloning, and thus the procedure could pose an undue burden on women. Second, there can be consequences to cloning that are harmful for the cloned person. For instance, it might be the case that clones have a shorter life expectancy. As a consequence, cloned persons could have a premature death, and it seems wrong to create persons under these conditions. Given our knowledge of cloning, then, Tooley would agree that until we perfect the procedure and understand the full consequences of cloning a person, cloning human persons remains too risky a medical procedure, and thus it ought to be prohibited. However, if these conditions could be improved substantially, then cloning should be permitted, since there is nothing intrinsically morally wrong with human cloning.

Intrinsic moral status of cloning persons

Tooley claims that there are two main arguments against the intrinsic moral permissibility of cloning persons: first, the right of a person to be genetically unique and second the right of a person to an open future. Let us examine each of this in more detail.

The right to a unique genetic code

Do we have a right to be genetically unique? Another way of thinking about this question is to ponder whether having another person that is genetically identical to you will affect the quality of your life. The answer to this question depends, in part, on whether having two persons with the same genetic code will result in the same identical person

First, we should point out that, in cases of identical twins, cloning already occurs naturally. From studying identical twins, we know that genetic identity does not mean that the twins will have the same personalities, even if they are raised in the same family. Genetic identity, therefore, does not equate to absolute identity of persons and personality traits. It appears that a person's lived experiences help shape his or her personality traits. Since identical twins experience different events, they will become persons with different personality traits. If genetic identity does not affect one's uniqueness as a person, then the argument for the right to be unique will have little force against cloning persons. Nevertheless, it has been demonstrated that identical twins' personalities will correlate more than fraternal twins (50 per cent correlation as compared to 25 per cent), more than non-twin siblings (11 per cent) and more than strangers (close to zero).[16] Can this degree of resemblance be sufficient to sustain the argument against cloning from the right to be genetically unique?

Tooley considers three thought experiments to contemplate further this line of argumentation: (1) Should one be a parent to identical twins? (2) What interest or right would a cloned person infringe upon? and (3) Would a world of clones be better than the actual world? First, consider the issue from a parent's perspective. If you know that you were going to have identical twins, would this be a good reason not to have children? If you believe that the existence of a genetically identical person would in some way deter from one's quality of life, then knowing that if one were to have children one would bring into existence identical twins, it might be a sufficient reason to reconsider having children. Certainly, it ought to give one reason to question the decision. Tooley argues that most parents who have identical twins do not believe that their children's lives have been compromised in virtue of being a twin. We could even reflect on anecdotal evidence since we all probably know of or are friends with some persons that are identical twins. It is difficult to see how and why having a genetically identical person to oneself would negatively affect the quality of one's existence. If the existence of a genetically identical person does not affect the quality of one's life, then there is nothing intrinsically wrong with producing a human clone.

Second, if a clone to oneself were to exist, what interest or right would he or she infringe upon? One's interests are connected to one's rights. Let's examine a little closer this connection. A basic right that people have is a right to life. Having the right to life makes sense because one has an interest in one's life and an interest in the continued existence of one's life. It would be absurd to contemplate the right to life of a rock since it has no life, and thus it cannot have an interest in sustaining its life. Consider another example. Would it make sense to advocate for a cat's right to vote? Why does this sound absurd? The reason is because the conception of voting is outside of the capabilities of cats and thus cats cannot have an interest to vote. Notice that the existence of an interests in x is not sufficient for having a right to x, but having an interest (or at least the capability of having an interest) in x does seem to be a necessary condition for having a right to x.

The purpose of rights is to protect not all interests but only those that are deemed worthy of protection. For instance, people have an interest in expressing their viewpoints, feelings and opinions. This interest is cherished in most democracies, and people believe strongly that such interests are vital and ought to be protected. As a consequence, we advocate in favour of people's right to free speech. However, notice that the right to free speech of plants would be absurd since plants do not have ideas, opinions or viewpoints, nor the ability to speak. The question therefore is what interests does the existence of a clone (to oneself) infringe upon for one to demand the right to one's genetic uniqueness be respected?

Let us rephrase the question. If there existed another person who was genetically identical to you, how would this affect your interests? Tooley argues that the existence of a clone does not seem to affect one's interests at all. For instance, imagine that there existed a person who was genetically identical to you in a distant land. Imagine that you were not even aware of the existence of your clone. It would seem difficult to find some legitimate interests or right that is in some way affected by the existence of such a clone. Tooley claims: 'A distant clone might have no impact at all on one's life.'[17] However, what if you were aware of the existence of such a clone? Would the knowledge that there existed a genetically identical person affect one's life? It might be somewhat disturbing to think that there existed a genetically identical person to oneself. Would we consider this person family? Should we love them the way we would love our mother, father and siblings? The thought does seem disturbing, but would it be sufficient to ban cloning of my genetic code based on the psychological effects it might have on me? It seems difficult to claim a right to genetic uniqueness based solely on psychological feelings of uneasiness.

Of course, we can imagine scenarios in which the existence of clones could have an impact on one's legitimate interests. For instance, imagine that there were fifty clones of you living in the same small city you live in. This could make living a decent quality of life impossible for many obvious reasons. However, Tooley will point out that this has to do more with the way, methods and procedures of cloning than with cloning itself. That is to say, the fact that cloning in principle is ethically permissible does not mean that all scenarios of cloning are ethically permissible. For instance, cloning persons to create an army to destroy the world is ethically wrong. However, this does not demonstrate that cloning itself is wrong, only that some uses of cloning are wrong.

Finally, imagine a world in which there is no genetic diversity. Imagine that God exists and decides to create a universe of genetically identical persons. The only genetic difference would be associated with gender and facial and hair traits so that we could distinguish people from one another. According to Tooley, such a world would be much better than the actual world for several reasons:

> First, unlike the actual world, one would be assured of a genetic makeup that would be free of dispositions to various unwelcome and life-shortening diseases, or to other debilitating conditions such as depression, schizophrenia, and so on. Second, inherited traits would be distributed in a perfectly equitable fashion, and no one would start out, as is the case in the actual world, severely disadvantaged, and facing and enormous uphill battle. Third aside from the difference between men and women, everyone would be physically the same, and so people would differ only with regard to the quality of their 'souls,' and thus one would have a world in which judgments of people might well have a less superficial basis than is often the case in the actual world. So there would be some serious reasons for preferring the alternative world over the actual world.[18]

Let us conclude with a theistic objection to human cloning. One might argue that God has created each individual being as a unique person, and this uniqueness has some intrinsic religious value. This argument, according to Tooley, will not succeed because if cloning were intrinsically evil, then certainly God would not permit its occurrence in nature in the form of identical twins. However, it does occur in nature and thus it cannot be intrinsically evil. A theist might respond by distinguishing between human cloning, as a process produced and directed by human beings, and the natural birth of identical twins. While the result is the same, for a theist the process is substantially relevant. What they might object to is not the creation of genetically identical individuals but rather to the process being performed and directed by human beings. However, if this is the issue, then it is not really about cloning but rather about all forms of human intervention in the procreation process, including all forms of Artificial Reproductive Technologies.

The open future argument

A second argument against human cloning is the right to an open future. This argument is based on the idea that if there are genetically identical individuals who have lived in previous generations, then, in many respects, their lives (achievements, failures, health etc.) deny the genetically identical individuals of future generations of an open future. Genetically identical individuals of future generations will acquire the knowledge of a set of limited parameters that have already been established by the genetically identical individuals of the previous generations. For instance, if you know that your clone could not finish a marathon under a certain time, or could not get into graduate school, or suffered certain genetic diseases throughout his or her life etc., then all of these events will foretell your capabilities, potentialities, and even your destiny to a great extent. Much of the unpredictability of my life, what I can and cannot achieve, and what will and will not happen to me will, to a great extent, be eliminated from my life. Knowledge of the lives of my previous generational clones, therefore, would be like having a crystal ball in which I can see much of my future. This argument has two important elements: (1) whether one has a right to an open future and (2) whether a person, A, denies its future clone (genetically identical person), B, of an open future, assuming that B has knowledge of person A's life.

Let us begin with the latter, because if this is false, then even if one has a right to an open future, such a right would not be denied by the previous existence of a genetically identical person. If we examined the life of a past clone of ourselves it seems that we could learn a lot about our own nature. However, the question here is whether this knowledge would in some way curtail our freedom and our ability to make decision and to live a very different life from our clone. The answer to this question depends on how much we believe is ultimately determined by our genes (things we cannot control) and how much is determined by our decisions and actions (or things we can control). There is an important balance here and if we lean towards the latter, then not only can we maintain that future clones will have an open future, but also that knowledge of their past clones will serve as a significant advantage to their decision-making in their own lives. The key here is whether knowledge of the life of a genetically identical person to oneself would constrain one's decisions in such a way that it would close off a valuable open future. Even if such knowledge could close off certain paths (which might actually be advantageous), it's difficult to see how it would constrain one's possibilities in such a way that it would reduce the quality of one's life. Tooley writes:

> In short, the idea that information about the life of a person genetically identical to oneself would provide grounds for concluding that only a narrow range of alternatives was open to one would only be justified if

genetic determinism, or a close approximation thereto, was correct. But nothing like genetic determinism is true.[19]

In conclusion, there are many ethical issues surrounding human cloning. Even if Tooley is right that human cloning is morally permissible in theory, there remain a myriad of moral concerns related to human cloning. For instance, how safe and efficient should the process of human cloning be before it is morally permissible? We have assumed that human cloning on non-human animals is perfectly ethical. However, given what we know about the process involved in cloning Dolly, it is also questionable whether cloning non-human animals is ethical? Moreover, if and when human cloning becomes feasible, the specific conditions of human cloning are ethically problematic. The problem might not be the right to genetic uniqueness but the right to be equally represented. One can imagine a world in which a few elite individuals, with similar ways of thinking and world views, decide to produce thousands of clones of themselves in order to influence the future geopolitical events of the world.

Summary

In this chapter, we considered ethical issues concerning prenatal testing, stem cell research and cloning. First, we analysed Adrienne Asch's argument that the current methods surrounding prenatal testing and screening are biased against the disabled, curtail women's freedom, implicitly encourage selective abortions when abnormalities are discovered and are based on misguided assumptions about the notion of disability and what it means to live with a disability. In effect, Asch argues that some of the major causes of the problems associated with disabled persons' living a quality life is not the disability itself, as some healthcare providers would have us believe, but rather the lack of accommodations society offers the disabled.

Next, we considered the ethical issues concerning hESC research. First, we investigated the ethics of hESC research focusing on embryos that are left over from IVF. We analysed Bertha Alvarez Manninen's argument that given the choice between throwing away embryos and using them for research, the latter option demonstrates more respect towards the living human embryos than the former, and that the former demonstrates disrespect towards the living human embryos. In addition, we examined the argument in defence of hESC research using left-over embryos from IVF based on the Principle of Waste Avoidance. Next, we contemplated the more contentious moral issue of producing embryos solely for the purpose of hESC research. Here, we analysed John Harris's argument based on the idea that we should maintain moral principles consistently throughout our moral reasoning. Harris goes on to focus on natural reproduction and IVF, noting that both forms of procreation entail and require the destruction of embryos. While the destruction of embryos in these cases are morally justified for a greater good, namely, the creation of new human persons, he argues that the destruction of embryos created for the sole purpose of research can also be morally justified for a greater good, namely, the alleviation of grave human suffering and death.

Finally, we considered whether it is morally permissible to clone human persons. This is probably one of the most controversial forms of cloning. We studied Michael Tooley's argument that, in principle, the cloning of human persons is morally permissible. We looked at two objections: first, the right to be genetically unique and second the right to an open future. We considered Tooley's responses to these objections and noted that while Tooley believes that, in theory, there is nothing unethical about cloning, there are many practical problems that make cloning a dangerous process and thus an unethical medical procedure at this time.

Study questions

1 Can some forms and methods of prenatal screening encourage abortions? Explain your answer. If they can, should they be eliminated or modified?

2 What is hESC research? Why is it so important for the future of human health and well-being?

3 What are the different sources and the moral relevancy of embryos for hESC research?

4 Why is hESC research morally problematic?

5 Explain the arguments in favour of hESC based on embryos derived from IVF. Is this a successful argument? Why or why not?

6 Explain the consistency argument in favour of creating embryos for the sole purpose of hESC research. Is this a successful argument? Why or why not?

7 What is cloning and what are the different possible ways of human cloning?

8   Is the cloning of persons morally unethical? Explain the argument against cloning based on the right to genetic uniqueness. Is this a successful argument? Why or why not?

9   Explain the argument against cloning based on the right to an open future. Is this a successful argument? Why or why not?

9

Law and Abortion in the United States

Throughout most of American history, abortion laws have been promulgated at the state level. It was not until the constitutionality of some of these laws was contested, and thus they were brought to the US Federal Circuit Court of Appeals and the US Supreme Court, that abortion law entered the national arena. In this chapter, we will consider five of the most significant Supreme Court cases that have influenced the abortion law in the United States: (1) *Griswold* v. *Connecticut* (1965), (2) *Roe* v. *Wade* (1973), (3) *Webster* v. *Reproductive Health Services* (1989), (4) *Planned Parenthood* v. *Casey* (1992) and (5) *Gonzales* v. *Carhart* (2007). The most important case, of course, is *Roe* v. *Wade* (1973) that legalized some forms of abortion in the United States. However, eight years prior, in 1965, *Griswold* v. *Connecticut* set important legal precedents that would play an important role in final opinion of the court in *Roe* v. *Wade*.

Griswold v. Connecticut (1965)

Griswold v. *Connecticut* was argued on 29–30 March 1965 and was decided on 7 June 1965. Justice Douglas delivered the opinion of the Court. In this case, the executive director of Planned Parenthood League of Connecticut, Griswold, and a licenced physician and professor of Yale Medical School, Buxton, were the appellants. Griswold and Buxton were arrested for counselling married women on the best form of contraception. According to the state law of Connecticut, 'Any person who uses any drug, medicinal article or instrument for the purpose of preventing conception shall be fined not less than fifty dollars or imprisoned not less than sixty days nor more than one year or be both fined and imprisoned.'[1] Griswold and Buxton were charged for abetting the married couple in breaking the law and thus were legally liable as if they were the principal offender.

The Supreme Court reversed the decision and found the Connecticut law unconstitutional. The central argument against the unconstitutional nature of the law was its broad sweeping scope that invades the privacy of married individuals. Justice Douglas argued using the First Amendment and the Bill of Rights as creating a 'zone of privacy' and the right of association. He writes:

> The right of freedom of speech and press includes not only the right to utter or to print, but the right to distribute, the right to receive, and the right to read and freedom of inquiry, freedom of thought, and freedom to teach—indeed the freedom of the entire university community … Without those peripheral rights the specific rights would be less secure. And so, we affirm the principle of the *Pierce* and the *Meyer* cases.[2]

The *Pierce* v. *Society of Sisters*, 268 U.S. 510 dealt with the right of parents to educate their children as they see fit. The *Meyer* v. *Nebraska*, 262 U.S. 390 dealt with the freedom of a private school to teach German as part of its curriculum. In addition to the First Amendment, Justice Douglas invoked the freedom of association and protection of privacy as peripheral rights to the First Amendment. He claims, 'In other words, the First Amendment as a penumbra where privacy is protected from governmental intrusion. … Various guarantees create zones of privacy.'[3] In addition he invoked the Due Process Clause of the Fourteenth Amendment that precludes states from passing laws that undermine basic constitutional rights of life, liberty and property without due process. Here is an excerpt of the Fourteenth Amendment of the United States Constitution and an emphasis on the due process clause upon which the Court based its opinion.

> **Section 1.** All persons born or naturalized in the United States, and subject to the jurisdiction thereof, are citizens of the United States and of the State wherein they reside. No State shall make or enforce any law which shall abridge the privileges or immunities of citizens of the United States; *nor shall any State deprive any person of life, liberty, or property, without due process of law* [my emphasis]; nor deny to any person within its jurisdiction the equal protection of the laws.[4]

The court, therefore, concluded that the Connecticut law went too far and invaded the privacy of married couples. Justice Douglas concludes as follows:

> The present case, then, concerns a relationship lying within the zone of privacy created by several fundamental constitutional guarantees. … We

deal with the right of privacy older than the Bill of Rights – older than our political parties, older than our school system. Marriage is a coming together for better or worse, hopefully enduring, and intimate to the degree of being sacred. It is an association that promotes a way of life, not causes; a harmony in living, not political faiths; a bilateral loyalty, not commercial or social projects. Yet it is an association for as noble a purpose as any involved in our prior decision.[5]

Roe v. *Wade* (1973)

Roe v. *Wade* is the most prominent of the Supreme Court decisions concerning abortion in the United States because it is the case that legalized abortion nationwide. The case was argued on 13 December 1971 and reargued on 11 October 1972. It was decided on 22 January 1973. Justice Blackmun delivered the opinion of the Court. Let us begin by providing some background to the case.

It began when a 21-year-old single woman, Norma McCorvey, got pregnant with her third child. McCorvey desired to terminate her pregnancy but abortion was illegal in Texas, except for cases of rape or cases where the pregnancy threatens the life of the woman. McCorvey's attorneys Linda Coffee and Sarah Weddington filed a suit under the pseudonym of Jane Roe in Federal District Court of Dallas County in March 1970. The defendant was District Attorney Henry Wade. In June 1970, the District Court, in a three-judge panel, ruled that the Texas law was unconstitutional. The case was appealed to the Supreme Court. Roe's case was based on the argument that the Texas law invaded her right to liberty, more precisely, her right to terminate her pregnancy, protected by Fourteenth Amendment's Due Process clause and her privacy protected by the Bill of Rights (as noted in *Griswold*).

Roe v. *Wade* produced four important legal and philosophical consequences concerning abortion in the United States. First, it clearly stayed away from the philosophical issue of personhood by declaring that it would not make any claim as to when human life begins. Nevertheless, it concluded that the use of the word 'person' in the constitution, specifically in the Fourteenth Amendment, does not refer to the unborn. Justice Blackmun writes, 'We need not resolve the difficult question of when life begins. When those trained in the respective disciplines of medicine, philosophy, and theology are unable to arrive at any consensus, the judiciary, at this point in the development of man's knowledge, is not in a position to speculate as to the answer.'[6] He later says, 'All of this ... persuades us that the word "person," as used in the Fourteenth Amendment, does not include the unborn.'[7]

Second, the issue at stake is the rights of the pregnant woman versus the right of the state, and the Court resolved this within a *framework of trimesters* of the gestation period. The Court found that the state has a compelling interest to protect the health of the pregnant woman and it also has a compelling interest in protecting the potential life of the foetus. However, the compelling interest of the state to protect the health of the pregnant woman does not begin until the end of the first trimester. The central argument for selecting this point in the pregnancy is based on the claim that the health risk of having of an abortion during the first trimester is equal to the health risk of giving birth. Thus, up to this point, a pregnant woman faces no considerable health risk in having an abortion, at least none higher than that of giving birth, and as a result she does not need the protection of state regulations. Justice Blackmun writes:

> With respect to the State's important and legitimate interest in the health of the mother, the 'compelling' point, in the light of present medical knowledge, is at approximately the end of the first trimester .... It follows that, from and after this point, a State may regulate the abortion procedure to the extent that the regulation reasonably relates to the preservation and protection of maternal health.[8]

The third important consequence of *Roe* v. *Wade* is the determination of the compelling point at which the state has an interest in the potential life of the foetus. The Court argued that this point should not begin until the foetus is viable (i.e. at the point at which the foetus can continue to live outside of the mother's womb independent of the mother). According to the Court, 'If the State is interested in protecting fetal life after viability, it may go so far as to proscribe abortion during that period, except when it is necessary to preserve the life or health of the mother.'[9] As a consequence, prohibiting abortion after the point at which the foetus is viable is constitutional.

Finally, the most important consequence of *Roe* v. *Wade* is that up to the end of the first trimester a pregnant woman has the right to have an abortion, in consultation with her physician, free of any interference from the state. Justice Blackmun writes,

> This means, on the other hand, that, for the period of pregnancy prior to this 'compelling' point [the compelling point to protect the mother's health] the attending physician, in consultation with his patient is free to determine, without regulation by the State, that, in his medical judgment, the patient's pregnancy should be terminated. If that decision is reached, the judgment may be effectuated by an abortion free of interference by the State.[10]

The Court, therefore, held that the Texas state statue and any state law that prohibited abortion without consideration of the stage of pregnancy is unconstitutional and violates the Due Process Clause of the Fourteenth Amendment.

Webster v. *Reproductive Health Services* (1989)

Webster v. *Reproductive Health Services* was argued on 26 April 1989 and decided on 3 July 1989. Chief Justice Rehnquist delivered the opinion of the Court. The importance of this case for the pro-life movement is significant. While it did not overturn *Roe* v. *Wade*, it significantly weakened it. As Justice Blackmun writes in the dissenting opinion:

> Today, *Roe* v *Wade* 410 U.S. 113 (1973), and the fundamental constitutional right of women to decide whether to terminate a pregnancy, survive but are not secure. Although the Court extricates itself from this case without making a single, even incremental, change in the law of abortion, the plurality and JUSTICE SCALIA would overrule *Roe* (the first silently, the other explicitly) and would return to the States virtually unfettered authority to control the quintessentially intimate, personal, and life directly decision whether to carry a fetus to term.[11]

In this case the state of Missouri passed a law that affected four central issues of the abortion debate: (1) a state's right to define personhood, (2) the prohibition of using public faculties for performing abortion, (3) the prohibition of using public funding for abortion counselling and (4) the requirement that physicians conduct viability tests prior to performing abortions.

The Missouri Act begins by stating that 'the life of each human being begins at conception'.[12] The Court of Appeals determined that stating a theory of life in the preamble of the statute was unconstitutional. However, the Supreme Court disagreed. The point of controversy concerns whether the theory has any substantive influence over the regulation of abortion law or medical practice. The Court of Appeals determined that it did. However, the Supreme Court claimed that the Missouri Act's statement about when life begins ought to be interpreted simply as a value judgement with no intended purpose to regulate abortion laws or medical practices. Rehnquist writes: 'The Court has emphasized that *Roe* v *Wade* "implies no limitation on the authority of the State to make a value judgment favoring childbirth over abortion." *Maher v Roe*, 432 U. S., at 474. The preamble can be read simply to express that sort of value judgment.'[13]

The Court of Appeals held that the state law that prohibited using public employees and facilities for performing abortions was unconstitutional. Their argument was that the law not only encourages childbirth over abortion but restricts women's ability to have abortions. Moreover, it would prevent a woman's doctor from performing an abortion if a hospital where the doctor works adopts this policy. And it would also make abortions more expensive and delay the timing of abortions. However, the Supreme Court disagreed and protected the state's law as constitutional. Rehnquist writes: 'We think that this analysis [of the Court of Appeals] is much like that which we reject in *Maher, Poelker,* and *McRae.* As in those cases, the State's decision here to use public facilities and staff to encourage childbirth over abortion "places no governmental obstacle in the path of a woman who chooses to terminate her pregnancy."'[14] He goes on to justify the use of public facilities in accordance with a strict anti-abortion policy: 'If the State may "make a value judgment favoring childbirth over abortion and ... implement that judgment by the allocation of public funds," *Maher, supra,* at 474, surely it may do so through the allocation of other public resources, such as hospitals and medical staff.'[15]

The Court held that the Missouri Act requiring a physician who has reason to believe that the pregnant woman has a foetus of twenty or more weeks of gestational age must first determine if the foetus is viable before performing an abortion is constitutional. The Court argued that, consistent with Roe, the state has an interest in protecting potential life. Moreover, the state of Missouri has chosen viability as the point at which it has a compelling interest in the potential life of the foetus. Therefore, testing for viability supports the state's interest in protecting potential human life. Rehnquist writes, 'But we are satisfied that the requirement of these tests permissibly furthers the State's interests in protecting the potential human life, and therefore believe [section] 188.029 [of the Missouri Act] to be constitutional.'[16]

In addition to a favourable conclusion towards the protection of potential human life, the Court presented a strong critique of *Roe's* trimesters framework and questioned the determination in *Roe* that the state's interest in the foetus's potential life begins at the point of viability. Chief Justice Rehnquist writes:

> In the first place, the rigid *Roe* framework is hardly consistent with the notion of a Constitution cast in general terms, as ours is, and usually speaking in general principles, as our does. The key elements of the *Roe* framework – trimesters and viability – are not found in the texts of the Constitution or in any place else one would expect to find a constitutional principle.

He goes on,

In the second place, we do not see why the State's interest in protecting potential human life should come into existence only at the point of viability, and that there should be therefore a rigid line allowing state regulation after viability but prohibiting it before viability.[17]

This decision eroded some of the protection that Roe had established for pregnant women who desired to terminate their pregnancy. Moreover, as Justice Blackmun's dissenting opinion states, it manifests a change in the attitude of the Court toward the abortion issue. Justice Blackmun writes, "I fear for the future. I fear for the liberty and equality of the millions of women who have lived and come of age in the 16 years since Roe was decided. I fear for the integrity of, and public esteem for, this court..."[18]

Planned Parenthood v. Casey (1992)

Planned Parenthood v. Casey was argued on 22 April 1992 and decided on 29 June 1992. Justices O'Connor, Kennedy and Scouter delivered the opinion of the Court. This case deals with the Pennsylvania Abortion Control Act of 1982 (as amended in 1988 and 1989). The issues at stake are as follows: (1) a woman seeking an abortion must give her informed consent prior to the abortion procedure and that she be provided with certain information twenty-four hours before the abortion is performed. (2) A minor requires the informed consent of one of her parents. (3) A married woman seeking an abortion must sign a statement indicating that she has informed her husband of the intended abortion. The Court of Appeals upheld all of the provisions of the Statute except for (3).

The Supreme Court's majority opinion starts by noting that, once again, the issues in this case affect the decisions of Roe:

Liberty finds no refuge in jurisprudence of doubt. Yet 19 years after our holding that the Constitution protects a woman's right to terminate her pregnancy in its early stages, Roe v. Wade, 410 U.S. 113, 93 S. Ct. 705, 35 L. Ed. 2d 147 (1973), that definition of liberty is still questioned. Joining the respondents as amicus curiae, the United States, as it has done in five other cases in the last decade, again asks us to overrule Roe.[19]

The Court begins by noting that the Constitution protects citizens from the state's interference in an individual's most intimate decisions concerning his or her family, as well as decisions concerning parenthood. The Court emphasizes the importance of the Constitutional protection from state's interference in the privacy of one's family life, including marriage, rearing of children and education. According to the Court, these decisions are central to one's dignity as a person and to one's autonomy, and they are decisions that should be left up to the individual person.

With respect to abortion, the Court introduces a feminist perspective that presents abortion not as simply another individual liberty but also as something pertinent to only women. It writes:

> Though abortion is conduct, it does not follow that the State is entitled to proscribe it in all instances. That is because the liberty of women is at stake in a sense unique to the human condition and so unique to the law. The mother who carries a child to full term is subject to anxieties, to physical constraints, to pain that only she must bear. That these sacrifices have from the beginning of the human race been endured by women with a pride that ennobles her in the eyes of others and gives to the infant a bond of love cannot alone be grounds for the State to insist she make the sacrifice. Her suffering is too intimate and personal for the State to insist, without more, upon its own vision of women's role, however dominant that vision has been in the course of our history and our culture. The destiny of women must be shaped to a large extent on her own conception of her spiritual imperatives and her place in society.[20]

The opinion, therefore, strongly reasserts the findings of *Roe* and a woman's right to an abortion during the early stages of pregnancy as protected by the Due Process Clause of the Fourteenth Amendment. According to the Court, the reaffirmation of the findings of *Roe* include the following: (1) The right of a woman to obtain an abortion before foetal viability without the interference of the state; (2) The right of the state to prohibit abortions after the stage of foetal viability, given certain exceptions are provided for when a woman's life is in danger and (3) 'the principle that the State has legitimate interests from the outset of the pregnancy in protecting the health of the woman and the life of the fetus that may become a child'.[21] The court says, 'These principles do not contradict one another; and we adhere to each.'[22] Of these three the Court writes, 'The woman's right to terminate her pregnancy before viability is the most central principle of *Roe* v. *Wade*. It is a rule of law and a component of liberty we cannot renounce.'[23]

On the other hand, the Court also concedes the state has a right to make sure that a woman who is planning on having an abortion is making a thoughtful and informed decision. This right is based on the legitimate right to protect both the pregnant woman and the potential life. As a consequence, the state has the right to create laws that will ensure that any woman having an abortion is properly informed about the procedure and that 'encourage her to know that there are philosophical and social arguments of great weight that can be brought to bear in favor of continuing the pregnancy to full term and that there are procedures and institutions to allow adoption of unwarranted children as well as certain degree of state assistance if the mother chooses to raise the child herself'.[24]

The key to reconciling a woman's right to an abortion and the state's right to protect the woman and the potential life is the concept of *undue burden*. If the laws or regulations present an undue burden on a woman from having an abortion, then the laws and regulations are unconstitutional. However, if the laws and regulations do not create an undue burden on a woman in her pursuit of an abortion, then the laws and regulations are constitutional. The Court defined the notion of undue burden as follows: 'An undue burden exists, and therefore a provision of law is invalid, if its purpose or effect is to place a substantial obstacle in the path of a woman seeking an abortion before the fetus attains viability.'[25]

The Court, then, needs to decide: (1) whether requesting a woman seeking an abortion to give her informed consent prior to the abortion procedure and that she be provided with certain information twenty-four hours before the abortion is performed (except in medical emergencies) creates an undue burden; (2) whether requiring a minor to obtain informed consent of one of her parents (with a judicial bypass option if the minor cannot obtain such consent) creates an undue burden and (3) whether a married woman seeking an abortion must sign a statement indicating that she has informed her husband of the intended abortion creates an undue burden. The Court concurred with the District Court and held that in cases (1) and (2) no undue burden is created on a woman's right to have an abortion. It also agreed with the District Court and found (3) unconstitutional. It concluded as follows:

> The spousal notification requirement is thus likely to prevent a significant number of women from obtaining an abortion. It does not merely make abortions a little more difficult or expensive to obtain; for many women, it will impose a *substantial obstacle* [my emphasis]. We must not blind ourselves to the fact that the significant number of women who fear for their safety and the safety of their children are likely to be deterred from procuring an abortion as surely as if the Commonwealth had outlawed abortion in all case.[26]

Gonzales v. Carhart (2007)

Gonzales v. *Carhart* was argued on 8 November 2006 and decided on 18 April 2007. Justice Anthony J. Kennedy delivered the opinion of the Court. This case deals with the Federal Partial-Birth Abortion Ban Act of 2003 H. R. Rep. No. 108–158, at 12–14. On 5 November 2003, President Bush signed the Act into law. The new federal law was a response to *Steinberg* v. *Carhart* (2000) in which the Court struck down a Nebraska law against Partial-Birth Abortions. In 2000, the Court held that the Nebraska Law against partial birth abortion was unconstitutional because it did not provide an exception for cases in which the mother's health was in danger, and because the law would create an undue burden for a woman to have an abortion using the procedure of dilation and evacuation (D&E).

It is important to understand the different abortion procedures in order to understand the case at hand. D&E is an abortion procedure that normally is done after about the thirteenth week of gestation age of the foetus. First the cervix is dilated and then the foetus is taken out in pieces. As the gestation age advances the D&E procedure becomes riskier. First, since the foetus is larger and the bones have become more rigid, the foetus will have to be taken out in more pieces, which means physician will have to introduce instruments into the woman more times for the extraction of the foetus. Therefore, there is greater risk of infection and uterus perforation. In addition, there are also more chances that foetal parts will remain inside the woman, increasing the risk of infection. Another abortion procedure known as dilation and extraction is also performed for later abortions. In this procedure the foetus is taken out intact and is killed outside of the womb. This procedure is known as 'intact D&E' or D&X or partial-birth abortions.

The Federal Law in *Gonzales* v. *Carhart* prohibits the specific procedure D&X or intact D&E but does not prohibit the standard D&E procedures. The law reads as follows:

(a) Any physician who, in or affecting interstate or foreign commence knowingly performs a part-birth abortion and thereby kills a human fetus shall be fined under title or imprisoned not more than 2 years, or both. …
(1) the term 'partial-birth abortion' means an abortion in which the person performing the abortion (A) deliberately and intentionally vaginally delivers a living fetus, in the case of a head-first presentation, the entire fetal head is outside the body of the mother, or, in the case of breech presentation [when the fetus comes feet first] any part of the fetal trunk past the navel is outside the body of the mother, for the purpose of performing an overt act that the person knows will kill the partially delivered living fetus.[27]

The District Court found the Federal Law to be unconstitutional. First, it held that the law does not include any exceptions for cases in which the mother's life is in danger. Second, it held that it covered more than just intact D&E procedures.

One argument in favour of the unconstitutionality of the law is the vagueness of the offence. Any law that criminalizes an act must describe the act in a definite manner so that 'ordinary people can understand what conduct is prohibited and in a manner that does not encourage arbitrary and discriminatory enforcement'.[28] The Court rejected this argument stating that the law indeed met both criteria. The Court writes, 'Doctors performing D&E will know that if they do not deliver a living fetus to an anatomical landmark they will not face criminal liability.'[29] In addition, the Act required for the doctor to perform the partial-birth abortion deliberately (i.e. *mens rea*). If the doctors don't pass the anatomical landmark (the navel if the fetus is delivered feet first), then the doctor cannot be held criminally liable.

The Court also found lower court's argument that the law is unconstitutional because it placed an undue burden on women as unfounded. The Court writes, 'The Act prohibits intact D&E; and, not withstanding respondents' arguments, it does not prohibit the D&E procedure in which the fetus is removed in parts. ... In sum, we reject the contention that the congressional purpose of the Act was "to place substantial obstacle in the path of a woman seeking an abortion."'[30]

Next the Court addresses whether the law is unconstitutional because it does not provide an exception for cases in which the mother's life is in danger. Or, to put another way, the question as to whether this new law 'has the effect of imposing an unconstitutional burden on the abortion right because it does not allow use of a barred procedure where "necessary, in appropriate medical judgment, for [the] preservation of the ... health of the mother"; *Ayotte*, 546 U.S., at 327–328.' The problem in this case is that the scientific evidence that supports the need of this procedure to protect the health of the mother is under dispute and thus remains uncertain. This uncertainty was enough for the Court to distinguish this case from the precedent set in *Ayotte*. The Court says, 'The question becomes whether the Act can stand when this medical uncertainty persists.'[31]

The Court instead appealed to other precedent in which the federal and state legislatures have been given wide and broad powers to pass laws in situations in which there is medical and scientific uncertainties. As a result, the Court held that 'medical uncertainty does not foreclose the exercise of legislative power in the abortion context any more than it does in other contexts'.[32] Here, again, the Court rejects the District Court's argument that the law is unconstitutional on the basis that the law excludes exceptions for the health of the mother. It concludes: 'The Act is not invalid on its face where there is uncertainty over whether the barred procedure is ever necessary to preserve a woman's health, given the availability of other abortion procedures that are considered safe alternatives.'[33]

Therefore, on all counts, the Supreme Court overturned verdicts of the District Courts and the Courts of Appeals. It sided with Congress and validated the Partial-Birth Abortion Ban (2003). The Court concluded as follows: 'Respondents have not demonstrated that the Act, as a facial matter, is void for vagueness, or that it imposes an undue burden on a woman's right to abortion based on its overbreadth or lack of a health exception. For these reasons the judgment of the Courts of Appeals for the Eighth and Ninth Circuits are reversed.'

Gonzales v. *Carhart* is a marginal win for the pro-life movement; it was more of a symbolic gain than a practical one. First, few abortions are performed after the thirteenth week of foetal gestation. For instance, in 2014, according to the Centers for Disease Control and Prevention, 91.5 per cent of all abortions were performed before the thirteenth week and only 7.2 per cent were performed between the fourteenth and twentieth weeks of the foetal gestation age.[34] In addition, this decision does not preclude late-term abortions; it only precludes the specific abortion method known as partial-birth abortion. Nevertheless, the Courts validation of this law upholds certain basic beliefs about the respect and dignity of human life. Part of the arguments within the law is that the partial-birth abortions kills the foetus once it is partially delivered, and thus it is very similar to infanticide or the killing of newborn babies. This practice, Congress argued, is inhumane, brutal and devalues human life. In addition, the legislature argued that this specific procedure is contradictory to the professed objectives of the medical professions: to protect and save lives. The ethical codes and standards of doctors are under the purvey of government, and, with this understanding, such procedures can come under the control and power of the government.

Summary

In this chapter we have discussed five of the most important and influential Supreme Court cases that have affected the abortion law in the United States: (1) *Griswold* v. *Connecticut* (1965), (2) *Roe* v. *Wade* (1973), (3) *Webster* v. *Reproductive Health Services* (1989), (4) *Planned Parenthood* v. *Casey* (1992) and (5) *Gonzales* v. *Carhart* (2007). All of these cases are important but the most important is *Roe* v. *Wade*.

The *Roe* v. *Wade* case found any law that prohibited abortion during the early stages of foetal development (first trimester) to be unconstitutional. Thus, in essence, making a woman's right to an abortion legal during her early stages of pregnancy. This liberty, according to the Court, is protected by the Due Process Clause of the Fourteenth Amendment of the United States Constitution, which states that 'no State shall make or enforce any law which shall abridge the privileges or immunities of citizens of the United States; *nor shall any State deprive any person of life, liberty, or property, without due process of law*'.[35] The *Roe* case also protected the state's interest in protecting and safeguarding the health of the pregnant woman and the potential life of the foetus. It establishes the trimester framework and used the criterion of viability or the third trimester as the point at which the state's interest in protecting the potential life of the foetus becomes compelling. During the second trimester, the state can promulgate laws to protect the health of the woman as long as the laws do not create an undue burden to a woman's right to an abortion.

In *Webster* v. *Reproductive Health Services*, the Court sided in favour of the states to allow them to encourage their preference that pregnant women not have an abortion. The Court determined that states are not obligated to use public funds, staff and resources to support abortion practices. The Court also determined that the state could reasonably establish laws to ensure that the foetus is not viable before an abortion is performed. The Court determined that these laws did not infringe on or create substantial obstacles to a woman's right and liberty to an abortion.

In *Planned Parenthood* v. *Casey*, the Court defined undue burden as follows: 'An undue burden exists, and therefore a provision of law is invalid, if its purpose or effect is to place a substantial obstacle in the path of a woman seeking an abortion before the fetus attains viability.'[36] The Court also strongly reaffirmed the findings in *Roe* v. *Wade* and claims that 'the woman's right to terminate her pregnancy without government interference during the first trimester is the most central principle of *Roe* v. *Wade*. It is a rule of law and a component of liberty we cannot renounce.'[37] Using the undue burden principle the Court surgically reconciled a woman's right to an abortion before viability with a state's interest in protecting a woman's health. Part of the states' rights include the right to inform pregnant women before they have an abortion about the procedures and its consequences to her and the foetus. The objective is to make sure that abortions are performed thoughtfully and reflectively.

Finally, in *Gonzales* v. *Carhart* (2003), the Court upheld the federal law banning Partial-Birth Abortions. The legal issue in this case was more about a specific procedure of abortion than about abortion itself. The procedure in question is known as intact Dilation and Evacuation (Intact D&E) or Dilation and Extraction (D&X). It is also referred to as Partial-Birth Abortions because the foetus is killed when it is partially outside of the women. While the effect of this ban on abortions is very limited, since it only affects late-term abortions of which there are few, and there are other procedures available that can be used for late-term abortions, it, nevertheless, represented a victory for abortion critics who defend the sacredness of human life.

Study questions

1 Explain the central legal issues in the Supreme Court case *Griswold* v. *Connecticut* (1965). What precedent was set in this case that influenced the landmark case *Roe* v. *Wade*?

2 Explain the central legal issues in the Supreme Court case *Roe* v. *Wade* (1973). How did the Court's decision affect the abortion laws in the United States? Explain the Due Process Clause of the Fourteenth Amendment and its relevancy to the Supreme Court's decision to make abortion legal.

3 Explain the central legal issues in the Supreme Court case *Webster* v. *Reproductive Health Services* (1989). How did this decision weaken the pro-choice position?

4 Explain the central legal issues in the Supreme Court case *Planned Parenthood* v. *Casey* (1992). What previous rulings were reaffirmed in this case? How did the Court reconcile a woman's right to an abortion with a state's right and interest to protect both the health of a woman and the potential life of a foetus? Explain the criterion of undue burden and its relevancy to the abortion law.

5 Explain the central legal issues in *Gonzales* v. *Carhart* (2007). In what ways was this a win for the pro-life movement?

Notes

Preface

1. David Boonin, *A Defense of Abortion* (Cambridge: Cambridge University Press, 2003).

2. See Bernard Gert, 'Moral Disagreement and Abortion', *Australian Journal of Professional and Applied Ethics* 6, no. 1 (2004): 1–19. He selects Don Marquis's deprivation argument and Mary Anne Warren's pro-choice arguments as two representative examples of opposing views that illustrate a 'classical unresolvable moral problem'.

3. 'Public Opinion on Abortion', Pew *Research Center*. Available online at http://www.pewforum.org/fact-sheet/public-opinion-on-abortion/ (accessed on 6 July 2018).

4. Available online at http://www.pewforum.org/2009/10/01/support-for-abortion-slips5/ (accessed on 6 July 2018).

5. Available online at http://www.pewresearch.org/fact-tank/2017/01/03/about-seven-in-ten-americans-oppose-overturning-roe-v-wade/ (accessed on 6 July 2018).

6. Jackie Calmes, 'Video Accuses Planned Parenthood of Crime', *New York Times*, 15 July 2015. Available online at http://www.nytimes.com/2015/07/15/us/video-accuses-planned-parenthood-of-crime.html?ref=topics (accessed on 6 July 2018).

7. Jackie Calmes, 'With Planned Parenthood Videos, Activist Ignites Abortion Issue', *New York Times*, 21 July 2015. Available online at http://www.nytimes.com/2015/07/22/us/with-planned-parenthood-videos-activist-ignites-abortion-issue.html?ref=topics (accessed on 6 July 2018).

8. David M. Herszenhorn and Julie Hirschfeld Davis, 'With Possible Shutdown Nearing, Obama Looks to Take Budget Fight to G.O.P', *New York Times*, 16 September 2015. Available online at http://www.nytimes.com/2015/09/16/us/with-possible-shutdown-nearing-obama-looks-to-take-budget-fight-to-gop.html (accessed on 6 July 2018).

9. Avantika Chilkoti, 'Planned Parenthood Battle Could Sway Fortunes of G.O.P. Health Bill', *New York Times*, 23 June 2017. Available online at https://www.nytimes.com/2017/06/23/us/politics/planned-parenthood-health-care-abortion.html?mcubz=0 (accessed on 6 July 2018).

10. 'Kansas Governor Signs Sweeping Ant-Abortion Bill', *USA Today*, 20 January 2013. Available online at https://www.usatoday.com/story/news/

nation/2013/04/20/kansas-governor-abortion-bill/2098801/. To access the new law online see http://www.kslegislature.org/li_2014/b2013_14/measures/documents/hb2253_enrolled.pdf (accessed on 6 July 2018).

11 '2012 Saw Second-Highest Abortion Restrictions Ever', Guttmacher Institute, 2 January 2013. Available online at http://www.guttmacher.org/media/inthenews/2013/01/02/index.html?utm_source=Jezebel±Newsletter&utm_campaign=a839b8334d-UA-142218-20&utm_medium=email (accessed on 6 July 2018).

12 For a more informed discussion see Bertha Alvarez Manninen, *Pro-life, Prochoice: Shared Values in the Abortion Debate* (Nashville, TN: Vanderbilt University Press, 2014), 12–13.

13 Peter Baker, 'A Conservative Court Push Decades in the Making, with Effects for Decades to Come', *New York Times*. Available online at https://www.nytimes.com/2018/07/09/us/politics/supreme-court-conservatives-trump.html (accessed on 11 July 2018).

14 Available online at http://www.pewforum.org/2013/01/16/public-opinion-on-abortion-slideshow/ (accessed on 6 July 2018).

Introduction

1 Most of the arguments we will examine have more than one premise, so I will continue to use the plural for brevity's sake.

2 Keith L. Moore et al., *The Developing Human: Clinically Oriented Embryology*, 9th edition (Philadelphia, PA: Saunders, 2013).

Chapter 1

1 Mary Anne Warren, 'On the Moral and Legal Status of Abortion', *The Monist* 57, no. 1 (1973): 43–61. See also her later works: 'The Moral Significance of Birth', *Hypatia* 4, no. 4 (1989): 46–65; 'Moral Difference between Infanticide and Abortion: A Response to Robert Card', *Bioethics* 14, no. 4 (2000): 352–359; and *Moral Status: Obligations to Persons and Other Living Things* (Oxford: Oxford University Press, 1997). Another similar personhood pro-choice argument comes from Michael Tooley's conception that a foetus is not a person because it lacks a desire for its continued existence. See Michael Tooley, 'Abortion and Infanticide', *Philosophy and Public Affairs* 2 (1972): 37–65, and 'Abortion: Why a Liberal View Is Correct', in *Abortion: Three Perspectives* (Oxford: Oxford University Press, 2009), 3–64.

2 Lynn Rudder Baker, 'When Does a Person Begin?', *Social Philosophy and Policy* 22 (2005): 25–48, and *Persons and Bodies: A Constitutive View* (Cambridge: Cambridge University Press, 2000).

3 Notice that this does not prove that the conclusion is false; it only shows that the argument is not a good one to demonstrate the truth of the conclusion.

4 See Judith Jarvis Thomson's justification for a third party to intervene and kill the foetus in Chapter 4, p. 108.

5 I intentionally use the word 'seems' because as we will see in Chapter 4, Thomson provides a provocative challenge to the argument that demonstrating the personhood of the foetus is a sufficient condition for the moral wrongness of abortion.

6 See Heather J. Gert, 'Viability', *International Journal of Philosophical Studies* 3 (1995): 133–142.

7 Warren, 'On the Moral and Legal Status of Abortion', 52.

8 Ibid., 54.

9 Ibid., 55.

10 Ibid., 56.

11 Ibid., 58.

12 Ibid., 59.

13 Baker, 'When Does a Person Begin', 27.

14 Ibid., 28.

15 Ibid., 30.

16 Ibid., 33.

17 Ibid., 34.

18 Ibid.

19 Ibid., 44.

20 See the discussion above concerning the truth or falsity of premise (1) of the Personhood Core Argument for the Moral Permissibility of Abortion: 'Killing a non-person human being is morally permissible.'

21 Ibid., 44.

22 Ibid.

23 It is important to point out that this is also true of most abortion defenders' personhood arguments.

Chapter 2

1 Stephen Schwarz, *The Moral Question of Abortion* (Chicago: Loyola University Press, 1990).

2 L. W. Sumner, *Abortion and Moral Theory* (Princeton, NJ: Princeton University Press, 1981).

3 See section 'Objection 1 against the potentiality principle' of this chapter (p. 61) for a discussion on Michael Tooley's symmetry principle.

4 See Gert, 'Viability'.

5 For a more detailed analysis of this view see Chapter 1.

6 Ibid.

7 Schwarz, *The Moral Question of Abortion*, 89.

8 Warren, 'On the Moral and Legal Status of Abortion', 55.

9 Schwarz, *The Moral Question of Abortion*, 89.

10 Ibid., 90.

11 Ibid., 91.

12 Ibid., 92.

13 Ibid., 94.

14 Aristotle, *Nicomachean Ethics*, translated by Terence Irwin (Cambridge: Hackett Publishing Company, Inc., 1999), 8, (1097b 20–30).

15 Tooley, 'Abortion and Infanticide', 60.

16 Warren, 'On the Moral and Legal Status of Abortion', 55.

Chapter 3

1 Susanne Gibson, 'The Problem of Abortion: Essentially Contested Concepts and Moral Autonomy', *Bioethics* 18, no. 3 (2004): 221–233.

2 D. Moller, 'Abortion and Moral Risk', *Philosophy* 86, no. 3 (2011): 425–443.

3 Gibson, 'The Problem of Abortion: Essentially Contested Concepts and Moral Autonomy', 223; see also W. G. Gallie, 'Essentially Contested Concepts', *Proceedings of the Aristotelian Society* 56, no. 1 (1956): 167–198.

4 Gibson, 'The Problem of Abortion: Essentially Contested Concepts and Moral Autonomy', 225.

5 See Chapter 7 for a more complete view of feminist theory on abortion.

6 Gibson, 'The Problem of Abortion: Essentially Contested Concepts and Moral Autonomy', 225 and 226.

7 Ibid., 227.

8 Ibid.

9 Ibid., 229.

10 Ibid., 230.

11 Ibid., 232.

12 Ibid., 230.

13 Ibid., 425.

14 Ibid., 432.

15 Ibid., 435.

16 Ibid., 438.

17 Ibid., 440.

18 Ibid., 441.

19 Ibid., 443.

Chapter 4

1 Judith Jarvis Thomson, 'A Defense of Abortion', *Philosophy and Public Affairs* 1, no. 1 (1971): 47–66.

2 Ibid., 48.

3 Ibid., 60.

4 See Chapter 1.

5 Thomson, 'A Defense of Abortion', 48–49.

6 Ibid., 55.

7 Ibid., 56.

8 Ibid.

9 Ibid., 55.

10 Ibid., 60.

11 Ibid., 51.

12 Ibid., 52.

13 Ibid., 53.

14 Ibid.

15 Baruch Brody, *Abortion and the Sanctity of Human Life* (Cambridge: MIT Press, 1975).

16 Ibid., 66.

17 Ibid., 53.

18 Ibid., 61.

19 Ibid., 60.

20 Ibid., 65.

21 Francis J. Beckwith, *Politically Correct Death: Answering the Arguments for Abortion Rights* (Grand Rapids, MI: Baker Book House, 1993).

22 Ibid., 64.

23 Brody, *Abortion and the Sanctity of Human Life*, 175.

Chapter 5

1 Marquis uses the term 'pro-life' to refer to those that are against the ethical permissibility of abortion. We will continue to use 'abortion critics' to remain consistency throughout the text, unless it is a direct citation from Marquis.

2 Don Marquis, 'Why Is Abortion Immoral', *The Journal of Philosophy* 86, no. 4 (1989): 183–202.

3 Ibid., 183.

4 Notice that Marquis's understanding of the abortion issue frames it only in terms of the moral status of the foetus and completely ignores what feminists take to be an essential element of the abortion issue, namely, the pregnant woman's interests, circumstances and rights.

5 Marquis, 'Why Is Abortion Immoral', 185.

6 Ibid., 185.

7 Ibid.

8 Ibid.

9 Ibid.

10 Ibid., 188–189.

11 Ibid., 189.

12 Ibid., 189–190. See also Jonathan Glover, *Causing Death and Saving Lives* (New York: Penguin, 1977) and Robert Young, 'What Is So Wrong with Killing People?' *Philosophy* I.IV, no. 210 (1979): 515–528.

13 Ibid., Marquis, 'Why Is Abortion Immoral', 192.

14 Ibid., 192.

15 See Lynn Rudder Baker's argument, *Supra*, 72.

16 Paul Bassen, 'Present Sakes and Future Prospects: The Status of Early Abortion', *Philosophy and Public Affairs* 4 (1982): 322–326.

17 Ronald Dworkin, *Life's Dominion* (New York: Vintage Books, 1993), 87.

18 Ibid., 87–88.

19 Gerald H. Paske, 'Abortion and the Neo-natal Right to Life: A Critique of Marquis's Futurist Argument', in *The Abortion Controversy: 25 Years after Roe v. Wade A Reader*, edited by Louis Pojman and Frank Beckwith (Boston: Jones & Bartlett, 1994), 362.

20 Ibid., 134–135.

21 Gerald H. Paske makes a similar point when he notes that 'the degree of harm, is not relevant to the wrongness of the murder *per se*'. Ibid., 265. However, Paske's conception of what makes murder wrong is that one is killing a person. This theory is different from the one proposed in this chapter as a solution and response to Marquis.

22 I am using 'innocent' here only to refer to the fact that the victim is not responsible in any way for the killer's decision and action, and thus he does not deserve to be killed.

Chapter 6

1 Aristotle, *Nicomachean Ethics*, 2nd edition, translated with introduction by Terence Irwin (Indianapolis, IN: Hackett Publishing Company, 1999).

2 Ibid., 19.

3 Ibid., 16.

4 Ibid., 8.

5 Ibid., 11.

6 Ibid., 8.

7 Ibid., 9.

8 Unfortunately, I have found this essential part of virtue ethics is missing in many published works on the topic as it relates to abortion. See, for instance, Rosalind Hursthouse, 'Virtue Theory and Abortion', *Philosophy and Public Affairs* 20, no. 3 (1991): 223–224; Justin Oakley, 'A Virtue Ethics Approach', in *A Companion to Bioethics*, 2nd edition, edited by Helga Kuhse and Peter Singer (Malden, MA: Blackwell Publishing, 2012).

9 Aristotle, *Nicomachean Ethics,* 20–21.

10 Ibid., 21.

11 Oakley, 'A Virtue Ethics Approach', 93. See also Hursthouse, 'Virtue Theory and Abortion', 223–246. She defines a right action under virtue ethics as follows: 'An action is right iff it is what a virtuous agent would do in the circumstances', 225.

12 Oakley, 'A Virtue Ethics Approach', 93.

13 Aristotle, *Nicomachean Ethics.*

14 Alasdair MacIntyre, *After Virtue*, 2nd edition (Notre Dame, IN: University of Notre Dame, 1984), 184.

15 Aristotle, *Nicomachean Ethics*, 98.

16 Ibid., 99.

17 Ibid., 49.

18 Ibid., 99.

19 Ibid., 69.

20 Ibid.

21 Hursthouse, 'Virtue Theory and Abortion', 234.

22 Ibid., 235.

23 Aristotle, *Nicomachean Ethics*, 50.

24 See Sumner, *Abortion and Moral Theory.*

25 Hursthouse, 'Virtue Theory and Abortion', 325–326.

26 Ibid., 326.

27 Ibid., 237.

28 Ibid.

29 Ibid., 238.

30 Ibid., 241.

31 Consider for instance the common interpretation of the theory of Act-Utilitarianism in which we ought to do the act that produces the greatest amount of happiness for the greatest number of people. Who the people are and how they are related to us is not taken into consideration.

32　Hursthouse, 'Virtue Theory and Abortion', 238.

33　Ibid., 242–243.

34　Ibid., 243.

Chapter 7

1　Since women's status around the world varies significantly, it would be impossible to address this topic in a way that includes all of the societies and countries in the world. We will here focus on feminism in the United States. For an introduction to feminist philosophy, see Noëlle McAfee "Feminist Philosophy: Introduction to the Feminist Philosophy Section" in *The Stanford Encyclopedia of Philosophy*, June 2018 available online at https://plato. stanford.edu/entries/feminist-philosophy/ (accessed on 14 October 2018)

2　Karen J. Warren, 'The Power and Promise of Ecological Feminism', *Environmental Ethics* 12 (1990): 139.

3　Ibid., 140.

4　Virginia Held, 'Feminism and Epistemology: Recent Work on the Connection Between Gender and Knowledge', *Philosophy and Public Affairs* 14, no. 3 (1985): 296–307.

5　Celia Wolfe-Devine, 'Abortion and the "Feminine Voice"', *Public Affairs Quarterly* 3, no. 3 (1989): 81–97.

6　Sally Markowitz, 'Abortion and Feminism', *Social Theory Practice Journal of Social Philosophy* 16 (1990): 2.

7　Ibid., 2.

8　Wolfe-Devine, 'Abortion and the "Feminine Voice"', 81–82.

9　Ibid., 83.

10　Stephanie Leland and Leonie Caldecott, eds., *Reclaim the Earth: Women Speak Out for Life on Earth* (London: The Women's Press, 1983), 72.

11　Wolfe-Devine, 'Abortion and the "Feminine Voice"', 88.

12　Ibid., 86.

13　Ibid., 87.

14　Ibid.,187.

15　Markowitz, 'Abortion and Feminism', 15.

16　Ibid., 7.

17　Ibid.

18　Ibid., 8.

19　Ibid., 9.

20　Ibid., 10.

21　Ibid.

22　Ibid.

23　Ibid., 11.

24 Ibid., 12.

25 Ibid., 7.

26 Ibid., 8.

Chapter 8

1 Adrienne Asch, 'Prenatal Diagnosis and Selective Abortion: A Challenge to Practice and Policy', *American Journal of Public Health* 89, no. 11 (1999): 1650.

2 Ibid., 1651.

3 Ibid.1.

4 Ibid., 1654.

5 John Harris, 'Stem Cells, Sex, and Procreation', *The Cambridge Quarterly of Healthcare Ethics* 12, no. 4 (2003): 353–371.

6 Ibid., 355.

7 Daniel Callahan, 'The Puzzle of Profound Respect', *Hasting Center Report* 25, no. 1 (1995): 39–40.

8 Bertha Alvarez Manninen, 'Respecting Human Embryos within Stem Cell Research: Seeking Harmony', *Metaphilosophy* 38 (2007): 226–244.

9 Ibid., 240.

10 Ibid., 233.

11 Ibid., 235.

12 Ibid., 234.

13 John Robertson, *On Cloning* (New York: Routledge), 2004. Cf. Harris, 'Stem Cells, Sex, and Procreation', 368–369; and Manninen, 'Respecting Human Embryos within Stem Cell Research: Seeking Harmony', 239.

14 Ibid., 362.

15 Ibid., 365.

16 T. J. Bouchard, 'Whenever the Twin Shall Meet', *The Science* 37 (1997): 52–57.

17 Michael Tooley, *Human Cloning*, edited by James M. Humber and Robert F. Almeder (Atlanta: Georgia State University, 1998), 80.

18 Ibid., 82.

19 Ibid., 85.

Chapter 9

1 Ian Shapiro, editor, *Abortion: The Supreme Court Decisions, 1965–2007* (Indianapolis, IN: Hackett Publishing Company, 2007).

2 Ibid., 2–3.

3 Ibid., 3.

4 Ibid., United States Constitution.

5 Ibid., 4–5.

6 Ibid., 40.

7 Ibid., 39.

8 Ibid., 42.

9 Ibid., 43.

10 Ibid.

11 Ibid., 161–162.

12 Ibid., 153.

13 Ibid., 154.

14 Ibid., 155.

15 Ibid.

16 Ibid., 158.

17 Ibid., 184.

18 Ibid., 162.

19 Ibid.

20 Ibid., 190.

21 Ibid., 186.

22 Ibid.

23 Ibid., 195.

24 Ibid., 196.

25 Ibid., 198.

26 Ibid., 207.

27 Ibid., 270.

28 Ibid., 271.

29 Ibid.

30 Ibid., 272.

31 Ibid., 275.

32 Ibid.

33 Ibid., 277.

34 Centers for Disease Control and Prevention, https://www.cdc.gov/reproductivehealth/data_stats/index.htm (accessed on 25 March 2018).

35 Ibid., United States Constitution.

36 Ibid., 198.

37 Ibid., 195.

Bibliography

Asch, Adriene. 'Prenatal Diagnosis and Selective Abortion: A Challenge to Practice and Policy'. *American Journal of Public Health*, 89(11) (1999): 1649–1657.

Baird, Robert M. and Rosenbaum, Stuart E., editors. *The Ethics of Abortion: Pro-life vs. Pro-choice*. Buffalo, NY: Prometheus Books, 1994.

Baker, Lynne Rudder. *Persons and Bodies: A Constitutive View*. Cambridge: Cambridge University Press, 2000.

Baker, Lynne Rudder. 'When Does a Person Begin?'. *Social Philosophy and Policy*, 22 (2005): 25–48.

Bassen, Paul. 'Present Sakes and Future Prospects: The Status of Early Abortion'. *Philosophy & Public Affair*, 11(4) (1982): 314–337.

Beckwith, Francis J. 'Arguments from Bodily Rights: A Critical Analysis'. In *The Abortion Controversy: 25 Years after Roe v. Wade: A Reader*, 2nd edition. Edited by Louis P. Pojman and Francis Beckwith. Belmont, CA: Wadsworth, 1998, 132–150.

Beckwith, Francis J. *Critically Correct Death: Answering the Arguments for Abortion Rights*. Grand Rapids, MI: Baker Book House, 1993.

Beckwith, Francis J. *Defending Life: A Moral and Legal Case against Abortion Choice*. Cambridge: Cambridge University Press, 2007.

Beckwith, Francis J. 'Does Judith Jarvis Thomson Really Grant the Pro-life View of Fetal Personhood in Her Defense of Abortion? A Rawlsian Assessment'. *International Philosophical Quarterly*, 54 (2014): 443–451.

Beckwith, Francis J. 'Potentials and Burdens: A Reply to Giubilini and Minerva'. *Journal of Medical Ethics: The Journal of the Institute of Medical Ethics*, 39(5) (2013): 341–344.

Bennett, Philip W. 'A Defense of Abortion: A Question for Judith Jarvis Thomson'. *Philosophical Investigations*, 5(2) (1982): 142–145.

Bloch, Ruth H. 'A Culturalist Critique of Trends in Feminist Theory'. In *Gender and Morality in Anglo-American Culture. 1650–1800*. Berkeley: University of California Press, 2003.

Boonin, David. 'Death Comes for the Violinist: On Two Objections to Thomson's "Defense of Abortion"'. *Social Theory and Practice: An International and Interdisciplinary Journal of Social Philosophy*, 23 (1997): 329–364.

Boonin, David. 'A Defense of "A Defense of Abortion": On the Responsibility Objection to Thomson's Argument'. *Ethics: An International Journal of Social, Political, and Legal Philosophy*, 107(2) (1997): 286–313.

Boonin, David. *A Defense of Abortion*. Cambridge: Cambridge University Press, 2003.

Bordo, S. *Unbearable Weight: Feminism, Western Culture, and the Body*. Berkeley: University of California Press, 1998, 71–98.

Brill, H. S. 'The Future-Like-Ours Argument, Personal Identity, and the Twinning Dilemma'. *Social Theory Practice*, 29 (2003): 419–430.

Brody, Baruch. 'Fetal Humanity and the Theory of Essentialism'. In *Philosophy and Sex*. Edited by Robert Baker and Fredrick Elliston. Buffalo, NY: Prometheus Books, 1984.

Brody, Baruch. 'Thomson and Abortion'. *Philosophy & Public Affair*, 1(3) (1972): 335–340.

Buckle, Stephen. 'Arguing from Potential'. *Bioethics*, 2(3) (1988): 227–253.

Callahan, S. and Callahan, D., editors. *Abortion: Understanding Differences*. New York: Plenum, 1984.

Cannold, L. *The Abortion Myth: Feminism, Morality and the Hard Choices Women Make*. Hanover, NH: Wesleyan University Press, 2000, chapter 3.

Clune, Alan. 'Deeper Problems for Noonan's Probability Arguments against Abortion: On a Charitable Reading of Noonan's Conception Criterion of Humanity'. *Bioethics*, 25(5) (2011): 280–289.

Cohen, Marshal, Nagel, Thomas, and Scanlon, Thomas, editors. *The Rights and Wrongs of Abortion*. Princeton: Princeton University Press, 1974.

Collins, Patricia Hill and Bilge, Sirma. *Intersectionality*. Malden, MA: Polity Press, 2016.

Cox, Damian and Levine, Michael. 'Violinists Run Amuck in South Dakota: Screen Doors Down in the Badlands!'. *Philosophical Papers*, 35 (2006): 267–281.

Cox, Daniel R. A. 'The Problems with Utilitarian Conceptions of Personhood in the Abortion Debate'. *Journal of Medical Ethics*, 37 (2011): 318–320.

Davis, Nancy. 'Abortion and Self-Defense'. *Philosophy & Public Affair*, 13(2) (1984): 175–207.

DeGrazia, David. 'Identity, Killing and the Boundaries of Our Existence'. *Philosophy & Public Affairs*, 31 (2003): 412–442.

Drum, Peter. 'Rights, Duties, and Abortions'. *Journal of Value Inquiry*, 33(4) (1999): 555–556.

Dworkin, Ronald. *Life's Dominion: An Argument about Abortion, Euthanasia, and Individual Freedom*. New York: Vintage Books, 1993.

Dwyer, Susan and Feinberg, Joel, editors. *The Problem of Abortion*. Belmont, CA: Wadsworth Publishing Company, 1997.

English, J. 'Abortion beyond the Personhood Argument'. In *The Abortion Controversy*. Edited by Louis Pojman and Frank Beckwith. Boston: Jones & Barlett, 1994.

Finnis, John. 'The Rights and Wrongs of Abortion: A Reply to Judith Thomson'. *Philosophy & Public Affair*, 2(2) (1973): 117–145.

Fischer, John Martin. 'Abortion and Ownership'. *Journal of Ethics: An International Philosophical Review*, 17 (2013): 275–304.

Feldt, Gloria. *The War on Choice*. New York: A Bantam Book, 2004.

Friedman, Michelle, Metelerkamp, Jo, and Posel, Ros. 'What Is Feminism? And What Kind of Feminist Am I?' *Agenda: Empowering Women for Gender Equity*, 1 (1987): 3–24.

Frowe, Helen. 'Killing John to Save Mary: A Defense of the Moral Distinction between Killing and Letting Die'. In *Action, Ethics, and Responsibility*. Edited by Joseph Keim Cambell, Michael O'Rourke, and Harry S. Silverstein. Cambridge, MA: MIT Press, 2010.

Gardner, R. F. R. and Stallworthy, J. A. *Abortion the Personal Dilemma*. Exeter, England: Paternoster Press, 1972.

Gensler, Henry J. 'A Kantian Argument against Abortion'. *Philosophical Studies*, 49 (1986): 83–98.

Gert, Bernard. 'Moral Disagreement and Abortion'. *Australian Journal of Professional and Applied Ethics*, 6(1) (2004): 1–19.

Gibson, Susanne. 'The Problem of Abortion: Essentially Contested Concepts and Moral Autonomy'. *Bioethics*, 18(3) (2004): 221–233.

Giubilini, Alberto and Minerva, Francesca. 'Abortion and the Argument from Potential: What We Owe to the Ones Who Might Exist'. *Journal of Medicine and Philosophy*, 37 (2012): 49–59.

Giubilini, Alberto and Minerva, Francesca. 'After-birth Abortion: Why Should the Baby Live?' *Journal of Medical Ethics: The Journal of the Institute of Medical Ethics*, 39(5) (2013): 261–263.

Giubilini, Alberto and Minerva, Francesca. 'Clarifications on the Moral Status of Newborns and the Normative Implications'. *Journal of Medical Ethics: The Journal of the Institute of Medical Ethics*, 39(5) (2013): 264–265.

Glover, Jonathan. 'Questions about Some Uses of Genetic Engineering'. In *What Sort of People Should There Be?* Harmondsworth: Penguin Books, 1984.

Hare, R. M. 'Abortion and the Golden Rule'. *Philosophy & Public Affair*, 4(3) (1975): 301–322.

Hare, R. M. 'A Kantian Approach to Abortion'. In *Essays on Bioethics*. Edited by R. M. Hare. New York: Oxford University Press, 1993, 186–184.

Harmen, Elizabeth. 'Creation Ethics: The Moral Status of Early Fetuses and the Ethics of Abortion'. *Philosophy and Public Affairs*, 28(4) (1999): 310–324.

Harris, John. 'Stem Cells, Sex, and Procreation'. *Cambridge Quarterly of Healthcare Ethics*, 12(4) (2003): 353–371.

Harris, John. *The Value of Life*. London: Routledge and Kegan Paul, 1985.

Hershenov, David B. and Hershenov, Rose. 'The I'm Personally Opposed to Abortion But..." Argument'. *American Catholic Philosophical Association Proceedings*, 83 (2010): 77–87.

Hopkins, Patrick. 'Can Technology Fix the Abortion Problem?" Ectogenesis and the Real Issues of Abortion'. *International Journal of Applied Ethics*, 22(2) (2008): 311–326.

Hursthouse, Rosalind. *Beginning Lives*. New York: Open University, 1987.

Hursthouse, Rosalind. 'Virtue Theory and Abortion'. *Philosophy and Public Affairs*, 20(3) (1991): 223–246.

Jagger, Alison. 'Abortion and Women's Right to Decide'. *The Philosophy Forum*, 5 (1973): 347–360.

Jensen, David. 'Decisions, Moral Status, and the Early Fetus'. *Ethics and Medicine*, 27(3) (2011): 155–163.

Kamm, F. M. *Creation and Abortion*. Oxford: Oxford University Press, 1992.

Kaposy, Chris. 'Proof and Persuasion in the Philosophical Debate about Abortion'. *Philosophy and Rhetoric*, 43(2) (2010): 139–162.

Kaposy, Chris. 'Two Stalemates in the Philosophical Debate about Abortion and Why They Cannot Be Resolved Using Analogical Arguments'. *Bioethics*, 26(2) (2012): 840–892.

Kornegay, Jo. R. 'Hursthouse' Virtue Ethics and Abortion: Abortion Ethics without Metaphysics?'. *Ethic Theory Moral Practice*, 14 (2011): 51–71.

Kenny, Anthony. 'The Beginning of Individual Life'. *Daedalus*, Winter, 137(1)
    (2008): 15–22.
Laing, Jacqueline A. 'Infanticide: A Reply to Giubilini and Minerva'. *Journal of
    Medical Ethics*, 39(5) (2013): 336–340.
Lappe, Marc. 'Ethical Issues in Manipulating the Human Germ Line'. *Journal of
    Medicine and Philosophy*, 16(6) (1991): 621–639.
Lee, Patrick. *Abortion and Unborn Human Life*. Washington, DC: Catholic
    University of America, 1996.
Lee, Patrick. 'Is Abortion Justified as Nonintentional Killing?'. In *Abortion and
    Unborn Life*, 2nd edition. Washington, DC: Catholic University of America,
    2013.
Lee, Patrick. 'The Pro-life Argument from Substantial Identity'. *Bioethics* 3(18)
    (2004): 249–263.
Levin, David S. 'Thomson and the Current State of the Abortion Debate'. *Journal
    of Applied Philosophy*, 2 (1985): 121–126.
Lockhart, Ted. *Moral Uncertainty and Its Consequences*. Oxford: Oxford
    University Press, 2000.
Manninen, Bertha Alvarez. 'Are Human Embryos Kantian Persons? Kantian
    Considerations in Favor of Embryonic Stem Cell Research'. *Philosophy, Ethics,
    and Humanities in Medicine*, 3(4) (2008): 1–16.
Manninen, Bertha Alvarez. 'Beyond Abortion: The Implications of the Human Life
    Amendment'. *Journal of Social Philosophy*, 43(2) (2012): 140–160.
Manninen, Bertha Alvarez. 'The Metaphysical Foundations of Reproductive
    Ethics'. *Journal of Applied Philosophy*, 26(2) (2009): 190–204.
Manninen, Bertha Alvarez. 'Pleading Men and Virtuous Women: Considering the
    Role of the Father in the Abortion Debate'. *International Journal of Applied
    Philosophy*, 21(1) (2007): 1–24.
Manninen, Bertha Alvarez. *Pro-life, Prochoice: Shared Values in the Abortion
    Debate*. Nashville, TN: Vanderbilt University Press, 2014.
Manninen, Bertha Alvarez. 'Respecting Human Embryos within Stem Cell
    Research: Seeking Harmony'. *Metaphilosophy*, 38(2–3) (2007): 226–244.
Manninen, Bertha Alvarez. 'Revisiting the Argument from Fetal Potential'.
    Philosophy, Ethics, and Humanities in Medicine, 2(7) (2007): https://doi.
    org/10.1186/1747-5341-2-7.
Manninen, Bertha Alvarez. 'The Value of Choice and the Choice to Value:
    Expanding the Discussion about Fetal Life within Prochoice Advocacy'.
    Hypatia: A Journal of Feminist Philosophy, 28(3) (2013): 663–683.
Manninen, Bertha Alvarez. 'Why Fetal Potential Matters'. *American Philosophical
    Association Newsletters: Philosophy and Medicine*, 11(1) (2011): 11–14.
Manninen, Bertha Alvarez. 'Yes, the Baby Should Live: A Pro-choice Response to
    Giubilini and Minerva'. *Journal of Medical Ethics: The Journal of the Institute
    of Medical Ethics*, 39(5) (2013): 330–333.
Markowitz, Sally. 'Abortion and Feminism'. *Journal of Social Philosophy*, 16(1)
    (1990): 1–17.
Marquis, Don. 'Why Abortion Is Immoral'. *The Journal of Philosophy*, 86 (April)
    (1989): 183–202.
McDonagh, E. *Breaking the Abortion Deadlock: From Choice to Consent*. Oxford:
    Oxford University Press, 1996.
McInerney, P. K. 'Does a Fetus Already Have a Future-Like-Ours?'. *Journal of
    Philosophy*, 87 (1990): 264–268.

McMahan J. *The Ethics of Killing: Problems at the Margins of Life*. Oxford: Oxford University Press, 2002.

Mohr, James C. *Abortion in America. The Origin and Evolution of National Policy*. Oxford University Press, 1978.

Moller, Dan. 'Abortion and Moral Risk'. *Philosophy*, 86 (2011): 425–443.

Noonan, John. *The Morality of Abortion: Legal and Historical Perspectives*. Cambridge, MA: Harvard University Press, 1970.

Norcross, A. 'Killing, Abortion, and Contraceptive: A Reply to Marquis'. *Journal of Philosophy*, 87 (1990): 268–277.

Olson, Eric. *The Human Animal: Personal Identity without Psychology*. New York: Oxford University Press, 1997.

Olson, Eric. 'Was I Ever a Fetus?' *Philosophy and Phenomenological Research*, 57(1) (1997): 95–110.

Parfit, F. *Reasons and Persons*. Oxford: Oxford University Press, 1984.

Parfit, F. 'Rights, Interests, and Possible People'. In *Bioethics: An Anthology*. Edited by P. Singer and H. Kuhse. Oxford: Blackwell, 2006, 108–112.

Parfit, F. 'Rights, Interests and Possible People'. In *Moral Problems in Medicine*. Edited by Samuel Gorovitz et al. Englewood Cliffs, NJ: Prentice Hall, 1976.

Paske, Gerald H. 'Abortion and the Neo-natal Right to Life: A Critique of Marquis's Futurist Argument'. In *The Abortion Controversy*. Edited by Louis Pojman and Frank Beckwith. Boston: Jones & Barlett, 1994.

Pavlischek, Keith. 'Abortion Logic and Paternal Responsibility: One More Look at Judith Thomson's 'A Defense of Abortion'. *Public Affairs Quarterly*, 7(4) (1993): 341–361.

Pavlischek, Keith. 'Abortion Logic and Paternal Responsibilities: One More Look at Judith Thomson's Argument and a Critique of David Boonin-Vail's Defense of it'. In *The Abortion Controversy: 25 Years after Roe v. Wade: A Reader*, 2nd edition. Edited by Louis P. Pojman and Francis Beckwith. Belmont, CA: Wadsworth, 1998, 176–198.

Petchesky, R. P. *Abortion and Women's Choice*. London: Venso, 1986.

Pojman, Louis and Beckwith, Frank, editors. *The Abortion Controversy*. Boston: Jones & Barlett, 1994.

Prijic-Samarzija, Snjezana. 'Abortion and Responsibility'. *Acta Analytica: International Periodical for Philosophy in the Analytical Tradition*, 19 (1997): 161–174.

Reader, Soran. 'Abortion, Killing, and Maternal Moral Authority'. *Hypatia*, 23(1) (2008): 132–149.

Reiman, Jeffrey. *Abortion and the Way We Value Human Life*. New York: Owman and Littlefield, 1999.

Resnik, D. B. 'The Moral Significance of the Therapy-Enhancement Distinction in Human Genetic'. *Cambridge Quarterly of Healthcare Ethics*, 9(3) (2000): 365–377.

Ross, Steven L. 'Abortion and the Death of the Fetus'. *Philosophy & Public Affairs*, 11(3) (1982): 232–245.

Roth, Paul A. 'Personhood, Property Rights and the Permissibility of Abortion'. *Law and Philosophy: An International Journal for Jurisprudence and Legal Philosophy*, 2 (1983): 163–192.

Schwarz, Stephen. *The Moral Question of Abortion*. Chicago: Loyola University Press, 1990.

Shapiro, Ian, editor. *Abortion: The Supreme Court Decisions, 1965–2007*. Indianapolis, IN: Hackett Publishing Company, 2007.

Sher, George. 'Hare, Abortion, and the Golden Rule'. *Philosophy & Public Affairs*,
    6(2) (1977): 185–190.
Shoemaker, David. 'The Insignificance of Personal Identity for Bioethics'.
    Bioethics, 24(9) (2010): 481–489.
Shrage, L. *Abortion and Social Responsibility: Depolarizing the Debate*. Oxford:
    Oxford University Press, 2003.
Singer, Peter. *Practical Ethics*. Cambridge: Cambridge University Press, 1993.
Solinger, Rickie, editor. *Abortion Wars: A Half Century of Struggle, 1950–2000*.
    Berkeley and Los Angeles: University of California Press, 1998.
Stroud, Sarah. 'Dworkin and Casey on Abortion'. *Philosophy & Public Affairs*,
    25(2) (1996): 140–170.
Sumner, L. W. *Abortion and Moral Theory*. Princeton: Princeton University Press,
    1981.
Tedesco, Matthew. 'Thomson's Samaritarnism Constraint'. *Philosophy in the
    Contemporary World*, 14 (2007): 112–126.
Thomson, Judith Jarvis. 'A Defense of Abortion'. *Philosophy and Public Affairs*,
    1(1) (1971): 48–66.
Thomson, Judith Jarvis. 'Turing the Trolley'. *Philosophy and Public Affairs*, 36(4)
    2008: 359–374.
Tooley, Michael. 'Abortion and Infanticide'. *Philosophy and Public Affairs*, 2 (1972):
    37–65.
Tooley, Michael. 'Abortion: Why a Liberal View Is Correct'. In *Abortion: Three
    Perspectives*. Oxford: Oxford University Press, 2009, 3–64.
Tooley, Michael. 'Mary Anne Warren on Abortion'. *American Philosophical
    Association Newsletter on Philosophy and Medicine*, 12(2) (1912): 9–14.
Tooley, Michael. 'The Moral Status of Cloning of Humans'. In *Human Cloning*.
    Totawa, NJ: Humana Press, 1998, 67–101.
Warren, Karen J. 'The Power and Promise of Ecological Feminism',
    Environmental Ethics 12 (1990): 125–146.
Warren, Mary Anne. 'Moral Difference between Infanticide and Abortion: A
    Response to Robert Card'. *Bioethics*, 14(4) (2000): 352–359.
Warren, Mary Anne. 'The Moral Significance of Birth'. *Hypatia*, 4(4) (1989): 46–65.
Warren, Mary Anne. 'On the Moral and Legal Status of Abortion'. *The Monist*,
    57(1) (1973): 176–198.
Watkins, Michael. 'Re-reading Thomson: Thomson's Unanswered Challenge'.
    Journal of Libertarian Studies, 20 (2006): 41–59.
Wertheimer, Roger. 'Understanding the Abortion Argument'. *Philosophy & Public
    Affairs*, 1(1) (1971): 67–95.
Wilcox, John T. 'Nature as Demonic in Thomson's Defense of Abortion'. *New
    Scholasticism*, 63 (1989): 463–484.
Williams, Melanie. 'An Ethics Ensemble: Abortion, Thomson, Finnis and the Case
    of the Violin-Player'. *Ratio Juris: An International Journal of Jurisprudence and
    Philosophy of Law*, 17(3) (2004): 381–397.
Wolfe-Devine, Celia. 'Abortion and the "Feminist Voice"'. *Public Affairs Quarterly*,
    3(3) (1989): 81–97.
Zaitchik, Alan. 'Viability and the Morality of Abortion'. *Philosophy & Public Affairs*,
    10(1) (1981): 18–26.
Zilberberg, Jill. 'Sex Selection and Restricting Abortion and Sex Determination'.
    Bioethics, 9 (2007): 517–519.

Index